What People Are Saying About Michael Hauge's *Writing Screenplays That Sell*

"An invaluable guide to taking a story on that long journey from your head to the screen."
—Kevin Wade, screenwriter:
True Colors; Working Girl

"Michael Hauge's encyclopedic book is magic—but unlike most other magicians, he shows you how it's done."
—William Link, screenwriter/co-creator:
Murder, She Wrote; Columbo

"Finally, a book I can recommend to all the young screenwriters who call me for advice."
—Jim Kouf, writer/producer: *Stakeout;* screenwriter:
The Hidden; writer/director: *Disorganized Crime*

"For the first-time scriptor and the down-in-the-trenches veteran, any writer who wants to be ahead of the game should read this book."
—Kathie Fong Yoneda, Vice President Creative
Affairs, Island Pictures; former Executive Story
Editor, Walt Disney/Touchstone Pictures

"A valuable step-by-step primer on the craft of writing a screenplay."
—Richard Fischoff, Senior Vice President
of Production, Tri-Star Pictures

"A concise, expert, and comprehensive guide . . . filled with ingenious devices, examples, checklists, charts, and definitions that lead the reader beyond completed screenplays into an awareness of the nature of the film industry and the writer's place in it."
—*Back Stage Magazine*

WRITING SCREENPLAYS THAT SELL

Michael Hauge

HarperPerennial

A Division of HarperCollins*Publishers*

FIRST HARPERPERENNIAL EDITION PUBLISHED IN 1991

Library of Congress Cataloging-in-Publication Data

Hauge, Michael.
    Writing screenplays that sell / Michael Hauge. — 1st HarperPerennial ed.
        p. cm.
    Reprint. Originally published: New York : McGraw-Hill, © 1988.
    Includes bibliographical references (p.   ) and index.
    ISBN 0-06-272500-9 (pbk.)
    1. Motion picture authorship.   2. Television authorship.
    I. Title.
[PN1996.H36   1991]
808.2′3—dc20   91-55005

96   RRD   19 18 17 16 15 14

Dedicated to the Memory

of

Art Arthur

and

Jerry Hauge

Acknowledgments

Since I know this is the section of the book you're going to skip over anyway (unless you think you'll recognize one of the names), please bear with me while I give some words of thanks to some of the many people whose knowledge, inspiration, support, and guidance made this book possible.

To my parents: my mother, who always believed in me and gave me her love of learning and teaching and the written word, and my dad, who used to sell popcorn to the movie theaters (and got me into the movies for free), gave me his love and support (both emotional *and* financial), and always stood by me, even when I know he thought moving to Hollywood was a pretty crazy thing to do.

To the people whose faith, enthusiasm, and effort made this book a reality: Esther Newberg, my literary agent; Bobbi Mark, Elisabeth Jakab, Lucia Staniels and Ann Craig at McGraw-Hill; Craig Nelson and Jenna Hull at HarperCollins; and especially my unofficial agent and good friend, Diane Cairns.

To Wendy Benjamin, Marty Chavez, John Deimer, Robert Mark Kamen, Lawrence Kasdan, Ivy Orta, Karen Rosenfelt, Jerry Weintraub, Jeremy Williams, and Wally Zavattero for their help and generosity in granting me permission to quote from *Body Heat, The Karate Kid,* and *The Sylmar Tunnel Disaster.*

To all those who have helped me in both my film and teaching careers, with particular gratitude to Gary Shusett and Sherwood Oaks Experimental College for getting me started; to producers

Michael Jaffe, Zev Braun, and Robert Guenette for giving me the opportunity to learn; to Mona Moore, Steve Waterman, Stephanie Mann, and Michele Wallerstein for their career guidance at critical times; to the many schools throughout the country who have sponsored my seminars; and to my publicist, Vicki Arthur, who keeps getting my name in the paper and drawing people into my classes even if I am her toughest client. And a special thanks to those at the Writer's Program at UCLA Extension, who gave me the credibility to take my show on the road and who prove you can have a great educational program and still be fun to work with.

To the many producers, agents, executives, teachers, screen-writers, and filmmakers I have worked with and learned from over the years, who have all contributed to the information in this book. And to six talented screenwriters who are now close friends: Paul Margolis, Frederica Hobin, Don Buday, Jewel Jaffe, Jill Jaress, and Eric Edson.

To two of my own teachers: William Cadbury, at the University of Oregon, who was the first to teach me to appreciate the deeper levels of meaning that film can achieve, and Art Arthur, who knew more about screenwriting than anyone I ever met and who was my biggest supporter, my mentor, and my dear friend.

To the many students I have taught over the last seven years. You have brought me joy and helped me achieve my own inner motivation.

On a more personal note, to all the members of my family, for their unending love and support and for always laughing at my jokes, with a special thanks for always being there to my brother Jim, Auntie Bon, Uncle Vince, Fritz, Jan, Bonnie Laurie, the Jacobsons, Jessica Arthur, and Pamela Steele.

To all my friends, with special thanks to Nancy Hicks and Cisci McGarry for years of concern and caring; to Eugene Webb, Dave Grill, and Bruce Derman for helping me through the emotional obstacle course of writing a book; to Marty Ross, Mitchell Group, Art Silverblatt, Michael Firmature, Nancy Pearson, and Dianne Haak for continued help and friendship; and most of all to Jim Hicks, John Hudkins, Earl Kamsky, Charles Moreland, and Bill

Trezise, who for thirty years have been willing to go to the movies with me, even on sunny days in Oregon.

And finally, thanks to my wife Vicki. Without her faith, support, commitment, inspiration, and love, I could never have written this book.

For Cookie

Contents

Introduction

Why Read This Book?

Screenplays have become, for the last half of this century, what the Great American Novel was for the first half. Closet writers who used to dream of the glory of getting into print now dream of the glory of seeing their story on the big or small screen.

After teaching about 7000 writers in more than forty-five cities in the United States, Canada, and England, I have found that the dream is by no means confined to Hollywood. People everywhere watch TV and think to themselves, "I could write better than that." Or they go to the movies and lose themselves in the magic of the dark, and they want to be a part of that magic or that glamour or that wealth that they see and read about. Or they just want to touch the pain and the wonder that comes from facing that blank page and turning it into something totally one's own.

So they decide to give it a shot. And then they meet The Great Destroyers: Everybody's writing a screenplay. You can't learn creativity. It's impossible to get an agent. You've got to live in southern California. It's who you know, not what you know. They'll rip you off. They'll ruin your script. Nobody knows what sells. All they want is teenage sex comedies. All they want is macho violence. All they want are established writers.

And you don't have any talent anyway.

So the dream gets changed or diminished or vanishes altogether. Or you forge ahead in blind, confused ignorance, assuming that there *are* no standards in Hollywood, that it's just a crap shoot. Or you refuse to consider commerciality at all, because that's a sellout. Or you decide *just* to go after the bucks because you can't hope to say anything meaningful anyway. And so on.

I don't buy it. After twelve years of working in Hollywood developing screenplays as a reader, a story editor, staff producer, and screenplay consultant for various production companies (including my own), and after having worked with probably a hundred or more screenwriters in acquiring and developing projects, and after listening to, talking with, working with, and interviewing another hundred or so writers, agents, producers, executives, and stars, I think all those notions listed above are myths. At the very least, they have grown way out of proportion to reality and need to be put in proper perspective.

I have now been teaching screenwriting for about eleven years, first at Sherwood Oaks Experimental College and then through UCLA Extension. And for more than eight years I have been conducting an intensive, two-day seminar on the complete screenwriting process. This book sets forth the principles that have evolved out of those classes and my own professional experience. The goal of this book is to destroy those common myths of failure and to replace them with the following ideas:

1. If screenwriting is a goal you wish to pursue, then you should go for it. And as long as you find the *process* of writing screenplays personally fulfilling, then you should keep at it, because anyone with talent who sticks around long enough will succeed.

2. Lots of us would like to have written a screenplay; what's important is whether you want to *write* a screenplay. If you get fulfillment out of the day-to-day work of putting a story to paper, then the additional rewards of money and success and fame can follow. But if it's those secondary rewards you're focused on, it probably won't happen, and success certainly won't be as golden as you think it will be if it does arrive.

3. Creativity is something we all possess. Your objective should be not to learn creativity but to stimulate it. This book is filled with methods of nudging, nurturing, and recognizing your own creativity, and funneling it into your screenplay.

4. No matter how much new technology can be thrown into a movie, no matter what new stars or concepts or directors are hot, and no matter how much Sylvester Stallone gets paid, the foundation of any successful film will always be a good, well-written story. A bad movie can be made out of a good script but never the reverse. Hollywood will always need the screenwriter.

5. Hollywood does have standards, and it is possible to know what those are and write screenplays that meet them. The most straightforward way is to look at successful movies and see what they have in common. And beyond that, to listen to the stated desires and needs of the people who are in the position of buying screenplays and making movies and TV shows. This book contains numerous checklists and outlines of those requirements and the methods for achieving them with your writing.

6. Commerciality and artistry are not mutually exclusive.

7. The screenwriting process can be broken down into a proven series of steps and stages which will enable you to achieve a salable, emotionally involving screenplay.

8. You can be a working screenwriter and live anywhere in the world.

9. You can launch a career as a screenwriter even if you don't know anyone within a thousand miles of southern California.

And finally:

10. You can make a bundle of money doing all of this.

Now before this list starts to sound like those no-money-down seminars, or those secret-way-to-riches ads at the back of *Writer's Digest* and *Family Weekly*, I'd better summarize:

If you want to decide whether screenwriting is a career for you, then do it on the basis of the reality of the work involved and the fulfillment you will achieve with your writing, not just on whatever delayed rewards may await you somewhere down the road. If you choose to pursue screenwriting on that basis, because it is your goal and your dream, you can empower yourself to do so by developing your own creativity, knowing what is required and helpful at each stage of the writing and selling process, and intelligently focusing on methods that have proved successful.

That is what this book will teach you.

Qualifications, Disclaimers, and Excuses

Finally, before launching into the meat of the book, a few words about my particular point of view in approaching this subject.

Even though working, experienced, living-on-the-beach-at-Malibu screenwriters can find value in the enclosed information and principles, I'm assuming that most of you reading these pages are beginning writers attempting to *launch* a career in feature films and television. Therefore the book is geared toward the screenwriter in the early stages of his or her* career. Certainly the book will be helpful to anyone writing screenplays, even if you've sold a dozen.

But don't worry if you've never even *read* a screenplay, let alone tried to write one. By the time you finish the book you will have sufficient information to know how to complete a screenplay, starting at square 1, and how to market it when it's done.

Similarly, though the principles included (particularly the artistic ones) apply to nearly all films and screenplays, many of the commercial considerations do not apply to established filmmakers.

If you are in fact at the early stages of your screenwriting career, you must understand that principles which apply to Woody Allen, William Goldman, and John Hughes do not necessarily apply to you. Particularly in the arena of commerciality, there are certain criteria, standards, and restrictions to which you must adhere, restrictions that those established filmmakers can ignore.

Woody Allen can write any screenplay he wishes and get it

---

* That's about the last time I'm going to use the phrase *his or her*. I think to say *his* all the time is sexist, and to always say *their* is grammatically incorrect (and poor grammar looks bad in a writing book). To always say *her* would be confusing and distracting. So from now on I'll just randomly use both masculine and feminine pronouns and hope the distribution evens out by the end of the book. Besides, it will keep you on your toes.

made. *Zelig* is a terrific film. But it is not a screenplay that would serve a novice screenwriter well in attempting to launch her career. Usually, those ground-breaking exceptions to the principles and standards outlined here, those films on the cutting edge of cinematic achievement, were written by established writers. Until you are in that situation, and can call your own shots, you must give much greater consideration to the tried and true rules of screenwriting.

This book also assumes that you are pursuing the American (U.S. or Canadian) film market, so the rules and standards for screenwriters working for the markets in France, Germany, Japan, or India do not necessarily apply to you. If you are a screenwriter in England or Australia, almost all of the writing principles will apply to your work, but some commercial considerations will differ, and you will need to research the current screenwriting market in your own country in choosing your story concepts and marketing methods.

To illustrate the principles I outline, I will be using American movies made within the last decade or two. Even though *Casablanca* can still turn everyone to mush, my assumption is that if you are reading this book, you are pursuing a screenwriting career today, and principles and commercial considerations apply to you that might not apply to screenwriters writing in other countries or other eras.

The book outlines screenwriting for what I call "mainstream film and television": fictional feature films that are distributed nationally, prime-time (network and cable) TV movies and episodic series, and short fictional films. We're not talking about documentaries, industrials, Saturday animation, daytime soaps, commercials, news, sports, or weather. But again, the goal of *all* of those forms is to create an emotional response in the audience, so many of the principles will overlap.

I will talk a lot about Hollywood in this book. By *Hollywood* I do not mean the city in southern California that could make Sodom and Gomorrah blush. Rather I mean the power structure and purse strings of the film industry. So if you're pursuing Hollywood, it could mean that you're approaching an investment group in Des Moines.

Finally, this book is filled with personal opinions. The principles which constitute good screenwriting can be verified by looking at those movies which have been commercially and financially successful by virtue of their box office returns or Nielsen ratings, or by looking at films which have garnered awards, strong word of mouth, cult standing, et cetera. But emotional response is purely personal, and in talking about how movies have succeeded in creating emotion, I'm obviously talking to a great extent about how they created an emotional response in me. So don't be overly concerned with your agreement or disagreement with my evaluation of a film. Focus on using the examples to increase your understanding of how the principles involved apply. And in turn, you should repeatedly verify the principles I outline by using your *own* favorite movies, those which created a positive emotional response in you.

Use and enjoy this book in whatever way is most helpful to you. Read it through once, then focus on the sections where you're feeling weakest. Or use the checklists after you have done one or two drafts of that facet of your own script. Or read the book just to decide if screenwriting is for you. Or lay it on your coffee table to convince the woman down the hall that you really *are* in show business. Or put it under the short leg of your typewriter stand to keep it from wobbling.

But at some point, put the book away. Screenwriting books, like screenwriting classes, run the risk of becoming a substitute for writing rather than a supplement to it. It's better to attempt your own screenplay, then go back to this book and its checklists after each draft. Then read other screenwriting books or take a writing class to get additional points of view prior to each screenplay you write.

In other words, somewhere along the line you've got to trust that you have enough information. Then you must call on all your courage, get out some paper, dig into your soul, and start writing.

Enjoy.

PART I

DEVELOPING THE STORY

CHAPTER 1

■ ■

The Goal of the Screenwriter

People do not go to the movies so they can see the characters on the screen laugh, cry, get frightened, or get turned on.

They go to have those experiences themselves.

The reason that movies hold such a fascination for us, the reason the art form has been engrossing and involving audiences for close to a century, is because it provides an opportunity to *experience emotion*. Within the safety and isolation of a darkened theater or in the privacy or comfort of one's own home it is possible to leave the real world behind or at a safe distance and experience emotions, thoughts, feelings, and adventures that would not be encountered in everyday life. In watching a movie or television show, we can experience the love, the hate, the fear, the passion, the excitement, or the humor that elevates our lives, but in a safe, controlled setting.

All filmmakers, therefore, have a single goal: to elicit emotion in an audience. Every director, every actor, every gaffer, and every production assistant has as his ultimate objective to elicit an emotional response from the audience. On the most basic level, when the movie creates that emotion in an audience, it is successful; when it doesn't, it fails.

The Primary Goal of the Screenwriter

The primary goal for the screenwriter is even more specific: *The screenwriter must elicit emotion in the person who reads the screenplay.*

The effect of a screenplay on a reader must be the same as the effect of the movie on the audience: to create an emotional experience. All of the stated considerations of commerciality, big stars, hot topics, low budgets, high concepts, and strong demographics go out the window if this single objective is not achieved.

If the producer, executive, agent, or star who can get your movie made doesn't smile, laugh, cry, get scared, get excited, or get turned on while reading your screenplay, then your script will never reach a real audience.

In other words, for the screenwriter, the term *reader* and the term *audience* are synonymous.

This book is about how to elicit that emotional response in a reader with your screenplay. From now on, whenever the book employs the word *audience*, translate that to mean *reader*, and vice versa. Every page of this book is designed to increase your ability to elicit emotion in a reader and in an audience and to make money with that ability.

How to Write a Screenplay in One Easy Lesson

Understanding what a screenplay needs to accomplish is simple; I can tell it to you in one sentence: *Enable a sympathetic character to overcome a series of increasingly difficult, seemingly insurmountable obstacles and achieve a compelling desire.*

That, in about two dozen words, is what almost every successful feature film has ever done. The few exceptions are those films where the character *fails* to achieve the compelling desire, as in *One Flew Over the Cuckoo's Nest* or *Out of Africa,* or a film where the hero learns that his compelling desire is a mistake, as in *Wall Street* or *Raising Arizona.* But the essence of all successful movies is still the same.

The difficulty is not in understanding what you must accomplish as a writer. Obviously, the tough part is knowing *how* to per-

form each of the facets of that objective. How do you make a
character sympathetic? How do you establish a compelling desire?
How do you create and arrange the series of hurdles that must be
overcome? How do you write this in such a way that the emotional
involvement of the reader is ensured?

And finally (and probably the reason you bought this book),
how do you make money doing all of this?

The Four Stages of Any Screenplay

Every aspect of writing your screenplay will be contained in one of
the following four stages:

1. **The Story Concept.** This is the single sentence that tells who
the hero of the story is and what he or she wants to accomplish.

2. **The Characters.** Obviously, these are the people who populate the story.

3. **Plot Structure.** This pertains to the events of the story and
their relationship to one another. In other words, this stage in the
process determines what happens in the story and when it happens.

4. **The Individual Scenes.** This stage pertains to the way the
words are laid out on the page: how one puts the screenplay in
proper format and how one writes the kind of action, description,
and dialogue that will increase the reader's emotional involvement.

This book will outline each of those four facets in detail, in the
above order. There are a couple reasons for doing this:

Beginning with a single-sentence story concept and developing
that into a full, 115-page screenplay is one way to write your
screenplay. It is very organized, logical, and left-brained. If you
are a very organized, logical and left-brained writer, or strive to be
one, it can be a very effective way of writing your own script. It is
a building process which allows each expanded phase of the
screenplay to grow out of the previous one.

Its big advantage is in its safety, so to speak. Since each step
logically proceeds from the previous one and since the book pro-

vides detailed instructions on what to do at each step, then the fear of moving into unknown waters of creativity is lessened by the preparation and security of the previously completed stages.

However, this logical, step-by-step approach is not the *only* way to write a screenplay. Of equal value, depending on what works for you, is the more free-form, right-brained method of putting a piece of paper in the typewriter (or booting the computer), typing FADE IN, and then simply seeing where the story takes you. In other words, letting the story "write itself."

Like any other journey of unknown destination, what you sacrifice in safety and security, you may get back in excitement and creativity. These unknown waters may enable you to tap into your unfettered creativity more easily and provide a more effective, fulfilling screenwriting experience.

I know about an equal number of writers who use the first method as use the second, each equally effective depending on the writer's methods and desires. The key is to use whatever method, or combination of the two, works for you.

But regardless of the approach you choose, sooner or later you're going to have to pay the piper. With either approach, the outcome must be a screenplay which effectively elicits emotion because the concept, characters, structure, and scenes are all excellent.

This book is going to give you a foundation from which you can depart in whatever direction improves your ability to get the screenplay written. If something's working, keep using it; if it's not working, find something better. My goal is to give you a method that prevents you from getting blocked at any stage of the process.

The second reason for using this method is that it is more conducive to teaching the process, since it takes things in a logical order, with each step growing out of the previous phase of the writing process. If I used a free-form, go-where-the-spirit-moves-me approach to *writing* this book, then the table of contents would be a mess.

Brainstorming, Editing, and Writer's Block

Throughout the process outlined in this book, you will repeatedly encounter words such as *brainstorming* or phrases such as *stimulating your own thinking*. There are periods of creativity within each of the four stages of your screenplay which require you to eliminate your critical and judgmental faculties in order to nurture your creativity. In other words, there are periods where you want to go for quantity and not quality, when you want to give your creativity free rein to extend its limits without fear of censure or criticism.

It is only after you have allowed your creativity to blossom through the nonjudgmental, brainstorming phase that you enter the editing phase of screenwriting. This is the critical, evaluative phase that will determine which of the multitude of ideas that your brainstorming generates will best serve your screenplay.

Art Arthur, who was a screenwriter for forty-five years, used to say that there are two secrets to success as a screenwriter. You'll have to wait until the end of the book to get the second one, but his first secret of screenwriting success was simply this: *Don't get it right, get it written.*

If you wait for something to be perfect before you write it, it's never even going to be good. You'll become so frozen with fear and judgment that you'll eventually give up on the entire process and start buying books on real estate. In other words, you'll become *blocked.*

Writer's block is the flip side of brainstorming. *Brainstorming* gives the mind freedom to go in whatever direction it chooses, holding back criticism and judgment so the writer can freely tap into her own creative source. *Block* is when the mind isn't going in any direction—creative impotence.

Writer's block doesn't mean that you are sitting at your typewriter, staring at the page for fifteen minutes until you find the line of dialogue that works best. Block is when you haven't worked on your screenplay in two weeks, and now you are watching *Wheel of Fortune* and eating Ding-Dongs instead of writing.

Block is the great pitfall of the writing process because it means that nothing at all is happening. And it possesses the added insidious talent of feeding on itself, so that the longer it continues, the less the chance of escape.

Therefore, even if you choose to follow the logical, ordered, step-by-step process of writing your screenplay which is outlined in this book, you will still need to depart from it occasionally and jump around a bit.

For example, there might be situations where you are working on the character development stage of your script, but you just can't get a handle on who your villain will be. Instead of waiting for perfection and blocking yourself, a better solution would be to jump over to the scene writing stage. If you know there's going to be a terrific confrontation between your hero and the bad guy, and you know how that scene should look, then go ahead and write it. Writing the scene will then reveal to you things about each of those two characters that you can take back to the character development stage in order to reprime your pump and keep the story flowing.

Similarly, working on story structure may reveal a need to go back to your original concept and give it greater depth or originality, or to lay in more background on your hero, and so on.

Eventually, the four stages of your screenplay will only form a general pattern, and you will actually be jumping all over the map in order to ensure the flow of ideas and creativity, alternating between your nonjudgmental brainstorming and your selective editing. This will both prevent writer's block and maximize your ability to elicit emotion in the reader and the audience.

Summary

1. The primary goal of any filmmaker is to elicit emotion in the audience.

2. The primary goal of the screenwriter is to elicit emotion in the person reading the screenplay.

3. In order to succeed, your screenplay needs to accomplish the following objective: enable a sympathetic character to overcome a series of increasingly difficult, seemingly insurmountable obstacles and achieve a compelling desire.

4. The four stages of any screenplay are:

Story concept

Characters

Plot structure

Individual scenes

5. The great pitfall of screenwriting is writer's block, which is rooted in fear of failure and desire for perfection. To prevent block, alternately brainstorm for a quantity of ideas and edit for quality.

CHAPTER 2

. . . .

Story Concept

My first job in the film industry was as a reader (aka story analyst) for a major Hollywood literary agent. This meant that it was my responsibility to read, evaluate, and write synopses for the numerous screenplays and novels which had been submitted to the agent for representation or for one of his acting clients.

When I reported for work on my first day, the agent told me, "Ninety-nine out of every hundred screenplays you read won't be worth considering. I just want you to find that one out of a hundred."

When I heard this, I thought the guy was either joking or awfully cynical. Being new to the business and just off the turnip truck from Oregon, I naively assumed that at least half of the people who would go to all the trouble of writing a screenplay would have *something* that had potential or showed writing talent, even if the screenplay wasn't fully realized. Giving the agent the benefit of the doubt, I figured at least 25 percent would be decent or worth further consideration.

I was wrong.

I discovered, after I had read a few hundred scripts myself, that if anything the agent had been too generous. It was a rare day indeed when I could give a screenplay even a mild recommendation.

Of the ninety-nine out of a hundred screenplays that can't be recommended, ninety fall apart in one or both of two very basic ways. The first is format: the writer has neglected to learn the very simple, straightforward rules for properly placing the words on the page. We will discuss format in detail in Chapter 6.

The other overwhelming weakness with these ninety-out-of-a-hundred rejected screenplays is with the initial concept. Repeatedly, after reading a screenplay, I ask myself in amazement how the author could possibly think that the story *idea* would be of interest to anyone besides him and maybe his Mom. Had the writer even chosen a *concept* that had the slightest degree of interest, uniqueness, or artistic and commercial potential, he would have already elevated his screenplay into the top 10 percent!

In this chapter, we will discuss those qualities which give a story idea both commercial and artistic potential, and how you can create, discover, acquire, or select such an idea.

Finding and Originating Story Ideas

Every story begins with a question: What if . . . ? The writer thinks of a character, situation, or event and begins to ponder: What if such and such happened?

What if a third-rate fighter had a chance to fight the heavyweight champion of the world? *(Rocky)*

What if an alien from outer space were befriended by a young boy? *(E.T.)*

What if a newspaper tycoon's mysterious dying words were investigated after his death? *(Citizen Kane)*

Even in true stories, there is the same implied question: What if an unknown Indian pacifist came up against all of the forces of the British Empire? The fact that such a situation actually occurred provides the writer with a specific answer, but it is still the provocative nature of the *question* which gives *Gandhi* its artistic and commercial potential.

Either your What if . . . ? pondering will lead you to a plot situation (a skyscraper fire in *Towering Inferno,* a town terrorized by a shark in *Jaws,* ghosts and demons plaguing New York City in *Ghostbusters*) or to a character or characters (a billionaire who is a lovable drunk in *Arthur,* an indestructible cyborg from the future in *The Terminator,* a group of former 60s radicals in *The Big Chill*).

Then you will begin looking for either the character to best enhance your plot or the plot situation to best bring out the qualities of your character.

Expressing the Story Concept

Any story idea can then be expressed in a single sentence: It is a story about a _____ who _____ .

The first blank of the sentence is your character or characters; the second blank is the action. For example: It is a story about a swashbuckling pirate who tries to rescue his true love from an evil prince *(The Princess Bride)*. Or: It is a story about a romance novelist who tries to rescue her sister and falls in love with a soldier of fortune *(Romancing the Stone)*.

If you didn't sleep through your junior high school English classes, you probably recognize this as subject and predicate. (And you hoped you'd never have to hear those words again. Shame on you.) Every movie or TV episode consists of somebody (character) who does something (action). When you have united those two elements, you have a story concept which can be expressed in the desired sentence: "It is a story about a _____ (character) who _____ (action).

Actually, the sentence is more specific than that; every movie and every episode of any TV series is about a character (or characters) who *wants* something visible. It is a story about a woman who wants to grow coffee in Kenya and have an affair with a big game hunter *(Out of Africa)*, or it is a story about three sisters who want to keep one of them from getting convicted of attempted murder *(Crimes of the Heart)*, or it is a story about a wealthy coat hanger manufacturer who wants to befriend a bum *(Down and Out in Beverly Hills)*.

This visible motivation on the part of the main character or characters is the cornerstone of the entire screenplay.

Every facet of your screenplay grows out of this marriage of character and motivation. Story concept, character development, plot structure, and even each individual scene must contribute to the main character's motivation.

Motivation will be defined and discussed in great detail throughout the book, and I will show how every element of your screenplay connects to what the main character wants. *The importance of an effective story concept, clearly defined, cannot be overstated,* since every word of the entire screenplay will grow out of that visible motivation.

For now, consider the starting point of your screenplay to be the uniting of character and action.

Finding Story Ideas

As you've probably figured out, expressing a story idea in a single sentence is no big deal. Creating the character and action in the first place is a big deal.

On rare and glorious occasions, the muse will be sitting on your shoulder and a story idea blossoms full-blown into your mind. When that happens, take full advantage of the situation, nurture the ability in any way you can, and enjoy it while it lasts. But don't be discouraged when this spontaneous creativity fails to occur. Most of the time, creativity is not so accessible, and it has to be given swift and repeated kicks in order to originate workable story ideas.

To originate story concepts for your screenplays, it is almost always necessary to stimulate your own thinking by observing, recording, and reacting to all of the potential material that confronts you every day, and to use that material as a jumping-off point for your own brainstorming and creativity.

I strongly recommend investing in a 49-cent notebook that you can carry at all times. Then, whenever you are confronted with a potential plot idea, character trait, or situation, write it down. The more you develop the habit of regarding *all* your experiences and *all* outside information as possible story material, the better you will ultimately be at "creating" story concepts.

Notice that you are not to find and record only good story ideas but any possible ideas at all. This is the brainstorming phase of story concept, and you're going for quantity, not quality. We'll discuss evaluating the concepts later, but at this stage you don't want to block the process in any way by judging your ideas. Just start noticing, pondering, and recording everything.

Simply recording ideas, characters, and situations as they present themselves to you is not enough. You must also actively search for story ideas. In other words, when you don't have a story idea to develop, go to the following sources to stimulate your own thinking and originate potential story concepts:

1. Adaptations. Perhaps the most obvious source of story material is the adaptation of other fictional forms: novels, plays, and short stories. These have the advantage of providing you with an already-created plot, as well as the added commercial strength that may come from identifying your screenplay as an adaptation of a published or produced work. If you think your weakness is in originating plots out of whole cloth but your strength is in your ability to mold a story into screenplay form, then adaptations can be a good starting point for your material.

Adapting novels, short stories, and plays requires acquisition of the right to do so from the original author or publisher. So unless you have googobs of money, you're probably not going to get the rights to adapt Stephen King's next book. (If you do have that kind of money, give me a call and we'll discuss the meaning of the term *coproducer*.)

But fictional and dramatic works can nonetheless be a good source of material for even the less-experienced screenwriter of modest means, since not all books and plays are big best-sellers. It could be that the material you have found never achieved a great deal of success or that it is ten or fifteen years old—still recent enough to be contemporary—and all of the interest and enthusiasm that accompanied the work's initial appearance has now faded.

The original material might not even be very good. But since you are using it only as a starting point for your own screenplay, it still might be appropriate for you to pursue the rights to it. Most of Alfred Hitchcock's career consisted of turning lesser-known works of fiction into great movies.

There are some crucial principles you must keep in mind, however, if you are considering adapting a play, novel, or short story:

Great literature doesn't necessarily mean great cinema. This is a lesson Hollywood never seems to learn. The qualities which constitute good literature are not the same as those which make for good screenplays. Ignorance of this principle has accounted for an abundance of movies which are literal translations of highly popular or critically acclaimed novels and plays but which fail in their film versions.

Those qualities which usually bring a book critical acclaim include rich, textured writing; lots of interior thoughts, feelings, and descriptions; an expansive, convoluted plot; and an abundance of symbol and allegory. None of these qualities translates readily to the screen.

As a screenwriter, you are getting only two things from your original fictional source: character and plot. You must then use those as a starting point for developing a screenplay that will meet all of the criteria for an effective movie (criteria which you will know in detail by the time you finish this book). Your screenplay must have a style, mood, texture, and structure of its own. Don't assume that just because you love reading a certain book, an audience will also love seeing the movie.

You must be truer to your screenplay than to your original source. If, in order to fulfill the requirements of film structure and character, you have to alter or eliminate parts of the original material, then do it. Of course, you'll suffer the anger and resentment of all those people who loved the book. But don't worry about that; nobody reads anymore anyway.

The problem with most unsuccessful film adaptations is that they take liberties with the original material and then make it worse. The result is a movie that fails to meet the standards of either film or literature and ends up pissing *everybody* off.

Be very wary of adapting your own novels and plays. I strongly recommend against it, particularly if your original novel or play is unpublished or unproduced. If you originally wrote the story as a novel or play, it is probably because that is how you envisioned it, and that is the best format for the story. If you want to write a screenplay, find *another* concept that is best suited to film.

I can usually recognize within five pages whether a screenplay is adapted from the writer's own novel or play. The play adaptations are consistently "talking heads" scripts (with a few outdoor scenes thrown in), and the novel adaptations lack the structure of a well-written screenplay. Books are books and movies are movies, and with your own original work, you should keep it that way. If you truly want to write both, develop separate stories for each medium.

If you find a piece of fiction which you want to adapt, you must then track down the author or publisher (or their representatives) and negotiate for the film rights to their creation. Your ability to do that will depend on what you are offering: how much money (up front and upon production of the film); how much talent and experience; how much respect for the original material.

2. Contemporary True Stories. The next source of possible story material is the contemporary true story, such as resulted in *Born on the Fourth of July, Silkwood,* and the TV movie *M.A.D.D.* I am talking here about the docudrama, the depiction of an actual event in dramatic form, using actors, actresses, and a full screenplay. This shouldn't be confused with a documentary, which is a filmed but not dramatized account of an actual event as it happens, using on-site footage, photographs, interviews, records, and so on.

The adaptation of true stories is similar to the adaptation of novels, short stories, and plays in that each requires you to obtain the legal rights to do so and each carries certain artistic pitfalls that must be avoided:

A story isn't necessarily appropriate for adaptation for a docudrama just because it is true. Real life seldom conforms to the neat, single-thrust nature of a movie, with the appropriate positive or uplifting outcome. Often real-life events and situations just go on and on, evolving or dissolving rather than resolving. Proper film structure is frequently lacking from the original true story.

A true story is often more effective as a documentary or a news item rather than as a ninety-seven-minute TV movie. *Often a true story achieves its most dramatic and effective portrayal as a segment of*

60 Minutes or an article in *Rolling Stone,* and adapting it to a feature-length screenplay means stretching it too thin.

Again, you must be truer to the screenplay than you are to the original source. You have much less leeway to do this with a true story than you do with fictional sources. Even to maintain that your screenplay is *based* on a true story requires quite a bit of allegiance to the actual events. You should, however, consolidate or amplify certain characters and situations when it increases the emotional impact of the screenplay and doesn't sacrifice the overall authenticity and spirit of the original event.

Keeping these cautions in mind, true stories can be a strong source of potential film material, feasible for even a beginning screenwriter. Since many of the most effective true stories depicted on film are not about legendary or well-known figures but rather about everyday individuals caught up in situations which bring out their courage and humanity, the possible sources for real-life story material are numerous.

This is also one arena where living outside of southern California is an advantage. Development people all over Los Angeles scour the pages of the *Los Angeles Times* and the national magazines for story ideas. But if you're in Portland, Oregon, or Syracuse, New York, you can be privy to stories of personal courage long before they make the NBC *Nightly News.*

Adapting a true story requires that you contact those involved in the event and negotiate for the rights to their life stories in the same way you would for the rights to a novel.

An added commercial benefit to adaptations of true stories is the ongoing appeal of the docudrama to television. The true story has been the backbone of any year's TV movie schedule since *Brian's Song. The Burning Bed, I Know My First Name Is Steven, Small Sacrifices,* and *A Family of Spies* were all given added potential because they were based on real events. If your screenplay meets the standards for any other script, then the phrase "Based on a True Story" on the title page will give it added commercial strength.

3. Historical Events. A variation on the adaptation of contemporary true stories is the screenplay dramatization of a historical event. While all of the considerations and pitfalls mentioned above for true stories certainly apply to the dramatization of historical events, there are a couple of additional considerations as well:

When all of the principle characters in your dramatization are deceased, then there is no need to obtain rights to the story. This places most historical events, at least those from many years ago, in the public domain category. If there is some question about the need to obtain rights, as when some of the characters in the story are still alive, then it is advisable to get legal help.

The greatest added difficulty with the historical adaptation is commercial. Except for miniseries, which is not an arena open to the beginning screenwriter, it is extermely difficult to sell a period piece to the studios or networks. This aversion to historical drama is based partly on cost and partly on the belief that audiences identify most strongly with contemporary characters and settings.

Using a single book as a source for a historical adaptation means going through the same process of obtaining rights as you would for a novel.

The strongest and most effective historical screenplays are those which involve some contemporary issue, theme, or plot situation placed in a period context. For example, contemporary issues of human rights and the morality of war are examined in the TV movie *The Execution of Private Slovik* even though the story takes place during World War II.

Often the best use of historical events is as a jumping-off point for a fictional story. You still face the great commercial difficulty of a period piece, but you will have far more latitude for giving the story both proper structure and contemporary application. *Amadeus, The Wind and the Lion,* and *Hoosiers* all grew out of such historical events.

4. Headlines. Story topics from newspapers, magazines, TV, and radio can provide an excellent springboard for creating your own fictional story concepts. Remember, at this brainstorming stage you're looking not for good story concepts but rather for any ideas, no matter how unlikely or absurd, that will get the creative juices flowing and might eventually result in something valuable.

With topics and headlines, you don't care at all about the facts or details of the original source material; you're going to take the subject matter in whatever fictional direction suits you.

The Karate Kid is an excellent example of how this process can work. The film's producer, Jerry Weintraub, saw a newscast about a boy in the San Fernando Valley who stopped getting picked on by the school bullies after he learned karate. The eventual story that grew out of this topic included a romance, an aging Okinawan instructor, a transplated high school student, and a climactic tournament. These elements probably had nothing to do with the true story. But the newscast served to stimulate the producer's thinking, eventually resulting in a screenplay that meets all of the criteria for an effective concept.

An even more effective use of headlines can result when you stimulate your thinking by trying to combine two totally unrelated story topics. Again, the goal at this stage is to achieve not a *good* story idea but rather a quantity of ideas, however absurd, which can in turn lead to others and stimulate further creativity.

Some time ago a headline in a Honolulu newspaper read GRAY LINE DRIVERS THREATEN STRIKE. Without reading any of the story at all, this might lead you in any of several directions, as long as you allow your creativity to roam freely. You might think of a story about a tour bus driver who goes on strike and the effect on her and her family, or you might consider a comedy about all of the bizarre jobs the driver must obtain to support herself during a strike, or the effects, economically and socially, on the children of a striking parent.

These ideas might in turn lead you to a story about economic hardship and its effect on children, which has nothing to do with strikes or bus drivers. Or you might pursue a strike story from the point of view of management or the tourists or a museum that was one of the stops on the tour, and so on. Your only goal at this stage is to get your creativity into fourth gear, so the further you wander from the original source, the better you are doing.

The same Honolulu newspaper also provided a good opportunity for combining two headlines. On the same day that the tour bus drivers were threatening to strike in Honolulu, another head-line read: HARE KRISHNAS SUED FOR $1 MILLION. In addition to brainstorming in many directions from that headline, it is worth-while to try to connect it to the earlier story.

The result might be a totally fictional comedy about a woman who inherits a small tour bus company. Because the drivers don't want to work for a woman, they go out on strike. At the same time that our hero is looking for bus drivers to save her company, a local religious cult must raise a lot of money for a pending lawsuit, so the members agree to go to work driving the tour buses, with hilarious results. (If anyone out there is interested in pursuing this obviously high concept, please give me a call and we'll talk option.)

The point of these examples is that the *process* of using head-lines as a starting point for your own brainstorming and lateral thinking is the real goal, because it will get your creative juices flowing. As long as you don't block, edit, or restrict yourself at the outset, the result can be a number of original ideas possessing strong potential.

5. Personal Experience. I have purposely put this category last on the list of sources for story concepts, even though the first piece of (usually misused) advice most writers get is, "Write about what you know." An old joke in the film business is that 90 percent of all screenplays are about someone who has just come to Hollywood to break into the movies, because that is what all of those screen-writers know.

There is a real danger in writing from personal experience, because most screenwriters just don't have lives that are all that exciting or interesting. Even though I am sure your first love affair was terrifying, passionate, glorious, and painful to you, it stands a good chance of being as dull as dust to the audience.

If you understand that piece of advice about writing what you know to mean that you should write about situations and emotions with which you're familiar, then you're on the right track. But the autobiographical screenplay, unless your life story puts Indiana Jones to shame, should usually be avoided.

The added difficulty with true personal experience is objectiv-ity. Being so close to your own life history can easily blind you to the needs of a well-structured story with believable, interesting characters. I repeatedly read scripts possessing severe problems of logic and audience interest, and the writers' excuses are often that the events really occurred. Sacrificing dramatic and artistic truth for historical fact is a great pitfall of the autobiographical screenplay, since blinding allegiance to what actually happened often destroys the possibility of proper structure and character development.

There is a much more effective and productive way to write about what you know. Use your personal knowledge and experience as a basis for a *fictional* story concept that gives you the freedom to meet all the criteria of an effective screenplay.

An excellent example of this principle is *Platoon*. *Platoon* is not the true story of Oliver Stone's tour of duty in Viet Nam. But the depth, richness, believability, and emotional impact of this fictional screenplay are obviously increased because the writer drew on his own personal experiences in the war.

If you've gotten the idea from this section that just about anything can be used as a source of possible story ideas, then you're right. Movies have been written that grew out of songs, song titles, myths, jokes, ads, and board games. The essential rule is that you never edit, judge, or block yourself as you search for, and record, ideas.

Selecting the Best Story Concepts

Searching for and recording What if . . . ? situations and characters should be an ongoing process that begins immediately and continues uninterrupted throughout your screenwriting career. But at some point you're going to need to select the single story idea which you will then begin developing into a complete screenplay. It is at that point that you will need to evaluate which ideas possess real potential and what qualities can be added to your initial ideas to make them fully realized story concepts.

I am talking here about both artistic and commercial potential. When deciding which ideas to pursue and develop into full screenplays or when deciding whether your terrific idea really is terrific, you must consider both.

Commercial potential is a fairly easy term to define. Generally it means that the motion picture based on your screenplay will earn more money than it costs to make it, promote it, and exhibit it. In other words, enough people will line up or tune in to see it to allow it to turn a profit.

More appropriate for you as a screenwriter, commercial potential means that the screenplay possesses qualities that will make the Hollywood agent, producer, star, or investor *think* that it can get made and turn a profit, thereby increasing the chances that this particular story concept can lead to a screenwriting deal for you.

Artistic potential is tougher to define. On one level, it means that the screenplay will succeed on its own terms and will fulfill whatever internal goals it has set out to accomplish in terms of plot, character, and theme. Beyond that, the artistic goals of the screenplay should be worth pursuing in the first place; a script could totally fulfill its goal of showing how to make a cheese sandwich, but that doesn't necessarily constitute artistic success.

Artistic potential implies the possibility of awards, critical acclaim, strong acceptance by some select audience, and so on. In other words, if a movie wins the New York Film Critics award and makes $14 at the box office, it had artistic potential. If it cost $14 million to produce and made $140 million at the box office, it had commercial potential. Artistic success is a matter of opinion; commercial success is a matter of dollars and cents. *One Trick Pony* was (I believe) an artistic success; *Friday the 13th* was (without question) a commercial success.

The following checklist contains those criteria you can use for evaluating a story concept at periodic intervals throughout the writing of the screenplay. The list is presented in order of priority, with the most important considerations given first.

Story Concept Checklist

The first five items are *essential* for both artistic and commercial success. *No movie can succeed without these five qualities:*

1. A hero. The story must possess at least one hero: a main character, who is on screen most of the time, whose visible motivation drives the plot, and with whom the audience is deeply involved. The hero can be a man, woman, boy, girl, or android, as long as this character (or characters) is the central focus and driving force of the story.

2. Identification. The reader must identify with the hero. That is, the reader must put herself in the shoes of the hero emotionally; she must experience emotion *through* that character. This does not mean that the hero is without flaws, shortcomings, or strongly negative qualities; often the opposite is true. It only means that there is sufficient sympathy and empathy with the hero that emotion will be elicited from the reader and from the audience through that character.

How one creates this emotional identification with the hero will be discussed at great length in Chapter 3.

3. Motivation. There must be a clear, specific, visible motivation or objective which the hero hopes to achieve by the end of the story. You can't just have your hero shuffle through life and call that a movie; you have to create something within the plot that the hero wants. That objective, in fact, is what your movie is about. Whether it's finding the treasure, getting the girl, stopping the killer, or winning the race, the hero's goal is what drives your plot forward.

Again, this desire on the part of your hero or heroes is the cornerstone of your entire screenplay. Not only is it necessary for creating an effective story concept but it is equally important to character development, plot structure, and each individual scene. In other words, there is no facet of writing your screenplay that doesn't hinge on your hero's motivation, and this motivation will be discussed in detail in each of those sections of the book.

By this stage in the development of your screenplay, the story concept *must* be expressed in terms of hero and motivation. Instead of "a story about the trials and tribulations of a depression-era farm woman," the concept should be expressed as, "a story about a depression-era farm woman *who wants to save her farm by growing cotton*" *(Places in the Heart)*. Or, "It is a story about a successful but uneducated clothing manufacturer *who wants to attend college with his son*" *(Back to School)*.

Putting the story concept in this form will better enable you to evaluate its potential with regard to the remaining items on this list.

4. Obstacles. The hero must face serious challenges, hurdles, and obstacles in pursuing his motivation. *Something* has to stand in the way of reaching the objective or there is no conflict and no movie.

By serious obstacles I mean challenges that are serious to the hero. If you write a screenplay about a 23-year-old woman who wants to be a police officer but is illiterate, that obstacle will be *very* serious to your hero, and that will make it serious (through identification) to the audience, even if they already know how to read.

5. Courage. In facing these challenges, hurdles, and obstacles in pursuit of his motivation, there must be the need for the hero to exhibit courage. This can be either physical courage or emotional courage or both. If nothing is at stake for the hero or if the hero does not regard the challenges as frightening on some level, the story will not work and the audience will not be emotionally involved.

Whether your hero ultimately *finds* whatever courage is necessary remains to be resolved by your screenplay; that is what the audience will stick around to find out. But creating the need for the hero to somehow muster that courage is essential.

The first five items listed above *must* be present in any screenplay for it to succeed either artistically or commercially.

The next items on the checklist are primarily commercial. These items have indicated greater potential for commercial success, greater likelihood that people will line up or tune in to see a film based on such a story concept.

Even more important, these are the qualities that agents, studio and network executives, producers, stars, and financiers seem to currently prefer in the screenplays they choose to develop, purchase, and produce. In other words, the more of these criteria that are met by your story concept, the fewer the hurdles *you* will have to overcome in getting it sold.

6. A high concept. *High concept* is a film industry term that gets tossed around fairly frequently and seems to take on a variety of definitions. Basically, it means that the story idea alone is sufficient to attract an audience, regardless of casting, reviews, and word of mouth.

If that single sentence describing your story idea (It is a story about a _____ who wants to _____) is enough all by itself to get people to line up or tune in to see the movie, then it has a high concept. High concept movies are those whose titles, newspaper ads, or *TV Guide* descriptions convey the promise of sex, violence, humor, or (particularly in television) some hot or taboo subject (nuclear war, incest, AIDS, and so on).

The best examples of high concept stories are found in television, particularly TV movies. Does anyone tune in to *The Dallas Cowboy Cheerleaders* and wonder what they're going to see? *The Day After, Something about Amelia, Oceans of Fire, Policewoman Centerfold,* and anything entitled *Portrait of a* _____ are all high concept stories. This doesn't mean that some of these films didn't have stars or didn't garner critical acclaim but merely that the initial audience for the movie was generated by the story idea alone.

High concept is becoming a much greater issue in feature films as well, with depressingly more producers and studios looking for story lines and subject matter that will attract an audience regardless of other considerations. If *War Games* epitomizes a high concept movie ("A teenage computer genius breaks into the Pentagon computer system and has to prevent World War III"), then *On Golden Pond* is the antithesis of high concept ("Two old people open up their summer home.") It was the promotion of the story idea alone that accounted for most of the initial audience for the first movie; it was the cast, the reviews, the word of mouth and the Oscars that led to the eventual success of the second.

   7. Originality and familiarity. Mentioning originality at all as a quality for commercial acceptance by Hollywood seems ludicrous in light of what is currently produced. Just look at the schedule of programs for any new TV season and *try* to find a wholly original concept. Or remove the sequels, remakes, takeoffs, rip-offs, and clones from any feature film production list, and it becomes evident that total originality scares Hollywood to death.

   Nonetheless, "lack of originality" is consistently a stated reason for the rejection by producers and studios of screenplays and story concepts. And it is true that while audiences seem to support "more of the same" in TV and theaters, people still want to see something they've never seen before when they go to the movies.

   As a screenwriter, you must therefore find some way to overcome this paradox and find a strong middle ground between never-been-anything-like-this-in-a-theater-before originality, and this-is-just-like-the-last-movie-I-saw familiarity.

   Your screenplay will be in big trouble if it is so original that your story concept is a total departure from what has consistently proven to be successful in Hollywood. The totally new, groundbreaking piece of cinematic art that you are dying to write should probably be postponed until your career is established sufficiently to give you the power and clout necessary to sell such a screenplay. Woody Allen had to make *Bananas* before he could make *Zelig*.

   In the meantime, you have to give executives and producers some precedent for the potential success and characters which have proven successful before. *Then* you can add the necessary elements of originality that will separate your screenplay from all the others and will give audiences some unique elements of plot, character, and theme to draw them to the film.

   Splash is an excellent example of a film that successfully combines familiarity and originality. Mermaid stories go all the way back to *Mr. Peabody and the Mermaid* and Hans Christian Andersen. But to this familiar situation, Lowell Ganz and Babaloo Mandel added the original elements of a comtemporary love story, evil scientists, and the mermaid's ability to transform temporarily into a complete human being.

All successful contemporary films draw on situations that have been explored before. We had seen lots of political thrillers, cop love stories, gangster movies, and war movies before *No Way Out, Stakeout, The Untouchables,* and *Good Morning, Vietnam* were released. Yet each of those screenplays added enough original elements or new combinations of familiar elements to take it to the top of the box office grosses.

Simply adding elements that haven't been seen before isn't enough to ensure success; these original elements to your story must be sufficiently provocative to entice and involve the reader. They can't just be different; they must be different in a way that will grab an audience.

Finally, you should be knowledgeable about any film that has ever drawn on a plot situation similar to that of your own story concept, so that when discussing your story idea, you can justify both its familiarity and its originality. And when you rip something off, rip off a winner. Saying that your story idea is the next *Heaven's Gate* is probably not your best sales pitch.

8. Second level of sell and subplots. These are both considerations that have to do with the depth and breadth of your story. *Second level of sell* is another bit of film industry jargon, only this one was only in vogue for about six weeks. However, its meaning and application are important in terms of giving your story concept added originality and depth.

A *second level of sell* is a second story line, of equal importance to your original story concept, which also involves your hero. It is a second, equally important, visible motivation for your hero.

The example I first heard cited by a network executive is a good explanation of how this principle can be applied to a story idea:

Several years ago, ABC was interested in developing a TV movie about weight loss: fad diets, exercise, Overeaters Anonymous, and so on. The network finally concluded that that plot line alone was too thin (so to speak) to sustain a full, two-hour movie.

At the same time ABC was trying to develop a story about an

older woman—younger man love affair (a notion that was much more original a few years ago). They finally decided to make the love affair concept the second level of sell for the story about weight loss. They combined the two plot lines, made their hero the main character in both situations, and gave each concept equal importance to the overall story.

The result was a story about a married woman with a weight problem who tries one method after another for losing weight, and is repeatedly unsuccessful. But when she then has an affair with a much younger man, who loves her in all her abundance, she is able to feel good enough about herself that the pounds just drop off (a diet plan that could easily put Weight Watchers out of business). This concept was eventually made into *A New Beginning* starring Patty Duke Astin.

Often, the second level of sell for a story concept will be the love story element of the plot. If *The Morning After* is about an alcoholic actress who wants to prove she's innocent of murder, the second level of sell is her desire for a relationship with the ex-cop who helps her. By adding this romantic element to the original concept, the story becomes much more provocative and possesses much greater potential, both commercially and artistically.

A second level of sell can also add originality to a story that might seem overly familiar if only the initial concept is used. A good example is *E.T.*, where two very familiar plot lines, "an alien from outer space" and "a boy and his dog," are combined and interwoven into a basic story concept and a second level of sell, resulting in a much more original, satisfying, and successful film.

A *subplot* is a secondary visible motivation for any of the characters in the screenplay. This story line will be of less importance than the original story concept but will run parallel to it and may or may not involve the hero. Subplots are added to give greater depth, texture, originality, and meaning to the plot and theme.

In the examples cited above, the desire of the hairdresser in *The Morning After* to marry a rich client is a subplot of that film; in *E.T.*, one of the subplots is the desire of the character "Keys," to capture and study the alien. These added elements certainly give the original story concepts even greater potential, but they aren't as important as the heroes' overall visible motivations, or the second levels of sell.

9. Familiarity of setting. Just as audience identification with the hero of your story is essential, it adds commercial potential if the audience, and reader, can identify with the *setting* of the concept—the time and place of the story.

This is one of the reasons contemporary stories which take place in urban or suburban America are so prevalent. Hollywood believes that the broad U.S. film and television audience will have a difficult time identifying with characters and situations which involve foreign or ethnic heroes, which take place in foreign countries (unless they involve transplanted Americans), or which occur in a time other than the present.

While this belief erroneously denies the ability of a skilled writer to create identification with *any* character in *any* period of history, it is one of the tenets of Hollywood and has to be considered in evaluating the commercial potential of any story concept.

Some settings may not be contemporary but have acquired greater familiarity through decades of film history. The old west, World War II, and outer space are all much more familiar to audiences than the Ming Dynasty or the time of the Spanish Inquisition.

10. Film category. Certain categories of film are currently very difficult to sell to Hollywood, and if your potential story concept falls into one of those, the struggle to get it sold will be greater. They are, in increasing order of acceptability:

> Musicals: All singing! All dancing! *Oklahoma*-type musicals are currently impossible to sell. Feature-length, MTV-inspired, *Flashdance*-type movies are not.

> Westerns

> Period pieces: This means anything pre-1970.

> Biographies

> Science fiction: The difficulty with sci-fi is that the big-budget special-effects films require more money than is usu-

ally risked on a newer screenwriter, and the rest are usually more metaphysical or abstract head trips and difficult to translate to the screen.

Horror films: The studios and networks will almost never produce original horror films. However, it is still a feasible way to obtain independent financing for a low-budget film, although the days have passed when any chop-your-body-into-hamburger movie could guarantee a profit.

There are, alternatively, certain categories of film which have consistently been strong commodities in Hollywood:

Action-adventure

Suspense thriller

Love story

Comedy

Drama

Or any combination of the above categories.

If your story concept falls into the latter group, it possesses much greater commercial potential.

11. Medium. It is crucial that you choose the best film medium for the particular story concept under consideration: feature film, movie for television, series episode, or short film. (If you are a beginning writer, you should not consider miniseries or pilot episodes for new series; those forms are developed by or assigned to established episodic or TV movie writers.)

Often, because of its lack of broader interest, its intimate nature, its familiarity, or its limited depth, a story concept will be more suitable as a segment of *Growing Pains, Murphy Brown,* or *Matlock* than as a feature film or movie for television. You must, based on your own story and your knowledge of what is currently in development in each of these categories, decide the best type and length of film to suit your concept.

Regarding the difference between feature films and TV movies, the best approach is to educate yourself to whatever is currently being developed for both arenas by reading *TV Guide,* the entertainment pages of your newspaper, and *Premiere* magazine. Then pursue the avenue best suited to your own story concept.

As a general rule, feature films are more expensive, more "panoramic," more graphic with regard to sex and violence, less formulaic, and more complex. *Dick Tracy, Total Recall, sex, lies and videotape, Havana, Brazil,* and *My Dinner with André* had to be made as feature films for those reasons.

Movies for television are generally more narrowly focused, more topical or issue-oriented, and more standardized in length, structure, and so forth. *Fallen Angel, Fatal Vision, Lois Gibbs and the Love Canal,* and *Mistress* seemed destined to be TV movies, by those criteria.

But there is so much overlap between these categories that a feature film will often be one which could have been a TV movie but was "elevated" to the big screen by the caliber of talent involved or by the quality of the execution. *Kramer vs. Kramer, Silkwood, Murder on the Orient Express, Ordinary People,* and *Roxanne* all have the topicality or high concept of TV movies; they became features primarily because of the artists involved in those projects.

12. Cost. While it isn't necessary to do budget breakdowns in order to be a screenwriter, you should have some sense of the cost of filming a potential story concept. Generally speaking, the more expensive the movie will be to make, the more difficult to sell the screenplay, particularly for a new screenwriter.

Five things make your screenplay more expensive to film:

Big special effects

A huge cast

Lots of exotic locations

A period or historical setting

Inclement weather

So if your screenplay shows the Mongol hordes thundering over the mountains of China in the snow to confront the alien space ship, you've probably just budgeted yourself out of a deal.

The thing you don't have to worry about is "above the line" cost —the fees for the major stars and talent who will make the movie. If you write a screenplay for a $3,000,000 movie and Dustin Hoffman wants to star in it, it will be a $30,000,000 movie. You should be so lucky.

Cost is purposely last on the list of commercial considerations, because generally speaking, if a studio wants to make your movie, they'll pay what it costs to make it. It becomes a more critical issue if you are pursuing independent financing, in which case a movie in the $1 million to $3 million range will be far easier to get off the ground.

Menachem Golen, president of Cannon Films, was once quoted as saying, "If a movie costs less than five million dollars and has a beginning, middle, and end, there is no way it won't make money." Of course, considering that this is from the man that brought us *Bolero,* I would take the quote in the spirit in which it was given. But generally speaking, the cheaper the film, the greater the possibilities for financing.

The final two items on the Story Concept checklist relate primarily to artistic considerations and do not necessarily add greater commercial potential. Many movies have been huge box office successes and many screenplays have been sold without exploring or developing these last two items. But in my opinion, stories that possess these two qualities are artistically stronger and more fully realized.

13. Character growth. Growth occurs when a character's search for courage results in greater self-knowledge, maturation, or actualization. If the story concept contains the potential for the hero to become, through the course of the plot, a better, more aware human being, then the artistic potential of the story idea is greater.

14. Theme. Closely related to growth for the hero is the notion of theme. By *theme* in a screenplay, I mean the universal statement the screenplay makes about the human condition. This is a level of meaning that goes beyond the plot of the film and applies to life in general. The theme is an idea that any member of the audience can apply to her own life, whether or not she's been in a similar situation. The theme gives the audience "words to live by."

Theme is not the same as the "message" of a movie. The *message* is a more political statement that connects directly to the plot, but has no obvious application to the average person's own actions. The message of *War Games* is, "The only way to win the nuclear game is not to play." The theme is, "If one moves toward the isolated and the technological at the cost of what is natural and human, tragedy will result."

Character growth and theme will be discussed in great detail in Chapter 4, and you will see how that particular message and theme were derived from the screenplay of *War Games*.

Artistry versus Commerciality

Consider, for a moment, *Chariots of Fire*. Other than a second level of sell, a subplot, and the combination of familiarity and originality, the story concept lacks every other commercial quality on the checklist:

1. It is not a high concept; a story about the 1920 English Olympic track team certainly didn't draw a huge initial audience on the basis of its one-line description.

2. The setting is not familiar or readily identifiable, since it is neither contemporary nor American, and neither are the heroes American.

3. The story falls into two of the taboo categories: period piece and biography.

4. It may not have even seemed the best film medium for the story; a documentary would have been more logical than a feature film.

5. The period nature of the story raises the cost.

Given all those considerations, it is no wonder the movie was such a failure. It only grossed about eleventy zillion dollars at the box office and only won umpty-dozen awards.

The point is that much of the time, Hollywood doesn't know what it's talking about. There are numerous films that fail to meet many of the above commercial criteria, yet attain immense success.

Nonetheless, the list is still valid, because we're talking about the potential for getting your story concept made in the first place. And *Chariots of Fire,* along with such movies as *Gandhi, One Flew Over the Cuckoo's Nest, The Killing Fields, Platoon,* and countless others, took years of struggle to get off the ground, and ultimately weren't produced by the major Hollywood studios.

While such exceptions to Hollywood's commercial standards are obvious and glaring, the above considerations have been shown over the years to indicate greater potential for big box office or high ratings.

These considerations raise an important issue with regard to your story concept: the seeming conflict between artistry and commerciality. It's pretty easy to become discouraged and antagonistic toward Hollywood's pursuit of the dollar and the rating point. Movies and television are often a cavalcade of slick mediocrity, attempting little and achieving less. And the big budget splurges on stars, special effects, and "sure things" always seem to be at the expense of story and screenplay.

Because the movies and TV shows coming out of Hollywood so often fall short of becoming anything moving, original, or meaningful, there is a prejudice among many writers against *any* commercial considerations. I repeatedly encounter the belief that any movie which strives for, or attains, commercial success is a superficial sellout.

This attitude is understandable but unrealistic and unfortunate. It is certainly possible, as *E.T., Chariots of Fire, When Harry Met Sally, Rain Man, Terms of Endearment, Roxanne, Platoon, Hannah and Her Sisters, The Big Chill, Kramer vs. Kramer, Tootsie, The Sting, An Officer and a Gentleman, War Games, Something about Amelia, Cheers, Hill Street Blues, The Wonder Years, M*A*S*H,* and lots of other movies and television programs illustrate, for a work of art to be both a commercial success and succeed marvelously on its own artistic terms. It is intellectual hogwash to maintain that any original or meaningful movie must be obscure, subtitled, or a financial failure.

As a potential screenwriter, you must accept this fact: if you want a *career* in screenwriting, you have to write movies that people want to see. It is certainly OK to write any movie you wish, but do not expect it to serve your career goals in the film business if only a select few people would ever pay money or tune in to watch it. You must (if you want to earn a living as a screenwriter) write movies or television series that have the potential to pay for themselves and turn a profit. Otherwise, you are writing only for your own personal satisfaction, with no realistic career goals in mind.

It is probably just as frequent a mistake to avoid *any* considerations of personal satisfaction or artistry and only pursue commercial success. This is even more unfortunate, because first and foremost, writing should be personally satisfying and fulfilling. Striving solely for the big bucks is just as unrealistic as disregarding commerciality altogether, because screenplays based on "hot" concepts which are devoid of any emotional involvement on the part of the screenwriter will almost never get sold or produced; the topic won't stay "hot," and the screenplay won't be that good. *Trixie: Portrait of a Teen-Age Nymphet,* or *Icepick in the Eye!* may sound like sure bets to make millions, but if you don't have any real love for such movies, then they won't make millions coming out of *your* typewriter.

To decide if any story concept contains the right combination of commercial and artistic potential, I recommend asking yourself the following questions:

1. Do I want to spend at least the next six months of my life working on this story idea? If the answer to this question is no, no matter how "hot" the concept is, go on to another idea. Otherwise you're in for six months of misery with little hope of a payoff.

If the answer to the first question is yes, then go on to question 2:

2. Does this story have commercial potential? This should be fairly easy to answer simply by applying the commercial considerations from the Story Concept checklist. If the story concept meets all, or all but one, of the primarily commercial items, then it possesses commercial potential.

If the answer to this question is also yes, then start developing the story, because you know it holds your personal interest and possesses commercial potential.

But if the answer to question #2 is no, then go on to question 3:

3. In spite of the fact that I know this story is commercially difficult, am I so passionate about it that I am determined to write it anyway? In other words, is this the story you were born to write, the one that's burning a hole in your soul and costing you sleep until you get it made?

If the answer to this question is no, then you should go on to another idea. Without that level of passion, it would be wiser to find a more commercial story to launch your career, and save this concept until you're more established.

But if the answer is yes, if you truly do possess that degree of passion, then you should go for it, for several reasons:

Writing should above all else be personally fulfilling, and you will gain the most pleasure and satisfaction from a story that holds your greatest emotional commitment.

Most screenplays don't get sold anyway. Rather, they serve as writing samples to get you other work. Commercial potential is not as important for a writing sample, and you will best exhibit your talent when you write from passion rather than just from mild interest.

Finally, *if you do a good enough job of writing a screenplay which grows out of your own passion for the story, then eventually you can find others who will share that passion, and the film can get produced.*

If you were to remove the sequels from the list of all-time box office champs, almost every remaining film took years of struggle and setbacks, as well as rejection by at least some of the major studios, before getting financed. This was true for *Star Wars, The Big Chill, Beverly Hills Cop, The Ten Commandments, Gone with the Wind, One Flew Over the Cuckoo's Nest, Platoon, Crocodile Dundee,*

E.T., and countless other blockbuster movies. Each eventually got made because its creators would not let their passion and determination die.

Modifying Your Story Concept

The Story Concept checklist is useful throughout the screenwriting process in helping you modify and develop your story so it meets more of the criteria on the list. Certainly you must, from the outset, turn your idea into a concept that meets the first five items: hero, identification, motivation, obstacles, and courage. You can also mold and modify your idea with regard to many of the other considerations:

1. If the concept is not provocative enough, can you add other elements to give it more immediate interest and a higher concept?

2. Can you combine the initial concept with another idea to give it a second level of sell or additional subplots?

3. If the setting isn't particularly familiar, could it be changed to contemporary America without destroying the other aspects of the story?

4. If the story is similar to other films, can you create elements that will add originality to the familiarity of the concept?

5. If the cost of filming the story seems prohibitively high, can the cost be lowered by changing the location or the period or by reducing the number of secondary characters?

In employing all of these story concept considerations, it is essential that the creation and development of your story and screenplay be an ongoing process. The criteria for story concept selection and development must be used very gently when first considering ideas, because at the initial stages, your concepts will of course seem ordinary or absurd. But if you keep returning at all stages of the writing process to this checklist, you can continually modify and build on the ideas and concepts you have selected until they become commercially and artistically successful screenplays.

Summary

1. Any story concept can be expressed in a single sentence: *It is a story about a _____ who wants to _____.*

2. The primary sources of story ideas are:

Adaptations of books, plays, and short stories

Contemporary true stories

Historical events

Headlines

Personal experience

3. *Commercial potential* means the ability to convince the people who make movies and TV shows that the movie of a screenplay will result in profits or high ratings.

4. *Artistic potential* means that a screenplay sets out to do something of value and can succeed on its own terms.

5. The five *necessary* elements for any screenplay are:

A hero

Identification with the hero

Motivation

Hurdles and obstacles

Courage

6. The qualities which increase commercial potential are:

High concept

Originality and familiarity

A second level of sell and subplots

Familiarity of setting

A commercial category: action-adventure, suspense thriller, love story, comedy, or drama

The proper medium for the story

Low cost

7. The qualities which increase artistic potential are:

Character growth

Theme

8. The three questions to ask before developing any story concept, in order to resolve any conflict between artistry and commerciality, are:

Do I want to spend at least the next six months of my life writing this screenplay?

Does this story concept possess commercial potential?

Even if it lacks commercial potential, am I truly so passionate about the story that I'm determined to write it anyway?

CHAPTER 3

. . . .

Character Development

Once you have selected a story concept for development into a screenplay, you must then create and develop the characters who will populate your story. As with all facets of screenwriting, your goal is to elicit the maximum emotional involvement from your reader and audience. While your initial story concept is evaluated on the basis of its *potential* for creating emotion and attracting an audience to the movie in the first place, the characters are the vehicles for taking the audience on the emotional ride you create. It is *through* the characters that your reader will experience emotion.

As with story concept, the cornerstone for the development of your characters is the hero's visible motivation. Just as the concept is defined as the statement identifying the main character and that compelling desire ("It is a story about a Navy flyer who wants to be chosen *Top Gun*"), so are all of the other characters defined by their relationship to that same motivation.

This chapter will give you the various components of effective characters; provide more specific methods of developing identification, motivation, conflict, and theme; and show you how to use those principles to create original, emotionally involving characters.

The Three Facets of Character

Any character consists of three basic facets:

Physical makeup: age, sex, appearance, disabilities.

Personality: intelligence, emotional makeup, and so on.

Background: everything that happened to the character prior to his appearance in the screenplay.

It is easy to see how these are crucial to your story. If you compare Rocky Balboa in *Rocky* to David in *War Games,* for example, you can see how each story would be changed and diminished if the characters did not differ as they do. David is young and fairly lacking in physical strength and possesses a somewhat nerdy personality. These things contribute to the degree of conflict in the story as well as the growth of the character, because if David were physically imposing, the hurdles he must face would not seem so great. It is his high intelligence that enables him to save the day and which gives the story its logic, originality, and interest.

Rocky, on the other hand, must possess a high degree of physical strength to give the story believability. But if he were as intelligent as David, so that other options besides fighting and breaking thumbs for a loan shark were open to him, the story wouldn't work. Further, each character's background is crucial to his overall makeup, the logic of each plot, and the sympathy and identification we feel for each hero.

You can examine countless other successful films and see how these three facets of character are consistent with the needs of the particular story. As the screenwriter, you must thoroughly understand your characters with regard to these three areas. If you don't know your characters inside and out, they will not function effectively in your story.

Many teachers recommend writing full biographies of all your characters, or at least the primary ones, before beginning the screenplay itself. At the very least, outline your main characters' lives from birth until their appearance in your story to ensure that you will know them at least as well as you know your best friends.

Even though much of this background material will never be revealed in the screenplay itself, your characters will function much more consistently, realistically, and effectively if *you* know the details of their lives.

At the outset, you will probably have a basic idea of at least who the hero for your story will be, based merely on the logic and dictates of the initial concept. You may also have a clear idea of who else will populate your plot and their physical characteristics, personalities, and backgrounds. But at some point you will need to know how to create a character from scratch.

There are two basic situations in which you might find yourself: (1) you will already have a character in mind, based either on reality (if it's a true story or adaptation) or on your original concept, in which case you must be sure that the character functions to maximum effectiveness; or (2) you will have to originate a character out of "whole cloth."

In either case, you will need to understand the categories of character and how each functions in the overall development of your story. I'll begin by outlining and examining the hero in great detail, along with all of the necessary considerations for that character. Then I'll go on to the other categories of primary characters (nemesis, reflection, and romance), and finally to secondary characters.

Developing the Hero

The *hero* of your story is that character (or characters) whose motivation drives the plot, who is the central focus of the story, who is on screen most of the time, and who is the primary means of identification for the audience. This is the character around whom the entire story revolves, making it essential that the hero be the center of attention, identifiable, and original. Since creating emotion in the audience is your goal, your hero must be the vehicle for leading your audience through that emotional experience.

In creating the hero who best suits your story concept, you must first determine those qualities the character should possess to suit the logic and reality of the basic plot. Then you must create the necessary identification with the hero for the reader, and finally you must add those individual facets to the character to make him or her original and provocative. Your goal is the interest that results from a character unlike any the audience has seen, combined with the emotional involvement that stems from audience and reader identification.

Creating a Rough Outline of Your Hero

You will certainly have some general idea of who your hero will be based on your story concept alone. There are certain qualities that are going to be dictated by the plot itself. If your basic concept concerns a woman gymnast, then the logic of the concept has already necessitated a certain sex, age range, and general physical makeup. If your concept is an adaptation of a true story, you will begin with an even more fully defined hero. Though you can vary and compress the truth somewhat even in a docudrama, at least 80 percent of your character will be dictated by the actual events you are dramatizing.

Let's assume, though, that you have no idea who your hero will be, and you have to create a character from scratch. What do you do?

First ask yourself, What limits are placed on this character by the plot situation itself? Must the character possess a certain age, sex, background, appearance, level of intelligence, or personality?

Then go to all of the sources outlined in Chapter 2 (headlines, true stories, personal experience), this time as a stimuli for character traits for your hero. As with story concept, the key is to brainstorm rather than edit; open yourself to lots of possibilities, no matter how seemingly ludicrous, before narrowing the focus of your potential hero.

Finally, *research* the area of your story concept. Whether you're doing a story about outer space, the old west, or a barber shop, read the appropriate literature and talk to the people (if possible) who have ever been involved in your story arena. Observing, interviewing, and researching can stimulate your own thinking and help you create and develop characters who suit your story concept and jump off the page for the reader.

As your character begins to take shape, you must then begin to focus on one of the most important functions of your hero: audience identification.

Establishing Character Identification

Identification with a character means that the audience, or reader, experiences emotion *through* that character. In other words, the audience puts itself inside the character emotionally to experience the story: if the character is in danger, the audience feels frightened; if the character suffers loss, the audience feels sad.

The audience and reader must identify with the hero of your screenplay. The methods for establishing identification are listed below in order of priority. Though your primary concern is with their application to the hero, these principles can apply to any other character in your screenplay as well, as long as these methods are used first and foremost for your main character.

1. Create Sympathy for the Character. This is by far the most effective and widely used method of creating reader identification with the hero. Often, in fact, the words *sympathy* and *identification* are used synonymously.

If you can get the audience to feel sorry for a character by making him the victim of some undeserved misfortune, then you will immediately establish a high degree of identification with that character. Examples of this device are so common that it is harder to find a film that does *not* employ this principle: C. D. in *Roxanne* is ridiculed for his big nose; *Gandhi* is first seen (after the assassination and funeral) getting thrown off a train because he's "colored"; in *Romancing the Stone*, Joan Wilder is alone and lonely, and then her sister is kidnapped and threatened; Gordy in *Stand By Me* is being ignored by his parents after his brother has been killed; *Yentl* is not allowed to study because she's a girl; Emma Greenway in *Terms of Endearment* loses her father, and her mother refuses to come to her wedding. Even in such a broad comedy as *Ghostbusters*, the hero loses his university position and is thrown out of the school before encountering the ghosts that he must eventually overcome.

The undeserved misfortune can originate either with a specific event (such as the shooting in *The Natural*, the husband's death in *Places in the Heart*, or the kidnapping in *Adam*) or with a hero's basic situation at the opening of the film (as in *White Palace*, *Full Metal Jacket*, or *The Verdict*).

In almost every case, the sooner you can employ this identification device, whether as background for your hero or as an early event in the plot of your screenplay, the more effective and stronger the audience identification will be. It is without question the most effective means of identification a writer can use.

2. Put the Character in Jeopardy. Closely aligned to creating sympathy for the character is getting the reader to *worry* about your character by putting her in a threatening situation. The Indiana Jones movies are prime examples, as each opens with a scene in which the hero's life is in great danger.

The threat of capture, exposure, embarrassment, or defeat can be similarly effective, depending on the tone of your film. *Robocop*, *Ferris Bueller's Day Off*, *Die Hard*, *Big*, and *Bonfire of the Vanities* all present physical or emotional threats to their heroes, thereby increasing audience identification.

3. Make the Character Likable. Getting the reader to like your hero will further strengthen identification, in the same way that in real life we sympathize and identify more strongly with those we care about. There are basically three ways to get a reader to like your hero, which can be used singly or in combination:

Make the character a good or a nice person, as with the heroes of *Norma Rae*, *Suspect*, *Crimes of the Heart*, or *Gremlins*.

Make the character funny, as in *Lost in America*, *Beverly Hills Cop*, *Nothing in Common*, *Radio Days*, or almost any sitcom.

Make the character good at what he does, as with the heroes of *Dirty Harry*, *War Games*, *Lethal Weapon*, *Tin Men*, or *M*A*S*H*.

You must employ at least one of these first three methods of establishing identification for your hero. Otherwise your reader won't care enough about your hero to remain emotionally involved in the story. And if you can use two or all three of the above principles, identification with your hero will be even stronger.

Additionally, you must establish identification with your hero *immediately*. Create sympathy, jeopardy, and/or likability for your hero as soon as she is introduced.

Only after you have established this identification can you begin to reveal flaws in the character. You can make a hero out of any character. Murderers, dictators, and child molesters have all been made into sympathetic heroes. But you must establish the identification first, before you reveal the negative side of your hero, or the audience won't maintain their identification with the character.

4. Introduce the Character as Soon as Possible. The audience is waiting for someone to identify with and root for. The sooner you get that person on the screen, the more effective the screenplay will be. It is hard to think of many films where the hero doesn't appear within the first ten minutes.

5. Show the Character in Touch with His Own Power. Power holds a fascination for an audience and creates identification on an almost fantasy level. We all would like to feel more powerful; through identification with a powerful character, we can.

Power in a character can take three forms:

Power over other people. This is illustrated by characters like J. R. Ewing in *Dallas*, Charles Foster Kane in *Citizen Kane*, and Don Corleone in *The Godfather*. Such characters connect with an audience not because they are likable but because their wealth, clout, and control exert a deep fascination, and there is a satisfaction in aligning oneself emotionally with the power they possess while distancing oneself from the evil or amoral actions they employ in gaining or exercising their power.

Power to do whatever needs to be done, without hesitation. The current popularity of heroes like *Rambo*, Arnold Schwarzenegger in *Commando* and *Raw Deal*, or anyone portrayed by Steven Seagal is not simply that the country has swung to the right politically but rather that these characters experience no ambiguity about their actions. They see what needs to be done, and they do it, regardless of the danger, the odds, or the political and moral implications. They possess a power over their own and other's destinies that the rest of us sorely lack.

When Rambo learns of the prisoners of war, his attitude is simply, "They have to be rescued, and I'm on my way." He doesn't care about politics, danger, or body count; he simply exercises his power. To an audience that feels increasingly powerless in the face of war, crime, pollution, the economy, politics, bosses, and the Internal Revenue Service, Rambo's power becomes irresistibly seductive.

Power to express one's feelings regardless of others' opinions is illustrated by many of Jack Nicholson's and Eddie Murphy's roles. They repeatedly portray characters who express anger, humor, or desire without editing it for social acceptance.

When Bobby orders the wheat toast in *Five Easy Pieces,* when MacMurphy stands up to nurse Ratchett in *One Flew Over the Cuckoo's Nest,* when the devil expresses his desire for the women in *The Witches of Eastwick,* or when Axel Foley yells at the hotel desk clerk in *Beverly Hills Cop,* the characters are expressing the power of their undiluted emotions. Such power is again seductive to all of us who worry about even raising our voices, and as such, it becomes a means of great identification with the character.

6. Place the Character in a Familiar Setting. The time in which a character lives, the place where she works, and her home and family situation all contribute to greater identification. For example, the Jessica Lange character in *Country* is a wife and mother who lives on a contemporary American farm. Obviously, this doesn't mean that everyone who identifies with the character has been in all of those situations but rather it means that the audience is likely to have known or heard a lot about people who are in such a setting. This would not be true for characters in a movie about a caveman or a Russian prince.

In a similar way, high school and college students, cops, doctors, secretaries, parents, and working stiffs are all easier to identify with than, for example, the characters in *Amadeus* or *Quest for Fire.*

Those two films depended on the other devices from this list for establishing character identification.

7. Give the Character Familiar Flaws and Foibles. This is closely related to both undeserved misfortune and creating a character who is funny. If your hero walks into walls like we all do from time to time, then identification can increase.

This is particularly true in the arena of social and sexual awkwardness. When Woody Allen's early comedies were achieving their success, I used to hear guys that looked like *Playgirl* centerfolds say how much they identified with his characters. I couldn't imagine how some 6-foot hunk could relate to the schlemiels Woody Allen portrayed, but I later realized it's because we all feel awkward around the opposite sex or in high-pressure social situations, so we will identify with a hero who suffers some of the same nervousness and embarrassment we do.

Those are the seven primary methods of creating identification with your hero. There are two additional ways that are unique to certain kinds of films and are used less frequently but still fall into this same arena:

8. The Superhero. The heroes of fantasy and adventure films, such as the Superman, Indiana Jones, or James Bond movies, tap into a viewer's subconscious and derive some of their emotional effect from the characters' similarity to heroes of myths, legends, and fairy tales.

Even if there is no real similarity between our lives and those of the heroes of these stories, we will identify with them on a fantasy level. It is our desire to imagine that *we* are performing the superhuman deeds of these characters that strengthens our identification with them.

9. The Eyes of the Audience. Identification is sometimes strengthened when the audience *only* learns information as the hero learns it. In a mystery, for example, the reader might only be given the clues as the detective gets them. *Body Heat* is an excellent example of the hero serving as the eyes of the audience, for we become aware of what's really going on only as Ned Racine does.

On occasion, a screenplay will include a character who is not the hero but who serves as the eyes of the audience. In coming-of-age stories such as *Honkytonk Man* and *Travels with My Aunt,* the story is told from the point of view of an adolescent who is observing the hero of the movie. And in *Sophie's Choice,* the hero is clearly Sophie, but the young man Stingo serves as the initial point of identification for the audience and the source of the gradually revealed truth about Sophie. The advantage of this device is to create immediate identification with the more familiar character, and then *transfer* that identification to the hero through the course of the film.

A good example of how effective and important these devices can be is *Tootsie.* Michael Dorsey, the hero of the movie, is actually a jerk, an actor who has little concern for the feelings of others, whose only interests are acting, picking up women, and saving face when caught in a line or a lie. Yet the audience is clearly made to sympathize and identify with him and overlook or accept his dishonesty and his self-centeredness.

The very first scenes of Michael (immediate introduction) show him rejected for a series of auditions, not because he is a poor actor, but because he is too short, too conscientious, or they don't pay attention to him (undeserved misfortune). We see immediately that he is a respected acting teacher (good at what he does), and is willing to help both Terry and Sandy (he is in that respect a nice person). He is also funny, lives and works in a familiar situation, and is in jeopardy of exposure when posing as a woman.

The combined use of all these devices within the plot is a sterling example of how a character can possess flaws, shortcomings, weaknesses, or negative characteristics but can still be the focus of reader and audience sympathy and identification.

Making Your Characters Original

After ensuring that your reader will identify with a character (particularly your hero), you must then give the character qualities that will add to her originality. A reader enjoys encountering characters he feels he has never seen before, who jump off the page and are not carbon copies of countless other characters from movies and television.

Just as with your story concept, your hero will draw on qualities that we have seen before in real life or on the screen; you don't want to create a hero who isn't grounded in some way in the reader's previous experience.

Indiana Jones is a literary and film descendant of Humphrey Bogart, Errol Flynn, Stewart Granger, Zorro, d'Artagnan, and Jason (the Argonaut Jason, not the *Friday the 13th* Jason). But these qualities are combined and supplemented in order to make the character something more than all of those others; Indy's hat, whip, job, knowledge, and relationships with women and children give him layers of originality that make him a unique, three-dimensional character.

Think of a clay sculpture. First the armature and the clay will identify the figure as human; then the details will be added that will identify the sculpture as a *particular* person. In the same way, when you create a character, you will draw on familiar qualities and identification devices to establish a common bond with the audience; then you will add the background material, personality traits, habits, speech patterns, attitudes, occupations, and appearance that will make that character original, unique, and entertaining.

There are several methods that will help you lay on these unique qualities for your character:

1. Research. The best device for fine-tuning your characters is extensive research of your subject area. If you are writing a movie about fire-fighters, then you should talk to lots of real-life fire-fighters, not only to get plot ideas but to observe individual personality traits as well. I have seen average heroes become unique and three-dimensional when the writers gave their characters the qualities observed in real people who existed in the same environment as their fictional counterparts.

2. Go against Cliché. Consider the epitome of a cliché character in the situation you have created. If it's a cop, the cliché would be a white male who is strong, tough, two-fisted, good with a gun, soft-spoken, a ladies' man, and a loner. If it's a nurse, the cliché would be a pretty, young, Caucasian, single woman. Then determine the opposite of that cliché, and incorporate those qualities into your character.

Here is where your physical makeup-personality-background outline (see above) can again be helpful. Go back through all of the traits you have assigned to your character and change each to its opposite. If your private eye is a 35-year-old, tough, good-looking, working-class male, make the character a 9-year-old rich girl who is blind.

Again, the purpose of this device is to facilitate brainstorming; you're not looking for good ideas, only ideas—quantity, not quality. You are altering your character to the point of absurdity in order to force yourself to be creative.

You will probably decide that a rich 9-year-old blind girl is totally inappropriate for your screenplay. But what qualities would such a character possess that could be incorporated into your hero, to make the character more original and interesting?

Perhaps the private eye could be a woman or come from a wealthy family or collect dolls or build doll houses or be blind or wear thick glasses or have some other disability or have a 9-year-old daughter or work part-time in a day care center or have a wife or husband who is blind or be hired to protect the blind 9-year-old witness to a murder.

You see? Once your brainstorming kicks into gear, the possibilities for originality are much more apparent.

One of the best examples of violating cliché is a TV cop who lacks almost all of the typical traits of that genre. He is married, polite, talkative, scared of guns, not particularly attractive, never gets into fights, and genuinely likes other people. Of course, I'm describing Columbo. One of the main reasons for the long success of Columbo is the way Richard Levinson and William Link broke the mold in creating their hero.

3. Play off Other Characters. You can often bring out unique and unexplored facets of your hero by pairing him with another character who is far different. If the next James Bond movie showed Bond protecting Punky Brewster, we'd probably see facets to the spy that hadn't emerged before.

Often, the story concept itself involves opposites being thrown together, resulting in greater depth and originality for the entire film. *Cheers, 48 Hours, A Fish Called Wanda, Driving Miss Daisy,* and *Pretty Woman* all employ this device in their basic concepts.

4. Cast Your Hero. Imagine a particular actor playing the role of your hero. (This device can also be used to create effective dialogue.) If your story is about a private eye, your hero will take on far more individualized traits if you imagine Arnold Schwarzenegger, Martin Short, Whoopi Goldberg, Jane Fonda or Pia Zadora in the role.

Never target your screenplay for only one possible actor, however. Putting all of your eggs in one casting basket will severely limit the possibilities of selling the script. Rather, you should imagine specific stars portraying a character merely to help make the character more unique, and then flesh out the character so that a wide range of possible stars could play the role. And never mention an actor's name in your script.

It is also true, of course, that both identification and originality will be added by the star who plays your hero. When an audience goes to see a Paul Newman movie or a Bette Midler movie or a Meryl Streep movie, the initial identification may have little to do with your screenplay. And those actors will each create characters like no others, due solely to their own personalities and talents.

But such a basis for audience identification has nothing to do with you as a writer. You can't leave anything up to the people who ultimately make your movie; you have to have it all on the page. Remember, if it doesn't get past a battery of readers who identify with your original characters just because of the way you've written them, then Paul and Bette and Meryl will never get to do their stuff.

This brings us to the final essential qualities for any character: motivation and conflict.

Motivation

Motivation is whatever the character hopes to accomplish by the end of the movie. Whatever your story concept, each of your characters must *want* something. These goals, desires, and objectives are what drive your story. This is the specific way, as is often stated, that character determines plot.

Most important, it is your *hero's* motivation that determines your basic, one-line story concept. This is the spine on which the entire plot, each of the other characters, and each individual scene will be built.

In other words, what your hero desires determines what the story is about. *Ghostbusters* is a story about a former university teacher who *wants to earn money by getting rid of ghosts. The Terminator* is about a waitress who *wants to escape a cyborg from the future who is trying to kill her.* The TV movie *Toughlove* is about two parents who *want to solve the problem of their uncontrollable, drug-involved son.* And one episode of *Newhart* is about Dick Louden *wanting to convince the people at his Halloween party that Martians haven't really landed in Vermont.* The story concept for *any* film or TV episode can similarly be expressed in terms of what the hero visibly hopes to achieve within the context of the movie.

Again, *this visible motivation for your hero is the most important element of your entire screenplay.* Every single facet of your script, from original concept to final draft, hangs on how clearly and effectively you create and develop the motivation for your hero. The problem with unsalable screenplays can almost always be traced back to poorly chosen, confusing, or nonexistent motivations for the heroes.

Motivation is not limited to the hero of your screenplay; as we will discuss, every character in your movie wants something. But I will first focus on the hero because that character's motivation forms the spine of your story and drives the plot. Then I will examine how the other characters all fall in line in relation to the hero.

Notice that the definition of motivation includes the phrase *by the end of the movie.* Characters can want all sorts of things in your screenplay, but their specific motivation is whatever they hope to gain by the time the story ends. Thus, in *An Officer and a Gentleman*, Zack keeps saying how he wants to someday fly jets. But that is not his motivation, because the movie is not about him attempting to do that. Rather, his motivations for that film are to become an officer, to have an affair with Paula, and to gain a sense of belonging. Those are the objectives that determine the plot and thrust of the film. "Flying jets" will have to wait to become the motivation in the sequel.

Motivation exists on outer and inner levels:

Outer motivation is that which the character visibly or physically hopes to achieve or accomplish by the end of the film. And, as I've purposely stated repeatedly, to the point of tedium, it is the *hero's* outer motivation which drives the plot of the story and determines the basic story concept.

In other words, outer motivation for the hero is the answer to the question, *What* is the story about? Solving a murder, winning the love of a beautiful woman, and holding a rich man's wife for ransom are all visible, plot-oriented outer motivations.

Inner motivation is the answer to the question, "*Why* does the character want to achieve his or her outer motivation?" And the answer to this question is always related to gaining greater feelings of self-worth. Inner motivation is a particular form of the character's desire to feel better about himself. Since this level of motivation comes from *within*, it is usually invisible and revealed through dialogue. It is also more closely tied to theme and character growth than a plot.

Comparing the two levels of motivation, then, reveals the following qualities for each:

Outer motivation	Inner motivation
Visible	Invisible
Desire for outward accomplishment	Desire for self-worth
Revealed through action	Revealed through dialogue
Answers question, What is this movie about?	Answers question, Why does he want to do that?

Related to plot   Related to character growth
                                          and theme

There is nothing particularly mysterious about this notion; real life works the same way. We all want to accomplish certain things, and those desires determine our actions: going to work, going to school, writing, going bowling, or spending time with a loved one. These are all visible outer motivations. But the *reasons* we go after these things can differ for each individual.

For example, your outer motivation right now is obvious: to read this book. This is the visible desire which determines your actions at this moment.

But your inner motivation, the *reason* you are reading this book, is impossible for me to determine without asking you. It could be to educate yourself; to be able to make a lot of money; to become a better writer; to cure insomnia. Whatever your inner motivation, though, it must be related to greater feelings of self-worth. Somehow, you believe that reading this book will enable you to feel better about yourself.

The process works the same way for the characters of your screenplay. For example, David, the hero of *War Games*, wants to beat Joshua, the NORAD computer system, at the game "Global Thermonuclear War." That is David's outer motivation. But the *reason* he wants to beat Joshua is initially to prove his ability at computers and eventually to save the world. These are his inner motivations, the ways his visible actions will make him feel better about himself, and give him greater feelings of self-worth.

Characters may not always be correct in believing that their inner motivations will bring self-worth. In *Stand By Me*, Gordy wants to find and report the dead body to achieve recognition, both from the town (by getting his picture in the paper) and from his parents. What he learns by the end of the movie is that the approval of others is *not* the best path to self-worth; self-worth comes from recognizing and nurturing one's own gifts regardless of others' opinions. His desire for recognition and approval is misguided. But as long as he *thinks* it is the path to self-worth, it qualifies as his inner motivation.

Similarly, many films are about heroes who believe that their inner motivations of revenge, greed, or power are paths to self-worth, and who learn otherwise in the course of the movie.

Outer motivation for your hero is an absolute necessity. It determines the story concept for your film; it is the cornerstone of your entire screenplay. Without a clear, visible outer motivation for your hero, you will have no screenplay and no movie.

Exploration of inner motivation is optional. All of your characters, including your hero, will have reasons for doing whatever they do, but you may choose not to examine their particular desires for self-worth.

Many successful films, including the James Bond and the Indiana Jones movies, do not explore the inner motivations for their heroes. We get a sense that these heroes like the excitement and are driven to do a good job, but the movies do not really examine this level of motivation in any significant way.

The important thing for you as the screenwriter is to get a clear conception of your characters' outer motivations and then, as your story begins to evolve, decide whether you are going to explore their inner motivations as well.

Later in this chapter you will see how inner motivation is also closely related to character growth and theme.

Conflict

Motivation alone is not sufficient to make your screenplay work. If Luke Skywalker says, "I want to overthrow the Empire," and Darth Vader immediately replies, "OK. We give up," you've got no movie. There must be something preventing the hero from getting what he wants. That something is the conflict.

Conflict is whatever stands in the way of a character achieving her motivation. It is the sum of all the obstacles and hurdles that the character must try to overcome in order to reach her objective.

Conflict, like motivation, exists on both an outer and inner level. *Outer conflict* is whatever stands in the way of the character achieving his outer motivation.

Outer conflict will be provided either by nature (as in *Jaws, Earthquake, The Andromeda Strain, St. Helens,* or *Krakatoa, East of*

Java) or by other characters (as in *Presumed Innocent, Scenes from a Mall, Misery, The Russia House,* ad infinitum). Many films, such as *Ghost, Splash,* and *Back to the Future,* involve outer conflicts for the hero provided both by nature and by other characters.

Inner conflict is whatever stands in the way of the character's achieving her inner motivation (if you have chosen to explore that aspect of your character). This conflict always originates from *within the character* and prevents her from achieving self-worth through her own inner motivation.

With inner conflict you begin to explore character growth, tragic flaws, and the like. Until the character can overcome her inner conflict, she will never be able to achieve the feelings of self-worth that are her objective.

For example, consider *Tootsie.* It is a story about an out-of-work actor who wants to pose as an actress on a soap opera and win the love of one of his costars. "Posing as an actress" and "winning the love of his costar" are, therefore, Michael Dorsey's outer motivations because they are visible, they drive the plot, they determine the story concept, and they are revealed through the action of the film. The hero's outer conflicts, which stand in the way of his achieving his outer motivation, are that he is really a man (conflict with nature), and if the other characters, including his costar, find this out, he'll lose his job and the possibility of winning her love (conflict with other characters).

The hero's inner motivation, the *reason* he wants to pose as an actress, is to achieve success as an actor; that is Michael's means of feeling better about himself and gaining greater feelings of self-worth. Posing as Dorothy Michaels will earn him the money to do a play, and more important, it will show what a great actor he is. Michael's inner conflict is that he doesn't know when to stop acting; this makes him dishonest and insensitive to others. He will never gain self-worth through the means he has chosen (acting), until he can become aware of and overcome his inner conflict.

The inner motivation is revealed through dialogue several times: he tells his agent what a great challenge this is, he tells his students how important it is to keep acting, and we hear him giving "lines" to women all through the first half of the film. The inner conflict is also revealed through dialogue: his agent tells him he's too hard to work with (insensitive to his directors), and when Jeff, his roommate, asks him why, if he can be a great actor and a great teacher, he can't just be himself, his response is, "What's my motivation?" Obviously, he sees no value in being himself, only in playing roles.

This inner conflict must be overcome before he is able to achieve the greater self-worth he desires and the love of Julie, his costar. A crucial scene occurs at the producer's party when Michael, as himself, tells Julie that he's attracted to her and would like to make love to her. Michael is "performing" the line that Julie had earlier told Dorothy she would like to hear from a man. The reason, at least thematically, that Julie throws a drink in Michael's face is that Julie had told Dorothy that statement sincerely, but Michael is just playing a role again and being dishonest.

This is the same reason that Sandy, near the end of the film, hits Michael with her purse when she learns he has been lying to her. Dishonesty, she tells him, is something she'd accept from a lover, but not from a friend. Friendship must be based on honesty and consideration, not lying and role playing.

It is only when Michael (through Dorothy) learns the value of honesty, and learns to grow out of and overcome his inner conflict and genuinely be himself that he is able to win Julie's love and friendship and thereby experience real feelings of self-worth.

This pattern is often used in love stories: it is only possible for the hero to win the love of the romance when the hero has realized and overcome his or her own inner conflict. *Roxanne, Working Girl, Pretty Woman, Tin Men, The Sure Thing,* and countless other love stories possess this typical resolution.

Developing the Other Characters of Your Screenplay

At this point in the development of your story, you have at least outlined the physical makeup, personality, and background for your hero; have found the means to create audience identification with the hero; and have added qualities and character traits to make the hero unique. You have also determined the hero's outer motivation and outer conflict and perhaps have begun to explore inner motivation and conflict.

But there is no such thing as a one-character movie, so now you must develop your other primary characters and your secondary characters. And all of them will be defined by their relations to your hero's outer motivation.

The Four Categories of Primary Character

In creating the other primary characters of your screenplay, you will be in one of two situations:

On one hand, you may already have a cast of characters in mind to populate your story because you've already thought it through, you're adapting a story from another source, or the logic of the plot dictates certain character types. In such instances, your characters will function most effectively if you know the basic function each fills in relation to your hero.

On the other hand, you may have your hero worked out but have no idea who the other characters in the story will be. Knowing the basic categories of primary characters is then helpful because you know you must originate people for your story who will fulfill specific functions.

The four basic categories for primary characters in your screenplay are as follows:

1. Hero. This is the main character, whose outer motivation drives the plot forward, who is the primary object of identification for the reader and audience, and who is on screen most of the time. As with all the primary characters, the hero must possess some outer motivation and conflict, while an inner motivation and conflict may or may not be revealed and explored.

2. Nemesis. This is the character who most stands in the way of the hero achieving his or her outer motivation. A nemesis can obviously be a villain in the movie but might also be an opponent, a rival, or even a good guy, as long as the character fits the above definition. While the killer in *Stakeout*, the evil prince in *The Princess*

Bride, and Al Capone in *The Untouchables* are obviously nemeses, so are Apollo Creed in *Rocky*, Keys in *E.T.*, and even Mozart in *Amadeus*, although those latter characters are not technically villains.

When creating your nemesis, it is important to remember the old maxim, "Good villains make good movies." The stronger and more formidable your nemesis, the more effective the story. Apollo Creed isn't just another palooka from down the block. The fact that he is the heavyweight champion of the world gives *Rocky* its emotional impact, because the challenges and hurdles he creates for the hero are so formidable. In the same way, Darth Vader's effectiveness as the nemesis of *Star Wars* arises from his ability to use the Force as powerfully as Obi-wan. And Arnold Schwarzenegger's cyborg character in *The Terminator* is an emotionally involving nemesis because he is seemingly indestructible.

The nemesis must be a visible and specific character, not a collective noun ("the Mafia"), force of nature ("cancer"), or quality of life ("the evil in the world").

The reason conspiracy stories are very difficult to write effectively is that the audience can't get its mind around a nemesis like "the CIA" or "the KGB" or "the phone company." One reason the conspiracy story *Three Days of the Condor* is emotionally involving is that the nemesis is a specific individual, played by Max Von Sydow. If your hero is coming up against "terrorists," then create a *specific* terrorist to represent the overall threat and serve as your nemesis.

Making your nemesis visible does not necessarily mean that the reader knows the identity of the person. In a murder mystery, for example, the audience may not know which character the hero is up against, but they know by the results of the nemesis's actions that there *is* a specific individual providing the obstacles to the hero's ability to solve the crime or stay alive. And the audience knows that when that character is revealed by name, the hero will have achieved his outer motivation.

You must also *show* the final confrontation between your hero and nemesis. Think about a Western in which the entire film has been leading up to a gunfight between the sheriff and the bad guy. Then all at once the sheriff runs into the saloon and declares, "You should have seen it! I shot him!" Nobody would sit still for that.

In most screenplays, this final confrontation is the climax of the entire movie because it is at this point that the hero either succeeds or fails to achieve his outer motivation. Even when this final confrontation occurs prior to the climax, as in *Body Heat* (where the murder of the nemesis occurs halfway through the movie) or *Jaws* (where the mayor is last seen before the three good guys head out to sea to find the shark), the confrontation remains a necessary element to the effectiveness of the hero and nemesis.

3. Reflection. This is the character who supports the hero's outer motivation or at least is in the same basic situation at the beginning of the screenplay. The reflection can be a friend, co-worker, sidekick, spouse, mate, lover, or any other character who adds support to the hero's objective.

Examples of characters who serve as reflections would be the Emilio Estevez character in *Stakeout* (who wants to help the Richard Dreyfuss character stake out the house to stop the killer), the John Candy character in *Splash* (who also wants his brother to have a love affair with Madison the mermaid), and Lowenstein, the DA in *Body Heat* (who is in the same basic situation as the hero—he's an attorney who "dreams of bigger things" and who "lives vicariously" through the hero, Ned Racine).

There are two main purposes for creating a reflection character in your screenplay. First, it adds credibility to your plot if your hero has help in overcoming the outer conflict (it is hard to imagine Daniel overcoming Johnny in *The Karate Kid* without Mr. Miyagi's assistance). And second, it gives the hero someone to talk to, making it easier to reveal background, inner motivation, inner conflict, and theme or to create anticipation ("Now here's my plan, Tonto . . . ").

4. Romance. This is the character who is the sexual or romantic object of at least part of the hero's outer motivation. When your hero's outer motivation includes as its objective winning the love of, or getting into bed with, another character, then that other character is the romance. Darryl Hannah, Ellen Barkin, Kirstie Alley, and Barbara Hershey play romance characters in *Roxanne*, *The Big Easy*, *Summer School*, and *Tin Men*, respectively.

Further, a romance must always alternately support the hero's outer motivation, and then be at cross-purposes with the hero's outer motivation. If the story is boy-meets-girl, boy-loses-girl, boy-gets-girl, then at first they share the outer motivation of wanting to be together; then something happens, and the romance doesn't want to be with the hero, so they are at cross-purposes; then they finally get back together and are again sharing the same outer motivation. It is the typical pattern for a love story.

A character is not classified as a romance just because there is sexual or romantic involvement between that character and the hero. In *War Games,* there is a clear sexual attraction between David and Jennifer, but she is a reflection, not a romance, because the movie is not about the hero trying to win her love. The same holds true for the spouses, friends, and loved ones in *Gandhi, La Cage aux Folles, Field of Dreams, Beverly Hills Cop,* and the TV movie *Adam.* A character serves as a romance only if the film is *about* the hero's motivation to win that character's love.

If your hero falls in love with a romance character, the audience has to fall in love with that character as well, or at least understand and sympathize with the hero's attraction. If the audience thinks the hero is falling for a real jerk, then sympathy and identification is lost for the hero, and the screenplay falls flat. We may know, for example, that the Michael Douglas character is headed for trouble when he has an affair with the Glenn Close character in *Fatal Attraction,* but we can understand why he desires her.

In creating your primary characters according to these categories, there are certain ground rules and qualifications you must understand:

1. Characters Must Be People. The characters we're discussing must be human or humanoid; a nemesis can't be an animal (unless it's an anthropomorphized animated creature), a situation (like the evil in the world), or a force of nature (like the fire in *Towering Inferno*). Nor can a reflection or a romance be any of these.

2. Inner Motivation and Conflict May or May Not Be Explored for Any of the Primary Characters. Usually, if your screenplay explores those levels of character development at all, it will be for your hero, adding inner motivation and conflict for the other primary characters as needed. This becomes especially important when developing character growth and theme, as will be discussed in Chapter 4.

3. It Is Not Necessary to Have a Character in Each Category. The hero is the only *essential* category. There is no nemesis in *The Killing Fields*, no reflection in *Amadeus*, no romance in *E.T.* or *Beverly Hills Cop*. You will always want to create at least one of the categories of primary character in addition to your hero; creating additional primary characters is optional and depends on the needs of your story.

4. A Character Cannot Fall into More Than One Category. If you say that your hero is "her own worst enemy," you are really indicating an inner conflict; she can't also be the nemesis. And a reflection can't also be a romance. One category per character only.

5. A Character Cannot Change Categories. Characters are defined by the way they function in the *beginning* of the film. When primary characters are introduced, their relation to the hero *at that time* determines whether they are nemesis, reflection, or romance characters.

It may turn out that the reflection ultimately opposes the hero, or that a nemesis isn't such a bad guy after all, but that doesn't alter the roles they play and the functions they serve in the film. The categories are defined when the characters first appear, which will always be by the beginning of act 2 (act definitions will be discussed in Chapter 5).

I get asked again and again if the nemesis can't become a reflection by turning into a good guy at the end of the movie or if the hero can't be his own nemesis, and so on. The answer is no, because thinking along those lines serves no purpose.

The function of these categories is to simplify the writing process and to bring your primary characters into focus so they will function more effectively. If you start worrying about switching categories, you're only going to muddy up the clarity and thrust of your story. Whatever the characters do in act 3, their categories remain the same, because this tool has already done its job.

When an audience sees a movie, they subconsciously ask themselves, "Who am I rooting for and what is she after?" (hero and motivation), "Who is she up against?" (nemesis), "Who is going to help her?" (reflection), and "Who will she fall in love with?" (romance). The purpose of these four categories is to guide you in creating and introducing characters who will meet the audience's expectations.

Even though characters can obviously change later in the screenplay, there is no advantage to thinking of them as changing *categories*. And because the categories are also important in determining and revealing theme and character growth (as we will discuss shortly), it is essential that each character fall into only one category.

6. It Is Possible to Have More Than One Character in Any of the Categories. There are two nemesis characters in *Lethal Weapon*, two reflections in *Ghostbusters*, and two romance characters in *Manhattan* and *The Sure Thing*. Dual and multiple heroes occur much more frequently. *Trading Places, When Harry Met Sally, Chariots of Fire, Driving Miss Daisy, Irreconcilable Differences, The Hunt for Red October, Lethal Weapon*, and the TV movies *When She Was Bad* and *Toughlove* all have two characters who fulfill the requirements for a hero: in each film, both characters are the object of audience identification, both are in a majority of scenes, and both possess outer motivations that drive the plot. Usually, each of the heroes in a dual-hero story functions as either the reflection or the romance for the other hero.

And of course, multiple heroes abound in episodic television: most episodes of *Hunter, Married . . . with Children, Perfect Strangers*, and *thirtysomething* provide at least two equal heroes.

The Big Chill, American Graffiti, Diner, St. Elmo's Fire, and *The Breakfast Club* are examples of *multiple* hero stories. Again, in these screenplays, each of the heroes fulfills all of the requirements of that category of primary character. In multiple hero screenplays, all of the heroes share one outer motivation, and each has his or her own separate outer motivation as well. Additionally, each of the heroes may serve as nemesis, reflection or romance for any of the other heroes. Thus, in *The Big Chill*, there are seven equal heroes in the story. Each shares the same outer motivation of wanting to spend the weekend together after their friend's suicide. But for the JoBeth Williams character, there is the added outer motivation of wanting to have an affair with the Tom Berenger character. So for her, he is the romance, her husband is the nemesis, and the Mary Kay Place character is the reflection (the other character who also wants to sleep with one of the men that weekend). For any of the other six characters, the breakdown would be different.

My strongest advice to those considering writing a multiple hero story is simply *don't*. Such a screenplay is hard to pull off, because multiple heroes tend to diffuse the focus of your story and make it confusing. It is also tough to sell such a screenplay, because it is often difficult for a reader to keep all of the characters straight in written form.

For newer writers in particular, the best approach is to stick to a single basic hero, nemesis, reflection, and/or romance and to maintain the dramatic and emotional thrust of the screenplay.

Secondary Characters

Secondary characters are all the other people in your screenplay, the characters you create to add logic, humor, complexity, depth, and reality to your screenplay after delineating your primary characters.

Let your secondary characters serve as many of the above functions as possible in order to keep each one as rich, unique, and emotionally involving as you can. But employ them only as needed in terms of your hero's outer motivations so you won't overload your screenplay with an abundance of walk-on characters who diffuse and complicate the plot.

I realize this section on secondary characters is pretty brief, but I've never seen a script that had terrific primary characters and then got rejected because the secondary characters were too weak. Create primary characters that function to maximum effectiveness and then create additional secondary characters as needed, and the overall character development of your screenplay will be fine.

Charting Character, Motivation, and Conflict

Now I will illustrate these principles of character, motivation, and conflict by filling in the chart below with regard to each of the primary characters in the film *An Officer and a Gentleman:*

	Outer motivation	Outer conflict	Inner motivation	Inner conflict
Hero				
Nemesis				
Reflection				
Romance				

An Officer and a Gentleman is about a young loner who wants to become an officer in the Navy and have an affair with a "Puget deb." That is the story concept.

The Hero is Zack Mayo because he is the main character, he's on screen most of the time, he is the one with whom the audience most identifies, and it is his outer motivation that drives the plot forward.

Zack's outer motivation is to become an officer and to have an affair with Paula. Those desires are visible, revealed through the action, determine the plot, and answer the question, "What is the story about?"

Zack's outer conflict is that the school is set up to eliminate cadets but he must get through school before he can be an officer. That meets the definition of outer conflict by providing the obstacle to his outer motivation. The outer conflict standing in the way of his affair with Paula is that she wants a permanent relationship.

Thus far, then, the chart would look like this:

	Outer motivation	Outer conflict	Inner motivation	Inner conflict
Hero ZACK MAYO	*Become an officer; affair with Paula*	*School; Paula wants marriage*		

To determine which characters meet the definitions of nemesis, reflection, and romance, always look at the hero's outer motivation. Remember, it is the cornerstone of the entire script, and each character is defined by his or her relationship to that square on the chart.

The nemesis is that character who most stands in the way of the hero's achieving his outer motivation. So ask yourself, "Who provides the greatest obstacle to Zack getting through school and becoming an officer?" The answer would of course be Foley. Foley's outer motivation is to get the cadets, particularly Zack, to D.O.R. (that is, drop on request). Foley's outer conflict is that the cadets (particularly Zack) are determined not to D.O.R. Again, these motivations are visible: you can see Foley try to push Zack into dropping out, and you can see Zack working to get his officer's bars.

As is usually the case, the nemesis's outer motivation provides the outer conflict for the hero, and vice versa.

The Reflection is Sid, the character who supports the hero's motivation (he also wants Zack to become an officer) and/or is in the same basic situation (he also wants to be a naval officer and have an affair with a Puget deb).

Sid's outer motivation, then, is to become an officer and have an affair with Lynette, and his outer conflict is that the school tries to weed him out and that Lynette wants a husband.

The Romance is that character who is the object of the hero's outer motivation, sexually or romantically. Since Paula's name is already in Zack's outer motivation square on the chart, and he does desire her sexually, she must be the romance. Another good clue is that any time two people spend half a movie in bed together, one is usually the romance.

Paula further meets the requirements of a romance character

by alternately supporting and being at cross-purposes to Zack's outer motivation. When he first tries to pick her up, she wants him too (supportive). Then he wants to break it off, but she wants the relationship to continue (at cross-purposes). Finally, he realizes he needs her, and she stands by him (supportive).

Paula's outer motivation is to have a permanent relationship with Zack. Don't fall into the trap of saying it is to escape her situation, because if that were her motivation, we would literally see her packing her bags and driving away. Outer motivation is what the character visibly tries to accomplish *within the context of the movie.* Similarly, her *outer* motivation cannot be to "better herself," because that cannot be revealed through action. Being with someone is visible; status is not.

Paula's outer conflict is that Zack wants a brief fling, not commitment. That is what most prevents her from achieving her outer motivation.

Those, then, are the four primary characters in the story, and the chart would now look like this:

	Outer motivation	Outer conflict	Inner motivation	Inner conflict
Hero ZACK MAYO	Become an officer; affair with Paula	School; Paula wants marriage		
Nemesis FOLEY	*Get Zack (cadets) to D.O.R.*	*Zack won't D.O.R.*		
Reflection SID	*Become an officer; affair with Lynette*	*School; Lynette wants marriage*		
Romance PAULA	*Relationship with Zack*	*Zack only wants affair*		

The right half of the chart, dealing with inner motivation and conflict, becomes a bit more complicated since these are often revealed through subtle bits of dialogue. Remember that the inner levels of motivation and conflict are optional; you may choose not to explore these. In *An Officer and a Gentleman,* determining these levels necessitates digging deeper into the characters' comments and attitudes to find the paths they have each chosen to achieving self-worth.

Inner motivation is the *reason* the character hopes to achieve his outer motivation. It is the path the character thinks will lead to greater feelings of self-worth, and it is usually revealed through dialogue.

For Zack, the key dialogue occurs when Foley is hazing Zack for hiding the polished shoes and buckles. Foley tries to get Zack to give up and D.O.R., but Zack refuses. When Foley finally threatens to kick Zack out, Zack finally screams that he has nowhere else to go. Zack's inner motivation, the path he believes will lead to self-worth, is a sense of belonging. In other words, Zack wants to find the family he never had as a child.

Zack's inner motivation for wanting an affair with Paula is simply that he desires her. As in real life, we all feel better about ourselves when we win the love or desire of the person we love or desire. So in any story involving a romance character, love or desire will be one of the hero's inner motivations.

Inner conflict is whatever within the character prevents him from achieving self-worth. Zack's inner conflict is revealed when he is in bed with Paula. He has told her about his mother's suicide and the fact that his mother never even left him a note.

When Paula sympathetically acknowledges how much that must have hurt, Zack responds that when you realize you're alone in the world, nothing hurts. But Paula doesn't believe that Zack really means what he says.

The dialogue shows that Paula understands Zack's inner conflict: he can't give himself to anyone. This is the quality within him that keeps him from achieving self-worth by belonging. Until Zack can learn to trust and give himself to others, he will never have the sense of family he longs for and which will enable him to feel good about himself.

Foley's inner motivation and inner conflict squares on the chart are blank. The movie doesn't really deal with the reason Foley wants to get the cadets to D.O.R. We might infer that he really likes Zack or that it's his job, but the movie doesn't explore this level of motivation and conflict for the character.

This is perfectly acceptable, because even though each primary character *must* possess outer motivation and outer conflict, a screenwriter can choose to explore inner motivation and inner conflict for only some (or none) of those characters.

It is interesting to note that in his original screenplay, Douglas Day Stewart did provide an inner motivation for the character: Foley had tried unsuccessfully to become an officer himself and as a result resented all the cadets and tried his best to beat them down. But in the translation to screen, this element of the character was omitted.

Sid's inner motivation, the reason he wants to become an officer, is, as is stated several times, to live up to his parents' expectations and fill his dead brother's shoes. And the reason he wants to be with Lynette is that he desires her.

Sid's inner conflict is that he has lived so long for others that he no longer knows what *he* wants. In the original screenplay (though it was eliminated from the film), one of the characters refers to Sid as "other-directed." He doesn't just give himself to others; he sacrifices himself.

At the end of the film, when Sid has dropped on request and given up the possibility of living for his parents, he goes to Lynette. When she rejects him, there is no one left for him to please, and it destroys him.

Paula's inner motivation is simply that she loves Zack. You might argue that her path to self-worth also involves escaping from a miserable job and home life, so that would be OK too, but it is apparent in the way Paula stands by Zack and refuses to trap him that her feelings run much deeper than those of a woman who just wants to snare a husband.

Finally, Paula's inner conflict square on the chart should be blank; there is nothing within Paula that prevents her from achieving self-worth and feeling good about herself through loving Zack. In other words, there is no inner conflict which she must overcome, as Zack must, in order to achieve her motivations.

This is a typical pattern for a love story. The romance character is the evolved person, and it is only when the hero recognizes and overcomes his own inner conflict that he reaches the level of his romance, wins her love, and achieves his outer and inner motivations. It is identical to the character development employed in *Splash*, *The Karate Kid*, *Defending Your Life*, *Innerspace*, *Tin Men*, and *Legal Eagles*.

The completed chart of motivation and conflict for *An Officer and a Gentleman* would therefore look like this:

	Outer motivation	Outer conflict	Inner motivation	Inner conflict
Hero ZACK MAYO	Become an officer; affair with Paula	School; Paula wants marriage	*Belong; desires her*	*Won't trust anyone or give himself to others*
Nemesis FOLEY	Get Zack (cadets) to D.O.R.	Zack won't D.O.R.	—	—
Reflection SID	Become an officer; affair with Lynette	School; Lynette wants marriage	*Live up to family's expectations*	*Other-directed*
Romance PAULA	Relationship with Zack	Zack only wants affair	*Loves Zack; escape*	—

The other characters in *An Officer and a Gentleman*—Byron, Lynette, Seeger, and the other cadets—fall into the secondary-character category. Though they are well drawn and important to the overall plot, they are not as essential as the four primary characters listed above.

An excellent exercise is to attempt to complete the above chart for other recent movies, particularly films such as *Tootsie*, *Body Heat*, *Splash*, *Rocky*, *War Games*, *Jagged Edge*, *Big*, *Stakeout*, *Platoon*, *Children of a Lesser God*, *Stand By Me*, and *Working Girl*, which possess clear outer motivations and are not complicated by multiple heroes or unexplored inner motivations. Chapter 7 of this book, which analyzes *The Karate Kid* in detail, should further clarify these principles.

Summary

1. The three facets of character are:

Physical makeup

Personality

Background

2. The major methods of creating character identification are:

Sympathy

Jeopardy

Likability

Immediate introduction

Possession of power

A familiar setting

Familiar flaws and foibles

An archetypal superhero

The eyes of the audience

3. The primary methods of ensuring *original* characters are:

Research

Go against cliché by altering the physical makeup, background, and personality

Pair with an opposite character

Cast the character

4. The two levels of motivation are:

Outer: What the character visibly hopes to accomplish by the end of the movie

Inner: The reason for the outer motivation, which the character thinks will lead to self-worth

5. The sources of conflict are:

Outer: Nature or other characters

Inner: Within the character

6. The four categories of primary character are:

Hero: The main character whose motivation drives the plot

Nemesis: The character who most stands in the way of the hero achieving her outer motivation

Reflection: The character who most supports the hero's outer motivation or is in the same basic situation

Romance: The sexual or romantic object of part of the hero's outer motivation, who must alternately support and be at cross-purposes to the hero

7. Secondary characters are added as needed for plot logic, hurdles or support for the hero, humor, texture, and depth.

Chapter 4

■ ■

Theme and Character Growth

I get frustrated evey time I hear someone imply that only foreign films say anything of significance and that American movies are too slick, too commercial, and too superficial. It is narrow minded intellectual snobbery to believe that if you're not reading subtitles, the movie you're seeing is devoid of intellectual or moral content.

The greatness of the best American movies is that they *can* be slick, entertaining, and appeal to the masses and, underneath, convey ideas, principles, and universal truths that reach audiences on an entirely different level. This underlying level of morality is explored through the film's *theme*.

Theme is the universal statement the movie makes about the human condition. It is the screenwriter's underlying prescription for how one should live one's life in order to be a more evolved, more fulfilled, more individuated, more moral person. It's the filmmaker's way of saying, "This is how to be a better human being." Theme is universal; it applies to any individual in the audience.

In addition to the action and subject matter of the story, some screenplays develop this deeper level, which can be directly applicable to any individual's life. For example, the theme of *Tootsie*, as you will see later in this chapter, deals with honesty and friendship and has nothing directly to do with putting on a dress, posing as a woman, or acting in a soap opera.

As with inner motivation and inner conflict, this is an arena you may choose not to explore with your own screenplay. It is perfectly acceptable to write a screenplay which involves only outer motivation and outer conflict and doesn't get into deeper thematic levels. Many immensely successful movies do just that. If you do choose to explore theme in the manner outlined below, you should do so only after you've written a draft or two of your screenplay. Then you can begin to explore whatever universal statement seems to be emerging from your own story. If you try to begin with theme and then lay a plot on top of it, the basic thrust of your story will fall apart. Theme *grows out of* plot; it should never be imposed on it.

At the very least, the method of determining and developing theme outlined below will enable you to see films in a new way and to recognize the deeper ideas that can emerge from popular movies.

Recognizing Theme

Theme emerges when the hero's similarity to the nemesis and difference from the reflection are revealed. When we recognize how the hero, at any point in the movie, is like the character he opposes (the nemesis) and unlike the character with whom he is aligned (the reflection), we begin to see the screenplay's broader statement about how one should live one's life.

Character growth begins when the hero recognizes his own similarity to the nemesis and difference from the reflection. Theme is recognized by the audience; growth is experienced by a character in the movie.

The easiest way to explain how this works is to illustrate the process using *An Officer and a Gentleman.* Then I will briefly show how the same process applies to a couple other recent films.

Here is the primary character chart for *An Officer and a Gentleman,* as developed in the last chapter:

	Outer motivation	Outer conflict	Inner motivation	Inner conflict
Hero ZACK MAYO	Become an officer; affair with Paula	School; Paula wants marriage	*Belong; desires her*	*Won't trust anyone or give himself to others*

	Outer motivation	Outer conflict	Inner motivation	Inner conflict
Nemesis FOLEY	Get Zack (cadets) to D.O.R.	Zack won't D.O.R.	—	—
Reflection SID	Become an officer; affair with Lynette	School; Lynette wants marriage	*Live up to family's expectations*	*Other-directed*
Romance PAULA	Relationship with Zack	Zack only wants affair	*Loves Zack; escape*	—

To discover the theme of *An Officer and a Gentleman*, begin by asking how Zack, the hero, is like his nemesis, Foley.

In Chapter 3 it was stated that outer motivation determines plot, but inner motivation is more closely related to theme. Often the similarity between hero and nemesis will be revealed by looking at the inner motivations and conflicts for the two characters.

In *An Officer and a Gentleman*, however, no inner motivations or conflicts are explored for Foley, so we have to go off the chart and ask ourselves in what other ways, at any point in the screenplay, Zack is like his nemesis.

There are lots of qualities and situations the two characters have in common. Both are men in the Navy, know martial arts, and use profanity the way politicians use doublespeak. But it's pretty clear that on a *thematic* level, Douglas Day Stewart isn't saying anything universal about manhood, the military, kung fu, or dirty language.

A stronger clue to their eventual similarity is in Foley's dialogue. Throughout the film, he represents the idea that Zack must give himself to others in order to succeed:

Foley tells Zack that he doesn't care about anybody but himself, and that other men would never want to fly with him.

Foley shakes his head in dismay at Zack when Zack sits by himself after winning the first obstacle race, while the other cadets urge each other on.

He sarcastically criticizes Zack for being a loner when the cadets are about to ride in the Dilbert Dunker.

And when Foley hazes Zack for a whole weekend after finding the shoes and belt buckles in the ceiling, he's punishing Zack because Zack is exploiting the other cadets rather than helping them.

There is even an additional scene in the shooting script that was omitted from the final film: Zack has been caught in a similar infraction, so Foley makes Zack sit and watch in a chair, sipping Coke, while all the other cadets are run ragged in the hot sun, punished for something Zack did. It forces Zack to feel compassion for his fellow cadets and to see how he is responsible for their well-being.

So Foley functions thematically as a representative of the concept of giving oneself to others. Yet it seems Zack is *unlike* Foley in this regard, since Zack so clearly stands alone, uninvolved with the other cadets in the scenes cited above. And I said earlier that theme emerges when the hero's *similarity* to the nemesis is revealed.

To find their similarity, consider the final obstacle race, near the end of the film. Here Zack sacrifices his personal record to help Seeger complete the course and become an officer as well. His priority is now support of the others over his own personal gain, as Foley has been urging him. When Zack then does his best to help Sid, and is able to expose himself emotionally to Paula, his growth in this regard is clear.

This follows a typical thematic pattern. A nemesis won't necessarily represent some bad quality that the hero also possesses and has to overcome. The similarity between hero and nemesis can involve either a positive or a negative characteristic and it can be revealed at the beginning of the screenplay, at the end, or anywhere in between. The only rule is to find that similarity.

When you read the analysis of *The Karate Kid* in Chapter 7, you will see an illustration of a hero who shares a negative quality with his nemesis at the beginning of the film. But *An Officer and a Gentleman* follows the opposite pattern.

So the theme of *An Officer and a Gentleman* has something to do with the need to give oneself to others. But there's more to it than that. Look now at how the hero is *un*like his reflection.

Here is where the chart is useful. Because even though Zack and Sid are identical in terms of outer motivation and outer conflict, their inner motivations and inner conflicts are quite different. While Zack simply wants to belong, Sid lives totally for other people; Sid's only path to self-worth is to fulfill others' needs and expectations. Zack may be learning to give himself to others, but Sid *sacrifices* himself for others.

The critical scene revealing their differences is in the cafeteria. Sid has told Zack that Lynette is pregnant and that he plans to D.O.R. and marry her. But Zack argues vehemently with Sid, saying that the reason he does anything is out of loyalty to his family, when his first responsibility is really to himself.

So thematically, the difference between the hero and the reflection is that Zack is not a martyr, and Sid is. The universal statement of the film now has something to do with the difference between *giving to* others and *living for* others.

When you combine these similarities and differences, the theme of *An Officer and a Gentleman* becomes: *In order to be better people (or more individuated or evolved or fulfilled), we must give ourselves to others but never sacrifice ourselves for others*.

Actually, you could carry the theme of *An Officer and a Gentleman* a little further by comparing Paula and Lynette. I don't want to make this issue of character categories too complicated, but it's fairly clear in this movie that Lynette represents Paula's reflection; both women possess the same outer motivation (to marry an officer), and the same outer conflict (Zack and Sid want affairs with no commitment). Plus Paula and Lynette are obviously friends who support each other's goals, are in the same basic situation at the beginning of the movie, and are aligned with each other throughout.

If you compare Paula to Lynette thematically, you see that Paula is unlike her reflection in one critical area: Lynette is dishonest, and Paula is not. Lynette's inner conflict is that she really is a Puget deb; she will lie to Sid in order to "catch" a husband. And this is the quality within Lynette that ultimately prevents her from realizing self-worth by trapping Sid. Her dishonesty keeps her from achieving either her inner or outer motivations.

When you add this element, the theme of *An Officer and a Gentleman* becomes: *In order to be better human beings, we must give ourselves* honestly *to others, but never sacrifice ourselves for others.*

One of the reasons that I think *An Officer and a Gentleman* is an excellent screenplay is that, in addition to creating emotion and entertaining so effectively, the movie develops a very insightful theme. I believe that the people who are willing to give themselves to others are the ones who make life worth living and who have led us to whatever humanity we have achieved. But it's the martyrs of the world who get us in a whole lot of trouble.

Whether you agree with this theme doesn't really matter. What's important is that you see how Douglas Day Stewart's particular prescription for living and statement about the human condition is developed in his screenplay.

This is not to say that the people who came out of the theater after seeing *An Officer and a Gentleman* were declaring, "I loved that movie! I, too, believe we must give ourselves to others, but never sacrifice ourselves." That would be absurd. If anything, they were saying, "Richard Gere! Hey, what a hunk!" But just because an audience doesn't verbalize a theme, doesn't mean they don't receive it. Theme in a movie is developed and revealed on a much deeper, more subtle level than that of the plot. I'm talking about a level of understanding that is subconscious but still very real and can still enhance the emotional effect of a film on an audience.

I don't even know if Douglas Day Stewart had anything close to this theme in mind when he wrote the screenplay for *An Officer and a Gentleman*. And actually, it doesn't matter. The critical issue is whether the theme is consistent with the character development of the movie, not whether it was intended by the author.

Theme grows out of the writer's unconscious (creativity), is delivered through the characters' unconscious (inner motivation and conflict), and is received by the audience's unconscious. It is, if you will, a soul-to-soul communication between screenwriter and audience.

Character Growth

As stated above, *character growth* occurs when the hero recognizes his own similarity to the nemesis and his difference from the reflection. The arc of Zack's growth toward giving himself to the other cadets is revealed throughout the film.

Zack is deeply moved when Sid, Paula, and Lynette cheer him on from the boat as he is being punished by Foley. After his weekend hazing, Zack secretly places the shined buckles and shoes in Perryman's locker as a gift. And in their final obstacle run, Zack sacrifices his record to help Seeger. It is after Zack has experienced this growth that he is able to achieve his *outer* motivation and become an officer.

Even more important, when Zack is able to face his own terror and risk giving himself to Paula, he is then able to realize a "belonging" with her that allows them to fulfill their relationship. I don't think those who criticized this film for its Cinderella ending were paying very close attention to exactly who had rescued whom in the final scene of the movie.

It is Sid's and Lynette's inability to grow and overcome their inner conflicts that makes them tragic figures.

Developing Theme in Your Screenplay

So how does all of this help your own writing? How are you going to use all of this complex information to develop a theme in your own screenplay?

Again, the first rule is to disregard theme until you've written at least one draft or, preferably, two drafts of your screenplay. You can't impose a theme on your script. It's absurd to think you could begin with a theme, such as the need for honesty and friendship in a relationship, and from that conclude, "Guess I'll write *Tootsie*."

Begin with a story concept that meets the criteria outlined in Chapter 2, and write your first draft focusing on the outer motivations and conflicts for your primary characters. Then begin exploring those characters' inner motivations and conflicts. Only then are you ready to see what more universal theme may be emerging.

If you try to impose a theme on your story, however, it may not be true for either you or your screenplay. I have had conversations with writers who insist that their themes are elevated messages for the world when what was actually emerging from the characters was something quite different. It is best to develop the *plot* and then see what underlying principles are emerging by analyzing your own creation with the method outlined above.

Once your theme begins to emerge, applying these principles can help you reveal and enhance the theme by clarifying the differences between your hero and your reflection, and the similarities between your hero and your nemesis.

Don't go overboard expounding your theme. Let it emerge subtly. The movie *Mean Season* beats the audience over the head with the idea that the reporter played by Kurt Russell is like his nemesis, the killer (played by Richard Jordan). It weakens the movie when the screenplay is so blatant about its theme of shared responsibility.

Theme versus Message

Theme is also not the same as message. A *message,* by my definition, is a political statement. It is a principle that concerns people in a particular situation and is not universally applicable to any member of the audience.

For example, the message of *Tootsie,* which kept cropping up in the promotion of the film, was, "A man puts on a dress and becomes a better man for it." This is certainly true for the movie, but unless one is willing to go out in drag, it's impossible to incorporate this message into one's own life.

By contrast, the theme of *Tootsie* is universal. By comparing Michael Dorsey (Dustin Hoffman) to his nemesis, the director Ron (Dabney Coleman), we see that they are alike in that both lie to women. Ron tells Dorothy Michaels that women are attracted to him and that they assume he feels more deeply about them than he really does. But he doesn't want to tell them the truth because it will hurt their feelings, so he continues to lead them on. Dorothy's response to this statement is that it's bullshit.

Yet only a few scenes earlier, Michael tells Jeff (Bill Murray) that the reason Michael won't tell Sandy (Terri Garr) that he was hired on the soap opera or that he doesn't really love her is that it would hurt her feelings.

When you compare Michael to Sandy, his reflection, you see that he is unlike her in that she is honest and a true friend. And she repeatedly asks Michael to be honest with her.

When Michael tells Sandy that he loves someone else, we expect her to say, "Oh, that's OK. At least you were honest, and we can still be friends." But instead, she hits him with her purse. Thematically, and comedically, that is the ideal response.

Sandy storms out of Michael's apartment, saying that she might take that from a lover, but never from a friend. She is saying that lovers are expected to play these dishonest games; Sandy's come to expect that. But Michael has claimed to be her friend. And friends don't lie to each other.

Put Michael's similarity to Ron and his difference from Sandy together and the theme of *Tootsie* becomes: *For relationships to succeed, they must be based on honesty and friendship.*

Michael's growth occurs when *he* recognizes how he is like Ron, whom he despises, and unlike Sandy, one of his closest friends. And, as in *An Officer and a Gentleman,* it is only when the hero overcomes his inner conflict and experiences the necessary growth that he wins the love of the romance character.

In *Tootsie,* the same theme emerges, perhaps even more clearly, if you choose to regard Dorothy as Michael's reflection. If Dorothy is regarded as a distinct character, then she fills the definition of reflection because she is the character who most supports the hero's outer motivation.

When Michael tells Jeff about Dorothy's first encounter with Ron, Jeff asks Michael how Dorothy reacted. Michael replies that Dorothy listened to what Ron said, agreed, and then did it the way she wanted to. And then he adds that Dorothy is much smarter than he is. This shows the beginning of Michael's growth away from someone who is dishonest, who sees everything as a part to play, and who disregards others' feelings, and toward someone who sees the value of honesty, consideration, and friendship. Of course, Dorothy has also been dishonest in her pretense of being a woman. But the *feelings* of love and friendship she expresses and her consideration of others are genuine.

At the end of the film when Michael tells Julie that, as a woman, he was a better man with her than he was as a man with other women, he is recognizing his own growth. He is now Julie's friend, just as Dorothy was.

A similar difference between message and theme can be seen by examining *War Games.* The message of the movie, the political statement applying to people in a certain situation, is: The only way to win the nuclear game is not to play. This is a great, important message. But it is still political; it still applies only to people in a specific, plot-related situation. (One might correctly argue that we're *all* in the grip of nuclear insanity, but the statement is still a political message.)

To discover the theme of *War Games,* follow the same process outlined above. Compare David, the hero, to the NORAD computer scientist, McKittridge (Dabney Coleman again—the man makes a great nemesis). Or compare David to Joshua if you believe the computer is humanoid enough to qualify as the nemesis. Then compare David to Jennifer (Ally Sheedy), his reflection.

I won't spell this one out for you, but your theme should end up including some statement about that which is natural and organic versus that which is mechanical, inorganic, and inhuman.

The method outlined above is not the only way to approach a movie's theme. There are other definitions of theme and other ways to find deeper levels of meaning in any film or screenplay. But this is a process I prefer, probably because I made it up, and it seems an effective way of giving greater depth to your own screenplay, and of finding added substance to the movies you see.

There can also be deeper levels of meaning beyond the theme and message of a screenplay: symbol, allegory, archetype, etc. *Stand By Me,* adapted by Bruce Evans and Raynold Gideon from Stephen King's novella, develops a theme of recognizing one's own gifts and pursuing them regardless of others' opinions or approval. But beneath that, it explores the terrifying but necessary death of one's childhood in order to pass into the unpredictable world of adulthood if one is to realize one's own gifts. And beneath that allegorical level, the film is a quest story, a Holy Grail myth portraying the journey from childhood to maturity, power, and individuation.

Lots of excellent, entertaining, emotionally involving, and profitable movies don't explore theme at all. I think *Raiders of the Lost Ark* is a terrific movie, but I don't see anything more there than what's on the surface. That's fine. It is your choice as the screenwriter to explore these underlying meanings or not.

And again, whatever the layers of meaning in your screenplay, your primary concern must always be to that cornerstone of your screenplay: the hero's outer motivation. It is only from that foundation that the depth and complexity of your screenplay can emerge.

Summary

1. *Theme* is a universal statement about the human condition that goes beyond the plot. It is the screenwriter's prescription for how one should live one's life in order to be more fulfilled, more evolved, or a better person.

2. Theme emerges when the hero's similarity to the nemesis and difference from the reflection are revealed.

3. *Character growth* occurs when the hero recognizes her own similarity to the nemesis and difference from the reflection.

4. Theme grows out of the writer's unconscious, is developed through the characters' unconscious, and is received by the audience's unconscious.

5. Theme must grow out of the story concept; it must never be imposed on it.

6. Theme is not message. A *message* is a political statement which applies to a specific group of people or a specific situation.

7. This chapter describes only one method of exploring theme; screenplays can reveal several underlying levels of meaning.

8. Theme is not a necessity for a screenplay; many successful movies choose not to explore deeper levels of meaning.

CHAPTER 5

. . . .

Structure

Think of your movie as a roller coaster at an amusement park: your story concept involves the way the experience appears initially —whether it looks like a ride that has the potential to be emotionally involving. In other words, is it a ride that will attract people in the first place? Your characters (particularly the hero) are the vehicles through which the audience experiences emotion, like the cars on the roller coaster. The plot *structure* involves the events of the story and the way they are positioned is like the curves and turns of the track on the ride. The layout of the track will determine whether or not the ride is exciting.

Plot Structure

Structure consists of the specific events in a movie and their position relative to one another. Proper structure occurs when the right events occur in the right sequence to elicit maximum emotional involvement in the reader and audience.

In other words, good plot structure means that the right thing is happening at the right time. If the events of your story lack interest, excitement, humor, logic, or relevance, or if they occur in an order that fails to create suspense, surprise, anticipation, curiosity, or a clear resolution, then the structure is weak.

Structuring your story effectively involves two stages of development: dividing your plot into three acts and making use of specific structural devices.

The Three Acts to Any Story

Any film story, of any length, can be divided into three acts. This division constitutes the first level of plot structure and is necessary to create an effective screenplay. These acts must satisfy the dramatic requirements of film and are not necessarily related to the acts of a play or the commercial breaks of a TV show, although there is often a close connection. The three acts of a film story can be defined in several ways, which will also help explain how to effectively divide your own screenplay.

The first method of defining the acts of a screenplay is in terms of the screenwriter's *objective* within each act: the goal of Act 1 is to *establish* the setting, characters, situation and outer motivation for the hero; the goal of Act 2 is to *build* the hurdles, obstacles, conflicts, suspense, pace, humor, character development, and character revelations; the goal of Act 3 is to *resolve* everything, particularly the outer motivation and conflict for the hero.

```
        ACT 1                 ACT 2                ACT 3
|------------|-------------------------|------------|
     Establish              Build              Resolve
```

The next means of defining each act is in the terms of the *outer motivation for your hero.* The three acts of the screenplay correspond to the three stages of the hero's outer motivation. Each change in the hero's outer motivation signals the arrival of the next act.

As discussed in the previous chapters, the hero's outer motivation determines your story concept and serves as the cornerstone of your entire screenplay.

This overall outer motivation always consists of three segments, three separate but connected goals and objectives for your hero. These three stages to the hero's outer motivation determine the three acts of your screenplay.

In *Stakeout*, the overall outer motivation for the hero is to stake out a woman's house to capture an escaped killer and to have a relationship with that woman. (The love story is the second level of sell, the equally important outer motivation for the hero.)

Dividing that overall outer motivation into its three stages provides the three acts of the story: act 1 is about a cop who wants to stake out a woman's house to watch for a killer, act 2 is about the cop wanting to continue the stakeout *and* have a relationship with the woman, and act 3 is about him wanting to stop the killer and save his own and the woman's life once the killer shows up.

Each of these stages is connected to the overall outer motivation that drives the story, and the replacement of one stage by another signals a new act. Therefore, act 2 of *Stakeout* begins when the Richard Dreyfuss character first meets the woman he's been observing, and act 3 begins when the killer arrives and captures them at gunpoint.

Similarly, act 1 of *War Games* is about a teenage computer genius who wants to break into a new computer system to play a game, act 2 is about him wanting to escape from the FBI and find the computer's creator in order to tell NORAD what's going on, and act 3 is about him wanting to stop Joshua, the computer, in order to prevent World War III.

Any properly structured episode of a TV series can be broken down in the same way. A past episode of *Cheers*, for example, is about Diane helping a psychopathic ex-con learn to act for the stage. Act 1 is about Diane wanting to get away from the man, act 2 is about her wanting to rehearse a scene from *Othello* with him, and act 3 is about her trying to get away from him during their performance when she discovers he's really trying to kill her.

The final way in which the acts of your screenplay can be defined corresponds to length: *Act 1 is always the first ¼ of your screenplay; act 2 is always the next ½; act 3 is always the last ¼.*

In a properly structured two-hour movie, therefore, act 1 should last about a half hour, act 2 one hour, and act 3 a half hour. The same holds true for episodic television. In a half-hour sitcom, the three acts should be about six minutes, twelve minutes and six minutes, and in a one-hour episode, the acts should be approximately twelve, twenty-four, and twelve minutes.

The acts to a series episode do not *necessarily* correspond to commercial breaks, but often a one-hour episode will place the first commercial at the end of act 1, the second at a big moment half way through act 2, and the third at the end of act 2.

A larger consideration in episodic television and TV movies is to leave the audience with a feeling of anticipation so they won't change channels during the commercial. Getting the audience to wonder, "What's going to happen next?" so they'll sit through the commercials is more important than getting the commercial breaks to correspond to the three acts of the story. But the necessary stages of the hero's outer motivation must still be there, following the $\frac{1}{4}-\frac{1}{2}-\frac{1}{4}$ formula.

The acts of your screenplay should conform to this formula in terms of the number of pages: If your screenplay is 120 pages long, then act 1 should end around page 30, and act 2 should end around page 90. The same formula ($\frac{1}{4}-\frac{1}{2}-\frac{1}{4}$) holds true regardless of the length of your screenplay.

The acts are the organic structural changes in your story, not in your written format. Never label the acts of a screenplay, as you would for a play.

Using the Three-Act Structure

How can all these methods of defining the acts help in writing your screenplay? At this stage of development, you have a clear idea of your basic story concept, your hero, your hero's outer motivation, the other primary characters, and their outer motivations. Possibly you have even created some secondary characters and begun to explore inner motivation as well.

Your next step is to divide the overall outer motivation for your hero into its three segments. That will tell you how the motivation will change twice and what the motivation for each of the three acts will be. You know that the changes from one act to the next need to occur at the one-quarter and three-quarter marks in the script, so you must now determine what specific event will signal that change in motivation. (These events, which turn the story in a new direction and signal a new act, are what author Syd Field [see the bibliography] terms "plot points.")

When you have determined how the overall motivation will break down into the three necessary acts, you can begin to list those scenes which you know must occur *within* each act in order to *establish* in act 1, *build* in act 2, and *resolve* in act 3. You won't know all of the scenes in your screenplay at this point, but you will know some of the key scenes, and this process will allow you to at least determine the act in which each occurs.

Assume, for example, that you're writing a film about a bank robbery. Your hero is a former employee of the bank who wants to get back at them for firing her. Your story concept, then, is about a woman who wants to rob the bank that fired her.

Divide that outer motivation into three stages. There are any number of ways this story concept could be laid out, so you must move back into your brainstorming mode to think of all the possible combinations of three stages to your hero's outer motivation.

In our bank robbery example, act 1 could be about a woman who wants to keep her job at a bank, act 2 about a woman who wants to plot a robbery of the bank that fired her, and act 3 about a woman who wants to carry out the robbery. Or, act 1 could be about a woman who gets fired and wants to plan a robbery, act 2 about a woman who wants to execute the robbery, and act 3 about a woman who wants to get away with the money she has stolen.

Let's use the first story line. Now that you know the three segments of the hero's outer motivation, you must decide on the scenes that signal these changes. Act 1 will end with her boss firing the hero and the hero declaring, "I'll get you for this!" Act 2 will end with her gang assembled and the hero announcing, "We're ready to go." Assuming your screenplay will be about 120 pages long, then you know that these two scenes *must* occur around pages 30 and 90.

Now you can brainstorm again by listing in your notes the scenes you already know will take place within each of the three acts. Act 1 will probably include scenes of her at the bank, in conflict with her boss, establishing her skill at computers (or whatever might enable her to pull off the robbery), and getting fired.

Act 2 will show her assembling the gang, getting romantically involved with her partner the safe cracker, the cops getting wise that
something is up, a trial run, a setback or two, and so on. Act 3 must
show the final robbery and getaway, the resolution of the romance,
and the final confrontation with her former boss.

You won't know *all* of the scenes at this stage, but you're beginning to structure your story by placing key scenes within their
proper acts.

The Structural Checklist

The following checklist contains the more specific structural principles and devices available to you, scene by scene, after you have
established the overall breakdown of the three acts to your story.
You should keep them in mind as you begin writing in scene format and return to the checklist with each successive draft to continually sharpen your plot structure.

**1. Every scene, event, and character in the screenplay must
contribute to the hero's outer motivation.** This principle again
shows how critical it is that you have a clearly focused outer motivation for your main character; it not only drives your plot and
determines your character breakdown but is the essential element
of structure as well. It determines the three acts of the screenplay
and then relates to *every single scene*.

You can write a hilarious mother-in-law encounter or a thrilling
car chase or any other provocative, moving, or side-splitting scene,
but if it doesn't relate to the central thrust of your story, you've got
to lose it, change it, or save it for another screenplay. This can be
excruciating, because sometimes these scenes are the ones you love
the most or are even those that you envisioned first when you
began developing the script. But no single scene can take priority
over your hero's outer motivation.

**2. Early in the screenplay, show the audience where the
story is going to lead them.** When you open your screenplay, you
want to create a question in the mind of your reader so that he will

stick around (emotionally) to find out the answer. Specifically, that question pertains to the resolution of the hero's outer motivation. Therefore, you must clearly establish, certainly within the first act, what that motivation is.

Viewers know very quickly that by the time the movie is over, they will have learned whether the attorney gets an acquittal for her client in *Jagged Edge,* whether Charley will win the love of Roxanne in *Roxanne,* or whether Elliot Ness will have stopped Al Capone in *The Untouchables.* Waiting to learn those things is what keeps the audience in the theater and keeps the reader turning pages.

It is sometimes possible to replace one question in the reader's mind with another as long as the new question logically evolves from the first and is more serious and provocative. In *Rambo,* the initial question in the audience's mind is, Will he get into the jungle and photograph the POWs? But eventually, this is replaced by the question of whether he can rescue them and escape, without any help from the CIA. The succeeding questions logically grow out of the initial one and are much more provocative.

In a biography, the question may simply be, How will this hero's life play itself out? But in the more effective biographies, the hero's life is linked to a more specific issue. In *Gandhi,* for example, the question is not simply, What's that old Gandhi guy gonna do next? The more focused, more effective question that drives the story is, Will Gandhi nonviolently overcome his oppressors?

3. Build the conflict. Make each successive hurdle and obstacle for your hero greater and more provocative than the previous one. In *Ghostbusters,* it would be ludicrous to imagine the Bill Murray character confronting all the demons in New York City in act 1, and then facing only the single ghost in the NYC Library in act 3. Each element of the hero's outer conflict must be more formidable and seemingly more insurmountable than its predecessor.

4. Accelerate the pace of the story. The momentum should steadily build as you drive the story to its climax. This applies not only to action films but also to comedies and straight dramas. Obviously, films like *The Road Warrior* and *Jaws* develop the plot so that the action scenes occur closer and closer together as the plot progresses. But the same can be said for films like *The Breakfast Club, Nuts, A Soldier's Story,* and *Planes, Trains and Automobiles.* In all of these films, the obstacles confronting the heroes occur with increasing frequency as the films move toward their climaxes.

This structural principle requires that the *exposition*—the factual information the audience must have to understand what is going on—must be provided as soon as possible. In *War Games,* for example, there is a lot of dry information about computers and NORAD that the audience has to understand for the plot to make sense. The writers skillfully present that information almost entirely within the first act of the film.

War Games also employs the added expositional device of delivering the information through emotion. Instead of a dry lecture about computers, we learn about "taking the humans out of the loop" during an argument between McKittrick, the computer scientist, and Berringer, the NORAD commander. This makes it much easier and more enjoyable for an audience to hear and absorb it. Had the writers waited until the climactic moments of the movie to explain what was going on, the accelerated pace would have been destroyed, and the audience would not have remained emotionally involved.

5. Create peaks and valleys to the action and the humor. High emotional moments in your screenplay must be followed by scenes with less emotional impact, so the audience can catch its breath or so you can build up to the next, even higher peak. There is no such thing as an effective thirty-minute action sequence or joke or car chase. Such a scene would ultimately dissipate emotional involvement, because the reader would eventually become bored with, and distanced from, the high emotional level.

The Road Warrior, which may seem to be nonstop action, is structured so that the car chases and action sequences are interspersed with quieter moments of preparation, conversation, humor, and the like. This maximizes the emotional impact of the action sequences when they do occur.

Similarly, there is a superb scene in *Jaws* that occurs on the boat, when the three men are comparing their scars, and Quint talks about the U.S.S. *Indianapolis*. The audience has just about reached the point where the shark encounters could become routine. So the writers give the audience a moment to catch its breath, while humor, sadness, and character revelation are added to the film. Then, just as the viewer is lulled into a false sense of security, the shark arrives and we're off to the races.

Humor follows the same principle. No matter how broad or hilarious the comedy, you can't have a ninety-minute joke. It is the principle of setup and punch line applied to screenwriting. Humorous action and dialogue must be interspersed with more serious scenes which serve other purposes and maximize the reader's emotional involvement.

6. Create anticipation in the reader. When a reader reads a screenplay or when an audience sees a movie, they try to guess what's going to happen next. They don't always want to be right, but it's the *anticipation* of where the story is going that keeps a reader or audience totally engrossed.

Jaws again serves as an excellent example. If you asked anyone to summarize that film in a single word, he would probably say, "Shark." But the fact is, the shark is only on screen a total of about fifteen minutes in the two-hour movie, and for much of that time, only the dorsal fin is seen. It isn't *seeing* the shark that keeps the audience riveted to the screen, it's the *anticipation* of the horrible, frightening, unknown things that will happen when the shark appears.

It is the anticipation of the battle with the cyborg in *The Terminator*, the showdown with the bad guys in *Beverly Hills Cop*, Mozart's murder in *Amadeus*, and the humor of the dual personality in *All of Me*, which sustains our emotional involvement in each film.

It is because of this principle that more audiences prefer suspense films to films of nonstop violence. Any time you set up anticipation, you have to pay it off, so there will eventually be some degree of violence in any suspense thriller. But a few hatchets in the skull go a long way, and splatter movies cease to be frightening and often just end up gross because they don't create anticipation of anything scary. They do create anticipation of what creative

method of slaughter will occur next, but for the majority of mov-
iegoers, that anticipation is more revolting than involving.

7. Give the audience superior position. *Superior position,* or
audience omniscience, occurs when the audience is given information that some of the characters in the film don't possess. *We*
know that Charley is responsible for the love letters in *Roxanne,* but
Roxanne doesn't. Similarly, the audience is given the information
that a murder is being plotted in *Body Heat,* that the wager has
been made in *Trading Places,* and that the Kevin Costner character
is the woman's secret lover in *No Way Out* long before the other
characters in those movies realize what's going on.

This device, when used in combination with anticipation, becomes extremely effective at eliciting emotion. It is the superior
position that *creates* the anticipation. The audience anticipates what
will happen when the characters learn or encounter what the audience already knows.

In many interviews, Alfred Hithcock cited an example of a
movie scene where two people are sitting at a desk, discussing some
banal subject. All at once, out of the blue, a bomb that was hidden
in the desk goes off, and the two people are blown to bits.

Now, such a scene *would* create high emotional involvement,
but only for a short time. After about sixty seconds of shock and
surprise, the audience would start wondering, "OK, what now?"

Imagine the same scene, however, if the camera cuts from the
two people's conversation to a shot of the bomb ticking away in the
drawer. You could milk that scene for a good five minutes, even
more if you cut away to the bomb squad rushing to save the people
at the desk. Because *we* know the bomb is there even if the characters don't (superior position), we imagine how horrible it will be
if the bomb goes off (anticipation).

The same principle can be equally effective in comedy. In *La
Cage aux Folles,* we know that the two main characters are gay men
and that one of them is in drag, but the visiting family does not
(superior position). The humor comes from the anticipation of this
secret being discovered.

8. Surprise the audience and reverse the anticipation. Even
though anticipation is arguably the strongest structural device you

can use, you don't *always* want your reader to be able to anticipate what might be coming. Occasionally, for humor, shock, and to avoid predictability, you must surprise the audience and jolt them out of their sense of security. Keeping the audience slightly off balance by reversing the anticipated action with something totally unexpected will further increase emotional involvement.

Examples of this device used to scare an audience abound: *Fatal Attraction, Wait Until Dark, Halloween, Friday the 13th, Carrie,* and *The Terminator* all have unexpected, jump-out-at-you moments which are designed to terrify the audience.

Reversing audience anticipation also heightens comic possibilities. *Raiders of the Lost Ark* offers a well-known example of this when Indiana Jones, after fighting off scores of bad buys with his whip, is confronted by a giant henchman wearing a black turban and whirling a huge scimitar. Everyone now expects to see a duel between the sword and the whip, so when Indy merely shrugs, pulls a gun and shoots him, it is a memorable comedic moment. (This reversal is even carried one step further in *Indiana Jones and the Temple of Doom.*)

A double reversal for humor is employed in *Tootsie,* when Michael, posing as Dorothy, is given a scene in which he is supposed to kiss the actor that the other actresses refer to as "the tongue." When Michael gets out of it by hitting him with the files instead, we laugh, because it wasn't what was anticipated. Then, when he gets kissed after all, it is doubly funny.

Remember, the reader and the audience want to *try* to guess and anticipate what's coming next; they just don't want to be right all the time.

9. Create curiosity in the reader. When a character, event, or situation is not explained fully at the outset or when the hero must find the answer to some question or mystery in the course of the story, the reader will "stick around" to learn the solution and satisfy his own curiosity.

Nuts provides lots of examples of creating curiosity in an audience: Why has Claudia, the Barbra Streisand character, been accused of manslaughter? Why do they think she's crazy? How did she get from Park Avenue to this horrible situation? Why won't she let her attorney bring in another pyschiatrist? Why won't she let him cross-examine her mother? What secret is everyone hiding? Will she win her competency hearing?

By gradually revealing the answers to these questions, rather than providing all the background information on Claudia right away, the film increases the audience's emotional involvement.

Other examples of this structural device include the unusual mountain shape that keeps recurring in *Close Encounters of the Third Kind*, the nature of the killer in *Predator*, and the question of what the Kim Basinger character will do if she does get drunk in *Blind Date*.

Obviously, curiosity is the *key* structural device in a whodunit; the entire film hinges on finding the solution to a murder. But murder mysteries are usually less successful commercially and produced less often than suspense thrillers because curiosity does not carry the emotional impact of superior position and anticipation. Curiosity is always most effective when used in combination with the other structural devices on the list.

This raises another key issue: the longer you withhold a secret from the audience, the more important it becomes, and the more satisfying it must be when it's revealed. A good example is *Silverado*. Throughout the early scenes of the movie, Paten, the Kevin Kline character, is repeatedly asked, "Where's the dog?" The audience has no idea what dog they're talking about, and the resulting curiosity increases the emotional involvement.

About a third of the way through the film, we learn that Paten was once captured after a robbery because he tried to rescue a dog. This creates additional sympathy for the character, and the audience's curiosity is satisfied. The device has been effective, because it increased emotional involvement until additional, more exciting events in the screenplay could occur. If the entire film had rested on the meaning of "Where's the dog?" the revelation would not have been sufficiently satisfying to sustain emotional involvement in the film. But instead, the structural device is very effectively used to *increase* emotional involvement until the other structural devices can raise it to an even higher level.

10. Foreshadow the major events of the screenplay. Foreshadowing means giving greater credibility to a character's actions or abilities by laying the groundwork for them earlier in the film. Foreshadowing is used to make the characters' actions believable, and to prevent contrived solutions to the major obstacles the characters face.

When you create your story, you are giving your hero an objective and then placing obstacles in the hero's path that will make it seemingly impossible to achieve that objective. Obviously, this puts you in a dilemma: if the obstacles are too easy to overcome, there is no dramatic tension or anticipation; if the obstacles are too hard, then you must make it believable that your hero can somehow overcome them. The audience has to be convinced that the impossible has become possible, but that the outcome is not contrived.

Foreshadowing is one solution to this dilemma. By laying in scenes early in the story which show the audience how the hero will finally achieve his objective, you give the necessary credibility to the climactic moments of the film.

In *Outrageous Fortune,* the Shelly Long character gets the best of the bad guys (in part) by effectively pretending to die, fencing with a master spy, and leaping across a twenty-foot canyon. It would be pretty hard for an audience to believe that an average person would be able to do all of that. But the screenwriter skillfully shows the character doing all of these things in earlier, minor scenes. Then when the important, climactic moments occur, the audience subconsciously says to itself, "Oh, yeah. I remember that she was the best jumper in her ballet class." And the final outcome becomes credible.

Had the screenwriter omitted the foreshadowing by having the hero leap over the canyon out of the clear blue, the audience wouldn't have bought it for a minute. The fact is, the ending of the movie *is* that contrived. The difference is that now it is *effectively* contrived.

Foreshadowing enables you to avoid endings in which the hand of God must come down to save your hero because you couldn't come up with any believable solution. If you sufficiently foreshadow your big resolutions, they will be much more credible and acceptable to the audience.

Foreshadowing is particularly important at the climax, where the hero is facing the last, seemingly insurmountable obstacle and you must persuade the audience that the means for your hero to overcome it are logical and believable. But the principle applies not only to the big climax of the film but to any actions or abilities which must be given added credibility.

The crossed laser beams in *Ghostbusters*, the Mel Gibson character's willingness to get out on a ledge with a potential suicide in *Lethal Weapon*, the hero's former job with the phone company in *Three Days of the Condor*, and the dagger throw in *Romancing the Stone* are all examples of foreshadowing.

When writing your screenplay, you will usually create your important and climactic scenes first, then go back to previous scenes and lay in whatever information is necessary to effectively foreshadow the later events.

11. Echo particular situations, objects, and lines of dialogue to illustrate character growth and change. Did you ever return to your old high school years after you'd graduated to be reminded of the old days and see how much the place had changed? Well, what you were actually doing was measuring your own growth. High school buildings never change; you're the one who had changed. And comparing yourself to the person you were the last time you saw the high school enabled you to see how far you had come, how much you had lost, or what a different person you were. This basic principle has kept high school reunion committees busy for decades.

The principle works the same way in movies. You can repeat an object or situation or line of dialogue in your screenplay at regular intervals through the course of the story, and it will illustrate the changes your characters have experienced.

For example, we see the cuckoo clock at least three times in *Out of Africa;* it never changes. But each time it appears, it indicates some new, changed facet of the hero. When Karen unpacks the clock, it illustrates the home and past she is clinging to in order to withstand the loneliness and isolation of Kenya. When the natives wait for it to cuckoo and then run in fear and surprise, it shows how foreign she seems to them, but also their growing acceptance of her. When she is finally forced to sell it, the clock illustrates how much she is having to give up and the inner strength that she has acquired to replace the outer trappings she clung to in the beginning of the film.

Echoing can also involve recurring situations, as with the three breakfast scenes in *Kramer vs. Kramer*, or the times Gib and Alison must sleep together in *The Sure Thing*. Or a screenplay can echo dialogue, as with "doing what is necessary" in *Body Heat* or the singing of the theme from *Have Gun, Will Travel* in the movie *Stand By Me*. In each case, the repeated words or images indicate growth or change for the characters.

12. Pose a threat to one of the characters. Putting any significant character of your film in jeopardy will increase emotional involvement in the story (as well as identification with that character). As long as there is impending danger for one of the characters, the reader will hang in there to see if she gets out OK. This applies not just to suspense thrillers, where the threat is to a character's life, but also to comedies and dramas where it might be the threat of exposure *(Splash)*, loss *(Country)*, or failure *(The Natural)*.

This device can work even if the threat is not to one of the principal characters of the screenplay. In the TV movie *Adam*, we are immediately emotionally involved by the unseen threat to the heroes' child, even though the child is not a primary character.

13. Make the story credible. In order to maintain maximum emotional involvement by your reader, your story must be logical and believable *with its own set of rules.*

Anything you choose can be possible in your screenplay; people can fly; disappear; travel through time and space; and defy death, gravity, and the Internal Revenue Service. But if you are going to alter the rules of real life in any way, the parameters and limitations of your fictional characters and universe must be clearly stated for the audience.

This is why fantasy and sword-and-sorcery movies are so tough to pull off. It is very difficult to clearly explain the rules of your make-believe universe and the limits to your hero's powers and still keep the story from becoming confusing. Yet if the limits to your hero's powers and abilities aren't clear, there will be no tension or conflict, since it will seem that your hero can come up with whatever superhuman skill is necessary to overcome the obstacles of the plot.

Since most of your screenplays are probably not going to be in the fantasy genre, this consideration will not be a problem. But logic and believability are still crucial. Your characters must talk and act the way we are accustomed to seeing characters talk and act, and their actions must be consistent with the background and situations you have given them.

The two greatest violations of this principle are: (1) Why don't they get out of the house? *and* (2) Why don't they call the cops?

Anyone who's ever seen a run-of-the-mill haunted-house (or haunted-campground) movie understands the first consideration. Most people, when presented with danger, will try to get away. Yet repeatedly, movies show characters who ignore killings, ghosts, blood seeping from the plumbing, and ominous warnings from John Carradine in order to stay put in an obviously unfriendly situation.

The solution to this dilemma is fairly easy: give the characters some compelling reason why they *cannot* leave. Perhaps they are trapped, or the survival of a loved one depends on confronting the evil force, as in *Poltergeist*. If it's impossible for your hero to flee the danger, then your story will become far more believable.

The second consideration is similar; most people who can't escape from a threat will try to get help. Rather than defying believability by ignoring the issue, make help inaccessible for your character. Either communication is cut off (*The Thing; Wait Until Dark*), the authorities *are* the opponents (*Three Days of the Condor, Witness*), the authorities are powerless (*The Terminator*), or the character can't go to the authorities because they suspect *him* of being the killer (*The Thirty-Nine Steps; North by Northwest; Frenzy; Hanky-Panky*).

When developing your story, ask yourself repeatedly, "Does this situation clearly fit the limits of the universe I have created?" and, "Given my characters' backgrounds and situations, is it logical and believable that they would behave this way?"

14. Teach the audience how to do something, vicariously.
Often a story will be more emotionally involving if the hero must
learn some particular skill, which the audience can then "learn"
through that character. In *The Color of Money*, we learn the skills
and philosophy of the pool circuit just as the Tom Cruise character
does. Similarly, the karate training in *The Karate Kid*, the boxing
training in *Rocky*, the military training in *Uncommon Valor* and *The
Dirty Dozen*, and all the dancing instruction in *Dirty Dancing*, serve
to involve the audience in the story.

Notice that this structural device is closely related to superior
position, anticipation, and foreshadowing in that the instruction
points to the later events when the knowledge will be used. The
reader anticipates the critical attempts to use the skills, and
the scenes in which the new skills are used are given greater credibility.

15. Give the story both humor and seriousness. This simply
means that even if you are writing a very heavy tragedy, give it
some moments of humor, lightness, and comic relief. In real life,
even the heaviest and saddest of situations will contain some elements
of humor, often as a necessary emotional release for those
involved. The same principle applies to film, as exemplified by
such tragedies as *Silkwood, Sophie's Choice, One Flew Over the Cuckoo's
Nest, Midnight Cowboy*, and *Dangerous Liaisons*.

The reverse is true as well: if you are writing a comedy, no
matter how broad, take your story and characters seriously. Even
in such seemingly off-the-wall movies as *Ghostbusters, Police Academy*,
and *Airplane*, the characters are presented as real, sympathetic
people in the midst of all the slapstick or satirical goings-on. The
films may be winking at the audience, but they're not copping out
with an attitude of "this is just low comedy so it doesn't matter what
we do." On an important level, we are meant to be involved in and
believe in the story and characters, and the humor grows out of
that emotional involvement.

The finest examples of this principle are those films which are
almost impossible to classify as comedy *or* drama. *The Big Chill,
Stand By Me, Broadcast News*, and all of Woody Allen's later films
combine hilarity with very serious moments and never get their

laughs at the expense of their own characters or the audience's emotional involvement.

16. Give the movie an effective opening. The first ten pages of your screenplay are the most important of the entire script. You must *immediately* grab your reader emotionally. Many executives will reject any screenplay that doesn't interest them within ten pages, and even readers who continue to the end of a script that didn't immediately capture their interest will read the rest of the screenplay with less than full involvement.

The most straightforward method of captivating a reader at the outset is usually the same one that will most easily grab an audience: thrilling action. An exciting action sequence right off the bat will usually get an audience, and a reader, immediately into your story. After the magnificent opening of *Raiders of the Lost Ark*, Indiana Jones could probably have read an insurance policy for the next twenty minutes and the audience would have stuck around to see if the movie returned to the excitement of those opening scenes.

However, heavy action is not always the most appropriate beginning for your particular story. Most movies are about everyday people thrust into extraordinary circumstances. So unless your hero is an everyday cop or spy or soldier of fortune, it is unlikely that she would immediately encounter some thrilling confrontation when first introduced. In those screenplays you must grab the reader with some other opening device: humor, a sense of foreboding, a provocative character, or even an unusual and interesting setting.

In addition to grabbing the reader, your opening must also establish the mood and tone of your screenplay. If you're writing a comedy, something funny better happen fairly quickly.

There are seven types of openings you can employ to begin your screenplay; you must choose the one that is most appropriate for your particular story:

The *hero action introduction* opens with your hero immediately involved in some thrilling action sequence. This is the opening used in *Beverly Hills Cop*, *Silverado*, *Batman*, *Rocky*, most of the James Bond movies, and the Indiana Jones movies.

The advantage of this kind of opening is that it both grabs the reader and establishes the hero immediately, which increases audience identification.

The disadvantage is that it will only be appropriate if you're creating a superhero or fantasy story or if your hero would logically encounter action as a part of his everyday life.

The *hero nonaction introduction* opens with your hero, living her everyday life, *before* she is thrust into the extraordinary circumstances. In *Back to the Future,* we meet Marty McFly on his way to school, stopping by to visit the home of the eccentric inventor, before he ever gets involved with time travel or any other excitement. *Look Who's Talking, Witness,* and *The Verdict* all employ the hero nonaction introduction as well.

The advantage here is that the films immediately establish their heroes, which is an important rule of identification. But since these openings lack heavy action, they must grab the reader emotionally in some other way: the humor in *Back to the Future* and *Look Who's Talking;* the unusual setting of the Amish community in *Witness;* the provocative character situation in *The Verdict.*

The *outside action opening* is used a lot in suspense thrillers and action-adventures. The screenplay opens with an action sequence which does *not* involve the hero, then cuts to the hero living her everyday life before she is plunged into these extraordinary circumstances. *Star Wars, Jaws, Romancing the Stone, The Big Easy, The Terminator, Lethal Weapon,* and at least every second episode of any cop show on television open this way.

This device is used in numerous action movies because it accomplishes so much all at once. The action grabs the audience, and the movie immediately establishes superior position (we know rebels are battling the Empire in *Star Wars,* but Luke Skywalker doesn't), anticipation (we anticipate Luke's encounters with the robots, Princess Leia and Darth Vader), and curiosity (about how this young man on some isolated planet will ever come up against the forces of the Empire).

The *new arrival* opens with a character arriving for the first time into a new situation, as in *The Year of Living Dangerously*, *The Secret of My Success*, *Children of a Lesser God*, *9 to 5*, and *E.T.*

The new arrival opening makes it easier to provide exposition for the audience. If we learn what's going on as the newly arrived character does, what could be a boring, "talking heads" scene becomes more emotionally involving.

This opening can also make your story more accessible to an audience by telling them, subconsciously, that they didn't miss out on anything, that they are entering a story right at the outset. As evidence of this, notice sometime how many TV shows open with airplanes landing.

The *prologue* is a sequence which occurs significantly prior to the main story—months or years before. This kind of opening is used in *Vertigo*, *Splash*, *Prizzi's Honor*, *Starman*, and *The Exorcist*.

The primary purpose of a prologue opening is foreshadowing: the early event give credibility to the characters' behavior in the main part of the story. If we don't hear the pledge made at the beginning of *Prizzi's Honor*, or don't know how Jimmy Stewart's character first gets vertigo in *Vertigo*, then the characters' actions in those films won't make any sense.

The prologue can also create curiosity and anticipation in the reader.

The *flashback* begins with a sequence in the middle or end of the story and then flashes back to reveal the events that led up to that opening scene. *Citizen Kane*, *Sunset Boulevard*, *No Way Out*, *Gandhi*, and *GoodFellas* open this way.

A variation on the flashback opening is the use of a narrator, particularly when the narrator is telling the story that occurred earlier in his or her own life. *Out of Africa*, *Stand By Me*, *Sophie's Choice*, *Annie Hall*, *Broadway Danny Rose*, and *Dirty Dancing* are all written this way.

The advantages to the flashback opening are that it allows the screenwriter to choose a sequence from any point in the story that will grab the reader, and it establishes superior position, anticipation, and curiosity.

The disadvantage to this kind of opening is the same disadvantage a flashback holds at any point in a screenplay: it's a hackneyed device. It *may* be the most effective way of opening the movie, but often a flashback simply means the writer is taking the easy way out.

The final type of opening is the *montage*. A montage is a series of events or actions, none of which by itself constitutes a scene, but which are strung together to speed up the exposition. *Tootsie, An Officer and a Gentleman,* and *The Electric Horseman* use montage openings.

The advantage of a montage opening is that it can provide necessary exposition very quickly. If each of the auditions and acting lessons at the beginning of *Tootsie* were presented as a full scene, they alone would take up the entire first act. But all we really need to know is that Michael Dorsey is a good actor who can't get work; the montage reveals that immediately.

The disadvantage of a montage is the same as the disadvantage of a flashback: the device has become a cliché. How many times have you had to sit through a montage sequence of two people falling in love as they ride a carriage, eat a romantic meal, and walk hand in hand down the beach while the Oscar-contending song plays in the background? If you employ the montage opening, be sure to create an *original* sequence of events to introduce your hero.

It is possible to combine two or more of the openings listed above, as with the flashback-montage at the beginning of *An Officer and a Gentleman*, or the new arrival-narrator flashback that opens *Dirty Dancing*. Your primary concern is choosing the type of opening that will grab your reader and establish the tone of your screenplay in the most effective, original way.

17. Give the story an effective ending. All commercially successful movies have two things in common: good word-of-mouth and repeat viewers. You won't achieve either if the audience doesn't find the ending of the movie satisfying and emotionally fulfilling. Choosing the best ending for your story is absolutely essential to its artistic and commercial success.

An effective ending involves two elements: the climax and the denouement.

The *climax* of the story is that scene in the latter half of act 3 in which the hero faces his greatest obstacle. The climax is the highest emotional point of the movie and must clearly resolve, once and for all, whether the hero achieves his outer motivation. The climax will almost always involve the final confrontation between hero and nemesis. There are exceptions, such as *Body Heat*, where the nemesis has been bumped off halfway through the movie, or *Jaws*, where the greatest obstacle is a force of nature, the shark. But the peak emotional moment of a screenplay will usually be that scene where the hero and nemesis confront each other for the final time.

If your screenplay contains a second level of sell, a second, equally important outer motivation for your hero, then you must include a second climax, resolving that outer motivation as well. The first climax of *Back to the Future* occurs when Marty McFly gets his future parents to dance together and fall in love, resolving that outer motivation. The second is when he reaches the city hall clock with the time machine, resolving his desire to get back to the future.

There can be no ambiguity to the climax of your screenplay. Either your hero achieves his outer motivation or he doesn't, but you can't leave that issue unresolved. The reader and the audience have been waiting at least an hour and a half to find that out; you can't leave them up in the air.

The end of your screenplay may still contain some ambiguous elements or some plot lines unresolved, to leave the audience questioning certain facets of the resolution. But these ambiguous elements must never include the resolution of the hero's outer motivation. *2001: A Space Odyssey, The Graduate, Body Heat, Manhattan, Five Easy Pieces, Places in the Heart, The Verdict, No Way Out, Broadcast News*, and many other superb films leave certain aspects of their plots or characters ambiguous or unresolved. But in each case, the audience knows by the end of the movie whether the hero achieved his or her overall outer motivation.

The *denouement* is the emotional tapering off period that follows the climax. After the peak emotional level of the climax, the denouement is the series of scenes that carries the story to the fadeout and allows the audience to absorb the impact of your ending.

Sometimes the denouement will be quite lengthy, as in *Broadcast News,* where the climax occurs in the airport and is followed by the reunion of the three main characters. In such films as *Rocky* or *The Karate Kid,* or in frequent episodes of *Miami Vice*, the denouement is very short, with the end of the film occurring just seconds after the climax.

Finally, the ending must be the one the audience accepts as the most emotionally satisfying resolution of your story.

This doesn't mean that you have to give your screenplay a happy ending; such a rule would eliminate decades of successful tearjerkers, all classic tragedy, all *film noir,* and half of Meryl Streep's career.

But the principle does mean that you cannot have a *defeated* ending. In some way, the conclusion of your film must preserve and convey the dignity of the human spirit and a sense of hope or growth or enlightenment about the human condition. *One Flew Over the Cuckoo's Nest* is a superb example of a classic tragedy that retains an uplifting sense of redemption, with the dignity and beauty of the human spirit preserved.

All I'm really saying here is that an audience is willing to hear that life is hard, that life is sad, or even that life is tragic. But they don't want to hear that life is shit. They probably already suspect that it is, and they certainly won't pay $7.00 to have the feeling reinforced.

Finally, given a choice, give your movie a happy ending. Because by and large, *happy endings sell.* This isn't just an arbitrary Hollywood choice. Audiences go to movies to see problems solved, and to identify with characters who overcome the seemingly insurmountable obstacles they face. It gives the audience a sense of hope and satisfaction, even if their own lives are in the crapper. Providing an audience with that emotional satisfaction, particularly if you are trying to launch your screenwriting career, increases your chances of getting work.

Summary

1. *Stucture* consists of the events in the plot of a screenplay and their position relative to one another. Proper structure occurs when the right thing happens at the right time to elicit maximum emotion.

2. A properly structured film story has three acts, determined by:

The screenwriter's goals of establishing setting, character, situation, and motivation (act 1); building up the hurdles and obstacles to that motivation (act 2); and resolving the outer motivation (act 3).

The three distinct segments or stages to the hero's outer motivation.

The necessary ¼-½-¼ proportion for the three acts.

3. The primary structural devices for maximizing emotion are:

Every scene, event, and character must contribute to the hero's outer motivation.

Show the audience at the outset where the story is going to lead them.

Build the conflict.

Accelerate the pace.

Provide peaks and valleys to the action and emotion.

Create anticipation in the reader.

Give the audience superior position.

Reverse anticipation and surprise the reader.

Create curiosity.

Foreshadow the major events of the story.

Echo particular events, objects, or lines of dialogue to show character growth and change.

Put a character in jeopardy.

Make the story credible.

Teach the audience something vicariously.

Give the story both humor and seriousness.

Grab the reader immediately, using the most appropriate of the following seven types of openings:

Hero action introduction

Hero nonaction introduction

Outside action

New arrival

Prologue

Flashback

Montage

4. Give the screenplay a satisfying ending:

An unambiguous climax

A denouement

A satisfying resolution

PART II

WRITING THE SCREENPLAY

CHAPTER 6

. . . .

Writing Individual Scenes

At this stage in the development of your screenplay, you are ready to write the individual scenes in proper screenplay format. The *way* you put the words on the page is as essential to eliciting emotion as are concept, character, and structure. And just as those three previous stages involved specific methods for grabbing and holding the reader and the audience, so are there underlying principles for writing action, description, and dialogue in a way that ensures the reader's emotional involvment.

The Basic Principles of Writing Scenes

These are the overall rules and guidelines for putting the words on the page and eliciting maximum emotion with your screenwriting style:

1. You must create a movie in the mind of the reader. If you have ever become so engrossed in a novel that you lost all sense of time and place in the real world, you know exactly the emotional experience you hope to create for the person reading your screenplay.

You must write your screenplay in such a way that the reader forgets she's reading words on a piece of paper because she is totally involved with the movie you are "projecting" in her head. Therefore, anything that slows the reader down or calls attention to the words themselves, such as awkward and confusing style, incorrect spelling and grammar, typographical errors, or a script that is twenty pages too long, works against you.

Conversely, whatever you can do to make reading your screenplay *fast, easy,* and *enjoyable* is to your benefit. If there is a single quality that distinguishes screenplays that sell from those that don't, it's this: *the people with the power to make movies choose the scripts that they enjoy reading.* When you crystallize your movie in the mind of the reader, that enjoyment is far more likely.

2. Nothing goes on the page that doesn't go on the screen. Screenplays are made up of action, description, and dialogue. That's all. Nothing can be included that can't be conveyed to an audience. There can be no author's asides, illustrations, interior thoughts of the characters (unless they are verbalized on the screen), or background information that isn't dramatized.

With each scene, ask yourself, "How will the *audience* know what I've just told the reader?" The reader can't be told anything the audience won't find out by watching the screen and hearing the sound track.

3. There are three uses for any screenplay. A screenplay can serve as a *proposal* for a movie you hope to get made, a *blueprint* of a movie that is being made (in other words, the shooting script), and a *record* of a film that has already been shot (for postproduction use by editors, composers, and the like). The only one of these three functions that concerns you is the proposal script.

At this stage in the writing process, your only concern is selling your script or using it as a writing sample. Some of the conventions of a shooting script are therefore unnecessary for your proposal script and actually slow down the reading process, thus violating principal number 1 above. Numbered scenes, capitalized sound effects, and the word *continued* at the bottom of most pages are all shooting script devices which should be eliminated from your proposal script.

Don't worry that your screenplay might sell and then you'll have to know how to write a shooting script; after paying you all that money, someone will be glad to show you how to number your scenes. But at the initial stage of marketing your script, streamlining the reading process is essential.

4. There must be nothing in the script which you know can be improved. When you finally begin submitting your screenplay, you are submitting it as a professional to other professionals. It must be as close to perfection as you can get it.

It is not a potential producer's or agent's job to tell you how to fix your submitted script. If you haven't done everything you possibly can to make your screenplay the best it can be, then it isn't ready to show.

Once I got a call from a writer in Columbus who was a friend of a friend of a friend of my brother and who wanted to submit a screenplay to my production company. He obviously understood the value of networking, and I was ready to take a look at his script until I asked him how long it was. "It's 145 pages," he replied. "I wanted to get your input before editing it any further." So I told him not to send it. I knew I could never get a deal to produce a screenplay that long, so there was no point in even considering it until the writer had done all he possibly could to make it commercial.

Agents and producers won't do your work for you. And since you often will have only one shot at a potential producer, agent, or financier, make sure your screenplay is as good as you can get it.

Similarly, don't leave anything undone because you figure someone's going to change your script eventually anyway. Leaving out dialogue for the actors to improvise or letting the special effects artists determine how the film will look is a huge mistake. You must write your screenplay as if every single moment of the film is your responsibility.

5. Improper format reduces the reader's emotional involvement. Readers in Hollywood do a great deal of inductive reasoning, which goes something like this: "I just read 99 screenplays, they were all horrible, and they were all written in improper format. Therefore, if screenplay number 100 is also in improper format, it must be horrible too."

This conclusion isn't necessarily true; a great screenplay could conceivably be handwritten on a roll of paper towels. But it's tough enough to get an agent or producer emotionally involved in your script. Why start out with that extra strike against you? Put the screenplay in current acceptable format.

The rest of this chapter will show you exactly *how* to write description, action, and dialogue in a style and format which adheres to the five principles listed above and which elicits maximum emotion in your reader.

Proper Screenplay Format

Unfortunately, screenplay format is not as cut and dried as English punctuation and grammar; there is no book like *Elements of Style* you can turn to for the exact rules of screenwriting. Screenplay format changes periodically, and within a general set of guidelines, acceptable screenplays vary somewhat. The variations are minor, however, and if you don't stay within the parameters of *current* accepted format, your chances lessen of getting the reader emotionally involved.

I can't say that every salable screenplay adheres totally to the following format, but if you follow these rules, your script should be acceptable to any reader in Hollywood.

The format I'm outlining is for feature-length films—features and TV movies. Episodic series use a somewhat different format, depending on the length of the show and whether it's filmed or videotaped.

If you're writing an episode of an existing TV series, it's a good idea to obtain, through a script library, the series' production company, or a company that sells screenplays, a copy of a past shooting script for the show. Then copy *that* format for your screenplay rather than the one I outline below. I know this violates my principle of writing a proposal script, but the writing staff of any series will be used to reading scripts in their own format, so copying their style will serve you better. If you can't get a script for the series for which you're writing, get a script for a very similar show, which would use the same format. That means a sample screenplay from a videotaped sitcom, filmed sitcom, or one-hour series, depending on the category of the series you have chosen to write, because each of those three categories uses a somewhat different format.

I'll begin with some overall rules and then use a couple sample pages to demonstrate how you put the words on the page.

The Basic Rules Of Format

1. The submitted screenplay should be photocopied on white, 8½ by 11 inch, three-hole paper. Never submit original or carbon copies, and never use legal-size or colored paper.

2. Screenplay covers should be 8½ by 11 inch, single color card stock, also three-hole punched. No polka dots, stripes, or pretty designs and no fancy leather bindings. Cheapest is best: a plain piece of card stock on the front and back of the script. But at least it can be any color you choose.

3. Nothing is printed on the cover. Don't put illustrations on the front of (or anywhere inside) your screenplay. Don't even put the title on the cover.

4. Bind the screenplay using either brass fasteners, Chicago screws, or an Acco two-piece fastener. Any office supply store will carry those items. Don't pay a fortune to have your script bound like a book, and don't use those plastic things that curl into a dozen rectangular holes on the side of the paper. Again, cheapest is best.

5. The first page inside the cover is the title page, followed immediately by the opening of the film. Omit from the screenplay any cast of characters, casting suggestions, table of contents, sales pitches, autobiography, or illustrations.

6. The feature film screenplay should be no more than 129 pages long. Studios want to distribute films that are ninety minutes to two hours in length so that exhibitors can have five showings a day. The rule of thumb for film length is that one page equals one minute of screen time. A script of 130 pages or more would last more than two hours. (The formula allows for a few more pages of screenplay than minutes of screen time.)

This rule isn't only for economic reasons. In my entire career, I've only read one submitted screenplay of more than 129 pages which elicited maximum emotion. The longer scripts all had too much dialogue and unfocused, convoluted stories. There is something intrinsically effective about a movie that lasts between ninety minutes and two hours.

Obviously, some great films have been longer, but if you're a newer writer, you stand a much better chance of selling your screenplay if you keep it under 129 pages. The *ideal* length for your feature film script is between 110 and 115 pages. And generally speaking, comedies will run closer to ninety minutes than to two hours.

This 129-page rule applies to feature films only. A movie for television should be 105 pages, which will translate to the necessary ninety-seven minutes. And television episodes should correspond to the proper shooting script length. Make your screenplay the same length as the sample episode script you've acquired as a format sample.

7. Omit parenthetical directions to the actors. It is your job as the screenwriter to give the characters action and dialogue. It is *not* your job to tell the actors how to deliver their lines. Such parenthetical directions distract the reader and irritate the actors.

Let's say a section of your screenplay reads as follows (don't worry if you aren't at all familiar with this way of indicating action and dialogue; it will be explained in detail later in this chapter):

INT - SUBURBAN HOUSE

Jim and Nancy are arguing.

                    NANCY
                  (angrily)
              You rotten bastard!

The direction "(angrily)" is unnecessary and improper. How else is Nancy going to deliver that line? Let the action and characters you have created stand on their own and trust that the director and actors will figure out how to convey them.

An even worse error, which I frequently encounter, is to place action within the parentheses. For example:

> NANCY
> (throwing a plate at Jim)
> You rotten bastard!

It *is* your job as screenwriter to give the characters action. But the proper place to indicate action is in the wide paragraphs, not parenthetically within the dialogue.

There are rare exceptions to the rule of omitting parenthetical directions. If a character is within a group, but a line of dialogue is spoken directly to one other person in the group, that would be indicated in parentheses:

INT - BILL'S HOUSE

Bill, Wendy, Charles, and Darcy are playing Trivial Pursuit.

> WENDY
> (To Bill)
> Hurry up and answer!

Similarly, if there might be some confusion about the intent of the dialogue, clarification could be put in parentheses. For example, if Mary called John a bastard in a joking way, the word "teasing" might be placed in parentheses above Mary's dialogue.

These exceptions are rare. If you include more than six such parenthetical directions within your entire screenplay, you've got too many.

8. Omit camera directions. This seems to be the toughest of these rules to swallow, especially for writers who want to direct someday. You must omit from your screenplay all references to FULL SHOT, TWO SHOT, TRACKING SHOT, CRANE SHOT, PULL BACK, PULL INTO, or ANGLE ON. If you don't know what those terms mean, don't worry about it; you shouldn't use them anyway.

As the screenwriter, it is your job to tell the story using action, description, and dialogue. It is *not* your responsibility to tell the director how to position the camera.

This doesn't mean that all those camera tricks and movements can't be emotionally involving on the screen. But *reading* all that terminology dissipates the reader's emotion and works against your script.

Again, there are a few exceptions, if the actual *meaning* of what is happening on the screen is conveyed by the camera direction. For example, if you wish to hide a killer's identity from the audience and from the reader you might say:

CLOSE-UP on a gloved hand as it picks up the letter opener and plunges it into the politician's back.

These instances of camera directions necessary for clarification are also rare, and there are other ways the same point can be made to the reader. Simply calling attention to the hand and knife in the action lets the reader know that the killer's identity remains unrevealed and that the scene will probably be shot in closeup. As with parenthetical directions to the actors, more than six camera directions per script is too many.

With these general rules of format in mind, I will now outline the way you should position the words on the page.

Here is the opening of an imaginary screenplay entitled *Bambi: Portrait of a Dental Hygienist*. First I'll write it in normal type size, so you won't go blind trying to decipher the text:

FADE IN

Sunlight spills through the narrow blinds of a large window and down onto a plush red carpet. A vibrator is heard humming in the background along with the voices of a man and a woman, FLOYD THURSBY and BAMBI SHARPSTEIN.

                    BAMBI O.S.
          Wider . . . Oh, please . . . Open wider!

The man's response is a garbled, inaudible groan.

                    FLOYD O.S.
Rowrafrooahara.

The camera moves up from the carpet to reveal the feet and
legs of the man, twisting and writhing in a horizontal position
on an extended lounge chair. They are clothed in black wing
tips, brown socks, and gray polyester slacks. Draped over the
man's legs is one of the woman's shapely calves, highlighted
by her sheer white hose and white shoes.

Moving up the two intertwined bodies, we see that the woman
is draped over the man's chest and is massaging his gums with
the rubber tip of an electric dental vibrator, while he squirms
apprehensively in a dental chair.

                    BAMBI
         You've got to start flossing more, Mr.
         Thursby.

She pushes her fingers deeper into his mouth.

                    BAMBI (Cont.)
         We don't want to let Mr. Plaque get the
         best of Mr. Molar now, do we?

                    FLOYD
                 (longingly)
         Fruhroorahayia.

We move into a CLOSE-UP of Floyd's hand as it grips the arm
of the chair passionately.

                                        CUT TO:

EXT - CITY PARK - NIGHT

Floyd is sitting on a lonely park bench, looking distraught and
disheveled. He is surrounded by pigeons and is clutching an
old toothbrush. He stares blankly into space.

FLOYD V.O.
My life dissolved the day I met her.

Margins and Spaces

Now I will use this excerpt to illustrate proper format, starting with
the rules for margins and spaces. Here is the same scene typed
exactly as it would appear in proper screenplay format, but reduced to fit the dimensions of this book. The circled numbers in
Figure 6-1 correspond to the numbered items in the list that follows.

1. The action and description in a screenplay are placed
within the wide-margin paragraphs. Set these outside margins on
your typewriter or word processor 1½ inches from the left-hand
edge of the paper, and 1 inch from the right hand edge.

2. The dialogue is indented on both sides, so create a second
set of margins 3 inches from the left-hand edge of the page and 2
inches from the right-hand edge for characters' dialogue.

3. The final indentation is for the characters' names above
their dialogue. Each such character name should begin 4 inches
from the left-hand edge of the page. Do not center the names;
begin each at this point, regardless of the length of the name.

The effect of these margin settings is to give the page a cen-
tered appearance. The purpose of the wider left margins is to allow
for the three holes in the paper.

Since typewritten screenplays are still the norm, it is probably
best not to justify the right margins for action or dialogue, even if
you are using a word processor that has that capability.

4. The page number is placed ½ inch from the top of the
page and 1 inch from the right-hand edge.

5. Whatever text begins the page is placed 1 inch from the
top of the paper. This could be a scene heading, action/description,
or a character's name above dialogue.

⑤
FADE IN:

①Sunlight spills through the narrow blinds of a large window ①
and down onto a plush red carpet. A vibrator is heard
humming in the background, along with the voices of a man
and a woman, FLOYD THURSBY and BAMBI SHARPSTEIN.

③BAMBI O.S.
②Wider . . . Oh, please . . . Open ②
wider!

The man's response is a garbled, inaudible groan.

FLOYD O.S.
Rowrafrooahara.

⑦The camera moves up from the carpet to reveal the feet and
legs of the man, twisting and writhing in a horizontal
position on an extended lounge chair. They are clothed in
black wing tips, brown socks, and gray polyester slacks.
Draped over the man's legs is one of the woman's shapely
calves, highlighted by her sheer white hose and white shoes.
⑫
Moving up the two intertwined bodies, we see that the woman
is draped over the man's chest, and is massaging his gums
with the rubber tip of an electric dental vibrator, while he
squirms apprehensively in a dental chair.

⑧
BAMBI
⑦You've got to start flossing more,
Mr. Thursby.

She pushes her fingers deeper into his mouth.

⑨BAMBI (Cont.)
We don't want to let Mr. Plaque get
the best of Mr. Molar now, do we?
⑩
FLOYD
(longingly)
Fruhroorahayia.

We move into a CLOSE-UP of Floyd's hand as it grips the arm
of the chair passionately.

⑬
CUT TO:
⑬

EXT - CITY PARK - NIGHT
⑪
Floyd is sitting on a lonely park bench, looking distraught
and dishevelled. He is surrounded by pigeons, and is
clutching an old toothbrush. He stares blankly into space.

FLOYD V.O.
My life dissolved the day I met her.

⑥

④1

Figure 6-1

6. The text ends about 1 inch from the bottom of the paper.
Rather than break a new scene or an individual speech as soon as
it begins, leave a wider space at the bottom of the page, and begin
the scene or dialogue on the next page. Or if you need only one

more line to end a scene or a speech, finish the passage, even if the bottom margin becomes a bit less than 1 inch.

7. Single-space the paragraphs within an action/description passage or within one character's dialogue.

8. Double-space between action/description and a character's name above dialogue.

9. Single-space between a character's name and his own dialogue.

10. Double-space between one character's dialogue and the name above the next character's dialogue.

11. Double-space between a scene heading and the action/description passage that follows.

12. If either action/description or dialogue continues uninterrupted for more than one paragraph, double-space between the paragraphs.

13. Double-space between the end of a scene and the words *CUT TO:*, and again between the words *CUT TO:* and the following scene heading.

Now let's examine what all of the words on the sample page mean and how they are properly written. The circled numbers in Figure 6-2 correspond to the numbered items in the list that follows.

14. FADE IN is a standard opening for a screenplay, although it isn't a necessity. It is equally acceptable to open with a standard scene heading (see number 15 below). If you do use FADE IN it will be the last time you use the word FADE until you write FADE OUT at the end of the script.

Don't put fades and dissolves within your screenplay; that's the editor's job. There might be a rare exception where you use a slow dissolve to introduce a flashback or to convey the long passage of time. But as a rule, remove the dissolves from your script.

15. EXT—CITY PARK—NIGHT is a standard scene heading, properly written entirely in capital letters at the beginning of each scene. A *scene,* in terms of format, is defined as action taking place in a distinct location. Every time your action moves to a different

---

⑭FADE IN:

⑯
Sunlight spills through the narrow blinds of a large window
㉖and down onto a plush red carpet. A vibrator is heard
humming in the background, along with the voices of a man
and a woman, FLOYD THURSBY and BAMBI SHARPSTEIN.

⑰
                    BAMBI O.S.⑰
          Wider . . . Oh, please . . . Open
          wider!

The man's response is a garbled, inaudible groan.

                    FLOYD O.S.⑳
          Rowrafrooahara.

The camera moves up from the carpet to reveal the feet and
legs of the man, twisting and writhing in a horizontal
㉖position on an extended lounge chair. They are clothed in
black wing tips, brown socks, and gray polyester slacks.
Draped over the man's legs is one of the woman's shapely
calves, highlighted by her sheer white hose and white shoes.

Moving up the two intertwined bodies, we see that the woman
㉖is draped over the man's chest, and is massaging his gums
with the rubber tip of an electric dental vibrator, while he
squirms apprehensively in a dental chair.

                 ⑲   ⑱BAMBI
          You've got to start flossing more,
          Mr. Thursby.

She pushes her fingers deeper into his mouth.

                    BAMBI (Cont.)㉑
          We don't want to let Mr. Plaque get
          the best of Mr. Molar now, do we?

                  ⑱FLOYD
              ㉓(longingly)
          Fruhroorahayia.
              ㉔
We move into a CLOSE-UP of Floyd's hand as it grips the arm
of the chair passionately.

                              ㉒CUT TO:

⑮EXT - CITY PARK - NIGHT

Floyd is sitting on a lonely park bench, looking distraught
㉕and dishevelled. He is surrounded by pigeons, and is
clutching an old toothbrush. He stares blankly into space.

                    FLOYD V.O.⑳
          My life dissolved the day I met her.

Figure 6-2

location, you must create a new scene and therefore a new scene heading.

This will sometimes differ from the dramatic definition of a scene. Let's say your characters John and Teresa start an argument in their kitchen, then continue it in the car, and finish at the golf course. Dramatically, that would be a single "scene"; your artistic concerns would apply to the three situations strung together. But proper format would be to place a new scene heading at the beginning of each segment—in the kitchen, the car, and the golf course.

A proper scene heading specifies the location of the scene: CITY PARK, CAR WASH, MOJAVE DESERT, FRITZ'S APARTMENT, or THE WHITE HOUSE ROSE GARDEN.

You *may* add two shooting script conventions which are so common that they are acceptable in your proposal script as well: INT or EXT to designate interior or exterior (indoors or outdoors); and DAY or NIGHT to indicate the time of day. These are optional, but if you think it makes your script look more like a real screenplay, go ahead and use either or both, in the order illustrated. For example, EXT—PARADISE, MONTANA—DAY.

Don't put character names or camera directions in the scene heading, such as ANGLE ON BONNIE AND VINCE. Stick to the scene locations only.

16. Go back to the top of the sample page and notice that screenplays are always written in the present tense.

17. When characters first appear, their names are written in all capital letters. This makes it easy for a reader who forgets who Bambi is to skim backward and find the scene where she's introduced. From then on the character's name within the action-description paragraphs is simply capitalized.

18. Characters' names are always written entirely in capital letters above their own dialogue.

19. Dialogue is never placed within quotation marks. Indenting on both sides and placing the character's name above is the proper indication for dialogue.

20. O.S. stands for "off screen." Add these letters to a character's name above her dialogue if she can be heard by the other characters in the movie, but isn't visible on the screen. A voice on a telephone or an intercom, a person in the next room, or a shout from outside the window would each require O.S.

A similiar designation is V.O. for "voice over." This is used when a character can be heard by the audience, but not by the other characters in the movie. The thoughts of a character or the voice of a narrator would require that the letters V.O. follow the character's name above his dialogue.

21. When a character's dialogue continues through action, or when a character is interrupted and then continues speaking, repeat the character's name, in all caps, followed by Cont. in parentheses above the second portion of dialogue. This alerts the reader that this isn't a conversation but that the same character is speaking.

Similarly, when dialogue is broken at the end of a page, you must end the page with the word *(Continued)*, then repeat the character's name at the top of the new page followed by *(Continued)* or *(Cont.)* before continuing the dialogue. Never begin a page with dialogue without repeating that heading.

22. CUT TO: is an optional ending for a scene. It isn't really necessary, since the new scene heading tells the reader that the previous scene is over. If you choose to include CUT TO: put it in all capital letters against the right-hand margin at the end of each scene, double space, and write the new scene heading.

If your script is running a little too long, taking out all of the CUT TO: indications could save you a page or two.

23. If you choose to include a parenthetical direction to an actor (in spite of my stern warnings to the contrary given above), center it under the character's name, before his dialogue.

24. Similarly, if you wish to risk putting in a camera direction, such as CLOSE-UP or PULL BACK, write it all in capital letters.

25. Always begin a scene with action and/or description; never follow a new scene heading with dialogue. And never give characters dialogue until they have been introduced in the action-description paragraph.

26. Finally, notice that the first three paragraphs of action-description in the sample show three ways you can convey what's happening on the screen *without* using formal camera directions.

The first paragraph illustrates what is by far the best way, and should *always* be used if possible: simply say what's going on and trust that the reader will understand that it's happening on the screen.

In the second and third paragraphs, the humor depends on the suggestion that something a lot more wicked is going on than what is really happening. Therefore other descriptive methods are used to ensure that the reader understands that only a limited amount of information is being revealed to the audience.

The second paragraph uses the phrase "the camera." This is not a camera direction, using specific terminology, but rather a statement in plain English of what the camera is doing.

The third paragraph uses the phrase "we see" in similar fashion.

If you're ever in doubt about proper format, simply copy the format illustrated above. If you follow the overall rules listed, minor details are not going to make or break your script. And if you remember that the most important principle is to create a movie in the mind of your reader, then you will describe what's happening on the screen as clearly and effectively as possible in your own language.

The Title Page

The title page is the only page of your screenplay which doesn't translate directly to the screen and the only one which varies from the format outlined above. Again, see the sample title page shown in Figure 6-3.

1. The title of your screenplay should be written in capital letters. You may also underline it, but that is optional.

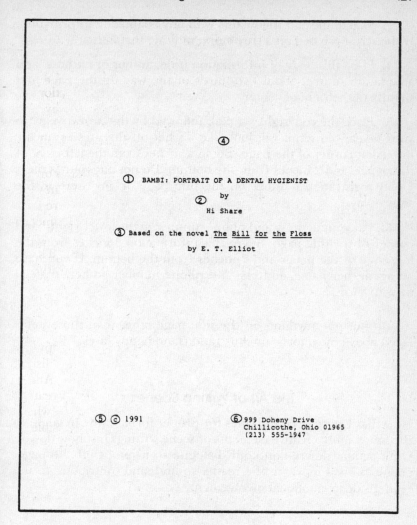

Figure 6-3

2. Skip a line and follow the title with the word *by*, then skip another line and write your name (or names, in alphabetical order, if you're a writing team). You can add the phrase *an original screenplay by* if your script is not an adaptation.

3. Skip a line and follow this with any adaptation information. If the script is based on a true story, indicate that here.

4. Place this body of information (title, author or authors, and adaptation source) about two-thirds of the way up the page and slightly to the right of center.

5. Place the copyright symbol, followed by the *current* year (so your 5-year-old script will look like it's hot off the presses) in the lower left corner of the page. Begin 2 inches from the left edge of the paper, and 2 inches from the bottom. Do not put your Writers Guild registration number on the title page or anywhere in the screenplay.

6. Put your address and phone number in the lower right-hand corner of the title page. Begin this information 5 inches from the left edge of the paper and 2 inches from the bottom. If you have an agent, her name, address, and phone number go here instead of your own.

Do not put anything on the title page other than those items listed above: no quotes, no illustrations, no happy faces.

The Art of Writing Scenes

Now that I've covered the rules for proper format, we can go on to the much more creative elements of scene writing. Just how do you write action, description, and dialogue so it jumps off the page, creates a vivid movie in the reader's mind, and contributes to the reader's deep emotional involvement?

Description

Original, clever, funny, provocative, vivid, and colorful descriptions add to the reader's emotional involvement by bringing the images into sharper focus and making your script more fun to read. Clear, concise writing is the goal. Two or three words or phrases which crystallize the image of the character or setting will work best, not long passages of endless prose.

The element common to all good descriptive writing is *detail*. The particulars of appearance, attire, decor, attitude, and manner which convey the essence and the uniqueness of a character or setting are the ones to employ. Such attention to detail will create and enhance the movie in the reader's mind and will contribute most strongly to his emotional involvement in each scene.

For example, "an aging, dusty Underwood" is a lot more vivid than simply "a typewriter," and "his sleek, newly polished Porsche" creates a more involving image than just "his car."

When introducing characters to your screenplay, instead of re-sorting to mere physical description, describe such things as cloth-ing, hair style, movement, surroundings, habits, or physical details (scars, deformities, or expressions instead of overall physical ap-pearance). Even attitudes and limited reference to background can be employed to enchance the clarity of a character description.

Description based only on physical appearance runs the risk of limiting casting possibilities. I have read far too many screenplays where the female lead is a buxom blonde of twenty-three. Yet there isn't one bankable star who could be cast in that role, at least not without a lot of makeup.

Effective description need not be lengthy. In *Body Heat*, Law-rence Kasdan give the following description of the man who pro-vides Ned Racine with a bomb:

TEDDY LAURSEN, rock and roll arsonist...

Those four descriptive words create a provocative, clever de-scription of the character which creates a sufficiently vivid image for the movie in the reader's mind. It's fun to read, and it conveys the essence of the character without limiting casting possibilities.

Occasionally, of course, you will *have to* provide a detailed phys-ical description of a character because the character's appearance is essentail to the plot. *Mask, The Terminator, The Elephant Man* and *E.T.* all portray characters whose physical appearance affects the plot, and in these circumstances detailed physical descriptions are appropriate.

In writing character description, you can cheat a bit on the rule that nothing can go on the page which doesn't go on the screen. It is OK to make *limited* reference to a character's background as part of the description. For example, you might say:

Earl's every movement projects the ten years he's spent pumping iron.

It's impossible to put "ten years" of "pumping iron" on the screen, but the vivid image created might be worth the gamble in your script. Just don't go overboard and replace character description with a biography.

And finally, never use an actor's name in describing a character.

Action

Your primary goal in writing action is *clarity*. You must convey to the reader exactly what is happening on the screen, so that there is no confusion, misunderstanding, or need for the reader to re-read the passage. Remember that anything that slows the reader's progress or takes the reader away from his "mental movie" will work against you.

Clarity is a very tough requirement. With screenwriting, as with any form of writing, it is almost impossible to know with certainty whether your ideas will be understood by the reader. But there are a few things you can do to help ensure the clarity of your action:

1. Use everyday, straightforward language. Your script should be comprehensible at a high school reading level. This will make it easy to read your script and will steer you away from convoluted words and phrases, excessive technical jargon, and an impressive but tedious vocabulary.

2. Lengthen the action and description passages. Most of the bad screenplays I read are too long. Almost without exception, they are too long because there is too much dialogue or because there are unnecessary scenes which don't contribute or relate to the hero's outer motivation. Screenplays are almost *never* too long because there is too much action and description. These sequences always seem shortchanged, while the dialogue and unnecessary scenes go on forever.

Remember the formula that one page equals one minute of screen time. It isn't an exact formula, but it certainly means that a five minute action scene can't be adequately described in half a page. The more detail to both the action and description, the better.

3. Use action words. Don't let the writing become static. There are at least twenty-five ways to say "go" in the English language. A character can walk, run, crawl, fly, leap, hurtle, dart, or shuffle down the street. Bring the action to life by letting the specific words convey the movement.

4. Give your action scenes to someone to read. It's the only way you can really check out whether you've achieved the necessary degree of clarity. Ask the reader to tell you what happened in the scene. If the reader misses or confuses any important detail, go back to the typewriter.

Pay special attention to certain kinds of action sequences in your screenplay. The first is the credit sequence. Omit it. Remove any reference to when and how the credits will be shown. Even though some films have striking, involving opening credits, *reading* about this sequence almost always dissipates emotion at a point when it is imperative that you grab the reader. Skip the credits and go right into the action of your story.

The words *special effects* should also be eliminated from the script. Your job is to describe exactly what happens on the screen. Let the filmmakers figure out when to call Industrial Light and Magic. If your script contains a thrilling space battle, a hallucination, or a terrifying creature from another dimension, then simply describe it in detail, creating as vivid a mental image as you can. It will be someone else's job to create the image on film.

The same principle holds true for action sequences such as car chases or lovemaking scenes. You must describe the action on the screen in specific detail. Don't simply say,

They jump into their cars and there's a terrific chase.

That sentence creates almost no clear image or emotion. Rather, describe exactly what is going on in the scene:

> As the black limousine comes racing toward Jimmie, he leaps onto the sideboard of a passing ice cream wagon. Opening the door of the moving truck, he pushes the startled driver off the seat and guns the accelerator.
>
> The limousine fishtails toward Jimmie and the truck, sideswiping a light pole and narrowly missing a young girl on her tricycle.
>
> Soon the limo is bearing down on Jimmie's truck at close to 90 miles an hour as he thunders toward an irrigation ditch...

Remember the rule about one page equaling one minute of screen time. That means that a car chase that you anticipate lasting five minutes on the screen will be close to four or five pages long. That would be a very lengthy scene, requiring some terrific writing. (If this rule prevents you from putting long car chases into your screenplay, then I've done my part for the improvement of civilization.)

Similarly, when writing lovemaking scenes, you can't just say:

> They look longingly into each other's eyes, and then they DO IT.

You must say exactly what's going on in detail. You don't have to get pornographic (although that would certainly brighten the days of lots of readers in Hollywood), but you do need to create clear images in the reader's mind.

An excellent example of this kind of detail is the screenplay for *Body Heat*. Consider the following scene, where Ned breaks through the window and makes love with Matty Walker for the first time:

> INT - HALL
>
> Racine crosses the dark living room fast. As he reaches Matty, she lifts her arms to match his embrace. They come together

hard and tight. They kiss. And kiss again. Her hands travel over his body, as though she's wanted them there for a long time.

They turn once slowly along the wall, into the dimness of the central hall. Then he rotates her body away from him, holding her close. For an instant he looks down her body from over her shoulder, then he puts his hands where only his eyes have gone—slowly, gently, then more desperately—first barely touching, then firmly palming her.

MATTY

Yes, yes . . .

Then she is just nodding. Racine puts his face deep into her hair, closing his eyes as the smell of her washes over him.

Matty turns in his arms and kisses him hard. She moves back a step and her hands are tearing at his shirt, fumbling with the buttons. Their hands are shaking badly. She parts his shirt and kisses his chest as her hands move down to work at his belt.

Racine's hands are moving up the backs of her thighs, pushing her skirt up ahead of them, lifting it out of the way. . . .

Matty is moaning, whimpering into his neck. Her hands down below, working on him. Sweat covers her forehead. She drops down to the floor and pulls him down with her. He is on his knees before her as she lifts her hips and bunches her skirt up around her waist.

RACINE

That's right . . . that's right!

Close on Matty's face, a look that might be anguish. She bites her lip in impatience, expectation, heat.

Racine's face, shiny with sweat. His eyes move down her.

Racine's hand appears in the light and Matty's silken panties slide off his fingers, into the corner. Racine moves over her.

                              MATTY
              Do it ... Please, please ... Yes! Do it.

She pulls him tightly to her, clinging like a drowning woman.

Bet you didn't expect to read that in some old textbook, did you?

Lawrence Kasdan was once quoted as saying that he wanted people *reading* the script of *Body Heat* to get turned on. If nothing else, that exhibits a great understanding of the principle of eliciting emotion in the reader.

Notice how much detail he gives to the action, while using simple, clear language and never resorting to four-letter words. The passage creates a vivid mental image but leaves much to the reader's imagination, never lapsing into vulgarity or repetition.

Of course, if you're going for a PG-13 rating, you'll dissolve away before the heavy stuff anyway. The point is that with any kind of action, thoroughly describe exactly what the audience will see, in a way that is as emotionally provocative and enjoyable as possible.

Music can occur in a variety of ways in a movie, each requiring slightly different handling within your screenplay:

1. The Score. This is the background music, which can be heard by the audience, but not by the characters in the film. *Omit the score from your screenplay.* No matter how much emotion is created and enhanced by the score of a movie, *reading* about music is a drag. The rule is: if music can't be heard by the characters in your film, make no mention of it in your script. Let your action, description and dialogue create the emotion, and John Williams will figure out how to add the orchestra.

2. Music Played by a Character in the Movie. If someone puts on a record, sits down at the piano, or plays some familiar song on the juke box, that is part of your story, and it is therefore your job to include it. For example, the characters in *The Big Chill* listen to "Ain't Too Proud to Beg" on the stereo while they all do the dishes. That scene, with the particular song identified, would have to be written into the script.

There are several pitfalls to watch out for when you name an existing piece of music. The first is that the reader won't recognize it. Don't assume a reader will recognize *any* tune besides "Happy Birthday To You" and "The Star-Spangled Banner." Precede or follow the name of any song with a phrase describing it:

> The lilting strains of Beethoven's "Moonlight Sonata" drift through the open window and up to her balcony.

Another danger of using existing music within the story is that the rights to use the music in the film may be costly. You don't want the reader to assume that the music rights will double the budget of the film.

Don't fill your screenplay with repeated references to specific music heard by the characters. Mention songs by title only when it's absolutely germane to the plot, and create emotion in the rest of the script with your own writing talent.

3. Original Music Written by One of Your Characters. Occasionally your screenplay will involve a character who writes original music. In this case, since it is part of the plot and will be heard by the other characters, you must describe it.

It is best to simply describe the kind of song being sung or played by the character, along with the reactions of the characters who are listening. Don't write in the lyrics to these songs. Reading lyrics in a screenplay is like reading poetry; the language is read in a different way and at a different pace, and the adjustment can be jarring. As a result, most readers will just skip over the lyrics anyway and go on with the story. But by then, they have already left the mental movie you are creating.

And whatever you do, don't enclose a cassette tape of you singing these original songs.

The one time you will want to include some lyrics is when the meaning of the song advances the plot of your film. For example, of all the songs in *Tender Mercies,* the most appropriate to the story line is sung by the Robert Duvall character to his new wife and son in the tavern. The lyrics are his way of expressing his deep love for them.

In such an instance, it is wise to put one or two stanzas of the song in the screenplay, since the lyrics themselves move the plot forward. Then say in your script that the character continues singing, and describe the subject of the song and the reactions of the audience. The song "I'm Easy" in *Nashville* functions the same way and would be handled similarly in the script.

The general principle for all music is that hearing it can be deeply moving, but reading about it diffuses, rather than increases, emotion.

Dialogue

When it's time to write dialogue, you will usually find yourself in one of two situations:

Perhaps you will begin by writing the scene heading, open with description and/or action, figure out who should speak first, write that character's name, and give that first character a line of dialogue. Another character will respond to the first, the first character will answer back or provide another statement or question, the conversation will begin to flow, and soon the characters will seem to be writing their own dialogue.

When this effortless creativity arises, nurture it. *Don't edit as you go.* In other words, when dialogue (or any other aspect of your writing) starts to flow, you are tapping directly into your creative source. You want to facilitate that process as much as possible, so don't stop to decide whether the dialogue is good or not. If you start to engage your critical, judgmental faculties, you will stifle the creativity you've been striving for.

Instead, let the words come, even if they seem awful or irrelevant and even if your three-minute scene gets to be twenty pages long. You can always go back and edit it to meet the overall needs of the script. But when you're in touch with your characters to this extent, they may reveal ideas to you which will take the scene, or the story, in a new and even better direction.

On the other hand, don't *wait* for that glorious burst of creativity to happen. As you probably know, you will far more often find yourself in the situation described below:

You write the scene heading, then open with some description and/or action, figure out who should speak first, write that character's name, stare at the blank page, and say to yourself, "What in the hell are these people going to say?" And you'll have no idea what the dialogue should be.

When you just can't think of any dialogue, the greatest danger is writer's block. For some reason, dialogue can be more frightening than any other aspect of your screenplay. So it's easy to allow your anxiety to crush your creativity and to start heading for the refrigerator rather than writing your screenplay.

To prevent writer's block while writing dialogue, you first must realize that what your characters say is *not* the most important part of your script. Dialogue is far less important than character development or plot structure, and any skilled filmmaker knows that dialogue is the easiest thing to change in a screenplay.

This doesn't mean that good dialogue can't help sell your screenplay and sometimes even cover up a weakly structured story. You certainly don't want your speeches to be boring or idiotic. But all dialogue doesn't need to sound as if Neil Simon or John Hughes wrote it, and sometimes "clever" dialogue isn't even appropriate. Your primary goal is for the dialogue to contribute to the overall thrust of the story and to the desired character development.

So if you're close to getting blocked, let go of your fear and go through the following steps, which will enable you to create effective dialogue for any scene in your screenplay.

Begin by asking the following questions about the scene, before attempting any dialogue at all:

1. What is my objective within this scene? This is the most important consideration, because this will link the scene to the spine of your story and ensure that the scene contributes to the outer motivation for your hero. You must know the purpose the scene serves within the context of the story. No matter how funny, dramatic, or original your dialogue may be, if the scene doesn't contribute to your hero's outer motivation, you've got to change the scene or get rid of it altogether.

2. How will the scene end? After deciding on your objective as described in question number 1, decide on the outcome of the scene. Almost all scenes should end with the individual issue in the scene resolved but with some element left unresolved which will compel the reader to turn the page and compel the audience to stay tuned. For example, in the scene in *Hannah and Her Sisters* where the Michael Caine character asks his sister-in-law (Barbara Hershey) if she is also attracted to him, his desire to get acknowledgment from her is resolved, but we are left wondering if they will actually have an affair.

3. What is each character's objective within the scene? Every character in every scene in your screenplay must *want* something. This desire will determine the character's actions and dialogue. For example, the boys' desire for food in the early scene of *Stand By Me* determines the dialogue concerning their money, who will go to the store, the coin toss, and so on.

4. What is each character's attitude within the scene? How does each character feel about what is going on? Often a character's attitude will remain hidden from the reader, but as the screenwriter, you must know your characters' true feelings at all times.

For example, when the Marlee Matlin character expresses aloofness and superiority in her first encounters with the language teacher (William Hurt) in *Children of a Lesser God*, she is actually feeling fear, anger, resentment, and pain. These attitudes are revealed to the audience later in the film. But the screenwriter had to have known them when writing those early scenes.

5. How will the scene begin? How are you going to get your characters into the situation you're creating? When Crocodile Dundee first appears in *Crocodile Dundee,* he bursts into the tavern clutching a crocodile and confronts several other characters before talking to the reporter. There are probably a dozen other meetings the screenwriters could have devised to get the two lead characters introduced, but this one serves to emphasize the contrast between the future lovers, to reveal much about the characters, and to add originality and tension to the dialogue that follows between the two.

When you have answered these five questions for your scene, you are ready to give your characters some initial dialogue. But before continuing to that stage of the process, here is an example of how the above questions can be applied to an original scene:

Let's say we want to create dialogue for a romantic comedy involving a two-character job interview. Frank, an advertising executive, is interviewing Janice, our hero, for the job of secretary. This provides a typical two-character situation which will rely heavily on dialogue.

To make the scene more interesting, let's say that Janice wants this job because her best friend, Bonnie, got fired from the same position after Frank made a pass at her and she wouldn't play along. Now Janice wants to get revenge on this sexist pig by nailing Frank when he tries the same thing with her.

Given that story line, how would we answer each of the above questions before attempting to write any dialogue?

1. What is my objective within this scene? To get Janice working for Frank. This will contribute to the hero's overall outer motivation of working for Frank and getting him fired or humiliated.

2. How will the scene end? To accomplish the above objective, the scene will have to end with Frank offering the job to Janice and Janice accepting.

3. What is each character's objective within the scene? Janice's is obviously to get the job. Frank's is to decide if this is the right woman to hire as his secretary.

4. What is each character's attitude within the scene? A person can have any number of feelings in a job interview: fear, trepidation, confidence, curiosity, ressentment. But from the story we've outlined, Janice's attitude and feelings must include anger, determination, and imposture.

Frank's attitude, given what we know about his past behavior, will probably include curiosity, lust, and anticipation.

5. How will the scene begin? A logical opening might show Frank dismissing the previous applicant, whose age, sex, or appearance are obviously not to his liking and then calling for the next secretarial candidate, Janice.

Now that you have the answers to all of the questions, you give your characters what is known as *on-the-nose* dialogue, where they say exactly what they think, feel, and mean. In other words, it's bad dialogue. *Nobody* says exactly what she thinks or feels or means. We all hide our true intentions, feelings, or desires, gradually tap-dancing our way up to what we really want. If you don't believe me, think back to the last time you were angry with a friend, bought a car, or asked someone out on a date.

But I am saying you *should* give your characters this bad, on-the-nose dialogue. Because when the process started, you had no idea what the characters would say and you were in danger of getting blocked. At least with on-the-nose dialogue you'll have a scene. From then on, you can tell yourself it's all editing, which is psychologically much easier than creating dialogue on a blank page.

So in this example, the on-the-nose dialogue would be as follows:

> JANICE
> I really want this job, Frank, because
> I'm angry about what you did to my
> friend, and I want to stomp on you for
> it.

> FRANK
> Well, since I've got the hots for you, I'm
> going to give you the job, and hope
> you'll be more cooperative than your
> friend Bonnie was.

Awful, isn't it? Not only are the words stilted and unrealistic but characters would never give away their true motives this way. But now we at least have something to fall back on. From now on we're simply rewriting.

Now we return to the original list of questions and develop the scene from the opening we chose in question number 5 above, this time allowing the characters to lead up to the on-the-nose dialogue, which will serve as the turning point of the scene. We'll assume that in the previous scene, Janice outlined her plan to Bonnie, so the reader already knows these characters and their true desires.

INT - FRANK'S OFFICE - DAY

Frank is sitting at his desk, interviewing RIVA KLUNK, Riva is not very attractive to Frank.

> FRANK
> Well thank you, Miss Klunk. We'll call you when we've made our final decision. Just leave your resume with the receptionist.

Miss Klunk leaves, and Frank speaks into his intercom.

> FRANK
> Gladys, could you send in the next applicant, please?

Janice walks into Frank's office, looking beautiful. Frank looks excited. He looks at her resume.

> FRANK
> Please have a seat, Miss Johnston. Could you tell me a little about yourself?

> JANICE
> Well, I've had eleven years of office experience, I was previously an executive secretary for the CEO of Moclips, Incorporated, and I type 80 words per minute.

> FRANK
> That's quite impressive. How soon would you be able to start?

                    JANICE
          I'm available immediately.

                    FRANK
          Wonderful. Be here Monday at 9:00.
          You've got the job.

It's still pretty bad, with stilted dialogue, awkward wording, and no emotion at all. But we've accomplished our primary objective (getting Janice the job), each character's individual objective is clear, and the dialogue is consistent with the attitudes of each character, even though the characters keep their feelings from each other.

Notice that we have thrown out that on-the-nose dialogue, which was just there to get us rolling and to pinpoint the necessary moment in the scene where the primary desire of the main character could be revealed.

Now we can really begin working with the scene. As it now stands, it's flat, familiar, and humorless. Our goal now is to go back and accomplish several things:

> Create more interesting, vivid description and action.

> Add humor to the scene (if the scene is supposed to be funny, as in the example).

> Reveal more of the inner motivations and attitudes of the characters.

> Create a few more obstacles for the hero (Janice).

> Make the dialogue more consistent with the speech patterns of the characters. If Janice and Frank are from the Fortune 500 crowd, they will have one pattern of word usage and slang; another if they are high school students, and still others if they are immigrants, factory workers, soldiers, or peasants in the French Revolution.

Given these considerations, the next rewrite might look like this:

INT - FRANK'S OFFICE - DAY

Frank is sitting at his desk, interviewing RIVA KLUNK. It is
clear from the glazed-over look in his eyes and the forced smile
sewn onto his face that this isn't his first interview of the day.
And since Riva has the face and body of Mrs. Potato Head,
it's pretty clear she's not going to get the nod from Frank
either.

> RIVA
>
> And another thing, I always prefer #2
> pencils for any office memos. I think
> ball points have been the scourge of
> the secretarial profession, not to men-
> tion the eyesight of America. I know
> Mr. Klunk, rest his soul, switched to
> ball points at his accounting firm in
> 1957, and he was blind as a bat when
> he died. I simply think you can't be too
> careful when it comes to office health
> and hygiene, do you?

> FRANK
>
> Huh?...Oh, yes, of course...#2 pen-
> cils. An excellent suggestion. Well,
> thank you Miss Klunk. We'll call you
> when we've made our final decision.
> Just leave your resume with the recep-
> tionist.

Miss Klunk leaves, and Frank speakes into his intercom.

> FRANK
>
> Gladys, could you send in the next ap-
> plicant, please? And try to find some-
> body from the planet Earth this time,
> will you?

Janice walks into Frank's office, and Frank almost slides out
of his chair. No longer the dress for success executive we saw
earlier, Janice is now the personification of old-fashioned fem-

inine beauty and demure sexuality. She's the Vargas Girl of
secretaries. He can barely take his eyes off her to glance at her
resume.

                    FRANK
          Well, let's see here, Ms. . . .

                    JANICE
          Johnston. And it's <u>Miss</u> Johnston. But
          you can call me Janice.

Her voice has gotten breathy, and her eyelashes seem to lower
seductively as she leans toward Frank's desk.

                    FRANK
          Well, Janice, I see that you were an
          executive secretary for the CEO at Mo-
          clips, Incorporated before they pro-
          moted you in-house to full office
          manager. And for the last four years
          you've been director of marketing for
          them.

                    JANICE
          That's right. I'm sure anyone there will
          vouch for me.

Now a trace of suspicion is entering Frank's voice. Maybe this
woman <u>is</u> too good to be true.

                    FRANK
          You know, this job is just as my per-
          sonal secretary. Don't you think maybe
          you're a bit overqualified?

A slight look of panic flashes over Janice's face, but she
catches it in time.

                    JANICE
          Well, Frank . . . can I call you Frank? . . .
          Those jobs were OK, but I found I was
          really happiest working under a
          strong, powerful man.

She's really laying it on thick now, and we can tell it's grating on her, but she's determined to reel this guy in. And Frank, who seems just short of panting out loud, is buying it. He decides to test the waters.

> FRANK
> I see. Well, I can certainly understand
> your feeling that way. But you know,
> this job isn't easy. For instance, there
> could be a lot of...uh...late hours.
> You know, the two of us, working
> closely together...at night.

> JANICE
> Oh, that would be fine. I'm sure I
> wouldn't be frightened about late hours
> as long as you were beside me, Frank.

She's got him, and she knows it.

> FRANK
> It's settled then. If you want the job it's
> yours. You can start Monday. Just tell
> Gladys to give you the necessary forms.
> Until that time, Janice.

> JANICE
> I can hardly wait.

Janice stands and swirls toward the door, but not before throwing Frank a last, lingering gaze to hold his interest over the weekend. After she exits, Frank is left staring dazedly at the closed door.

Not exactly Woody Allen, but it's reading a lot better than it was.

At this point, if you're going full steam ahead and *want* to do a rewrite of the scene, go ahead. Otherwise, leave the scene and go on with the rest of your script.

By the time you complete this first draft, you will be much more familiar with your plot and characters. So when you return to this scene on your second draft, you'll be able to make it more consistent with whatever new directions your plot and characters might be taking.

With each successive draft, concentrate on accomplishing more with the scene, making it more consistent with your plot and characters, and improving the writing style. If there is an opportunity to employ some added structural devices, then do so: reveal more about inner motivation, conflict, character background or theme; strengthen character identification; or add the appropriate humor, action and conflict.

Eventually you will reach a point where you don't think you can make it any better. That's when you need a tape recorder, a friend, and as many actors as there are characters in your scene. (If you can't find any willing actors or acting students, just use other friends.)

Assemble this group with copies of your scene or scenes and tell them only what they would know from having read the previous scenes in your screenplay. From then on you have to keep your mouth shut. *You can't play director in this exercise.* You have to see if the scene and dialogue will stand on its own, since you won't have the opportunity in the future to talk to the readers of your screenplay and "explain" what they missed.

After giving your group the necessary background information only, turn on the tape recorder, and have the actors do a reading of the scene.

When they finish, ask your friend what she thought of the scene. Was the dialogue clear, interesting, real, true to the characters, funny? A good clue is this: if your friend laughed during the reading, it was funny. If your friend didn't laugh but tells you it was funny, it wasn't that funny.

Then ask the actors their opinions of the scene. Get any suggestions for improvement they have as a result of performing the scene.

And finally, if the actors are trained and willing, ask them to put the pages away and, knowing what they now know about the scene, improvise it.

When you have all the performances and everyone's comments

and suggestions on tape, thank everyone, go home, and in light of all that you heard, do another rewrite and polish of the scene.

The most important considerations for your dialogue are that it contribute to the overall thrust of your story, that it be true to your characters, and that it sound "real." And the above process will accomplish all of that.

A Scene-by-Scene Checklist

The following checklist can now be applied to each scene in your screenplay to ensure that the scene is as effective as possible.

Use this list *after* you have completed your first draft. Although you will have these principles in mind as soon as you begin the writing process, it is helpful to have new tools to employ with successive rewrites. The longer you have been working on a screenplay, the more likely you are to lose your critical objectivity, to feel frustrated, foggy or burned out, and to begin settling for scenes which aren't eliciting maximum emotion. Approaching your screenplay in new ways can help you figure out additional improvements. This is when the following checklist and the later screenplay chart can be most helpful.

1. How does the scene contribute to the hero's outer motivation? I hope you're getting weary of hearing about this by now because I want to drive home the idea that every single scene, event, and character in your entire screenplay must connect to your original story concept.

Even when the scene doesn't involve the hero, it can contribute to the spine of the story. For example, *Platoon* is about a young soldier who wants to survive his year in Viet Nam and bring one of his sergeants to justice. The scene in which Elias is finally confronted in the jungle by Barnes doesn't include Taylor, the hero. But it contributes to Taylor's outer motivation nonetheless because it creates additional conflict for Taylor later in the story and helps determine his actions in the climax of the film.

2. Does the scene possess its own beginning, middle and end?
Each scene in your screenplay is like a minimovie: it must establish, build, and resolve a situation. The scene doesn't necessarily follow the $\frac{1}{4}-\frac{1}{2}-\frac{1}{4}$ layout of the full script, but it must employ that same basic emotional arc.

For example, in the previously mentioned scene in *Hannah and Her Sisters* in which the Michael Caine character first confesses his attraction for the Barbara Hershey character, the situation is established when he encounters her, builds as he tells her of his desire, and is resolved when she agrees to see him again.

Occasionally, you may choose to break this rule in order to keep an audience curious and emotionally involved. Let's say you have a scene in which a baby-sitter goes into the house where a killer is lurking. We follow the baby-sitter into one room after another, until she hears a sound coming from behind a closet door. We see her open the door and let out a scream, a look of terror on her face.

The screenplay then cuts away to another scene and *later* reveals the horrifying body of the baby-sitter. By cutting away, that first scene ends in the middle, with no resolution. The resolution (her murder) is then revealed in the later scene, and in the meantime, the audience emotion has been heightened through curiosity and anticipation.

Even though this can occasionally be an effective device, you don't want to overdo it; once or twice in a script is probably enough.

3. Does the scene thrust the reader into the following scenes?
At the end of each scene, you must compel the reader to turn the page; any time a reader doesn't care about what happens next, your screenplay has failed. So each scene must have the reader wanting more.

For example, in *Outrageous Fortune*, the scene of the two women in the morgue is resolved when they realize the body is not that of their lover. But the scene then propels the audience into the following scenes by their decision to try to find him.

4. What is each character's objective in the scene?

5. What is each character's attitude in the scene? These are the same two questions we asked in the dialogue exercise earlier in this chapter. But even if a scene contains no dialogue at all, this remains an important principle: *Every* character in every scene wants something. It may be as simple as observing what's going on or spending time with another person, but every character will possess some motivation at all times. That visible objective must be clear in each scene.

Additionally, every character in every scene *feels* a certain way about what's going on. Whether happy, sad, angry, bored, scared, uninterested, or turned on, everybody has an attitude about the action.

While the characters' objectives will always be revealed, their attitudes may not be apparent to the audience or reader. But as the writer, *you* must know how your characters feel.

For example, in the scenes in *Ishtar* where the Arab woman and the CIA agent give the two heroes directions for crossing the desert, everyone's objective is clear: to give or to receive these instructions. But the attitudes of the woman and the CIA agent are unknown to the audience at this point; either person may want Rogers and Clark to survive, or they may wish to lead them to their deaths. Even though the audience doesn't yet know the characters' true feelings, the screenwriter had to know them in order to write the scene effectively and consistently.

6. Does the scene contain action, and not just dialogue? Hollywood is not looking for talking heads movies. They're called movies because they're supposed to *move*. When you create a scene which revolves around what the characters say, rather than what they do, it's a sign of danger. Obviously, some scenes in any film will be primarily dialogue. But when the majority of scenes fall into that category, you're in trouble.

Here's an effective trick: imagine the movie of your screenplay with the sound track turned off. Ask yourself if an audience would still understand the characters' motivations, the conflict, the resolutions, and the relationships among the characters. If the honest answer is no, your screenplay is talk-heavy, and you have to focus on more action or find a more action-oriented story concept.

Even in movies like *The Big Chill* or *The Breakfast Club,* which contain a great deal of dialogue, watching only the action will clearly reveal who the primary characters are, what is happening, and how the story is resolved. The films will no longer be particularly entertaining, but the thrust of the story will be clear for each.

This is a good concept to try out on an airplane. Instead of renting those obnoxious headphones, watch the movie without listening to the sound track and see how much comes across through the action alone. This exercise has the added advantage of keeping you from supporting one of the most effective ways ever devised to diminish the art of film viewing.

7. Does the scene serve multiple functions? Does the scene accomplish as much as possible to keep the audience emotionally involved? Some scenes can accomplish a great deal in addition to simply moving the plot forward. The following can all be employed in a single scene: character background, inner motivation, inner conflict and identification; theme; humor; exposition; and structural devices (superior position, foreshadowing, echoing, and so on).

Some scenes should contain nothing but action. For example, when the boys are running for their lives across the bridge in *Stand By Me,* it would be detrimental to the emotion, and ludicrous as well, to have them stop in the middle of the tracks and discuss their inner motivations. When the emotion is high from the action alone, don't burden the scene with added objectives.

It is in those scenes eliciting a *lower* level of emotion that these other objectives are usually accomplished. For example, consider the earlier scene in *Stand By Me,* when the kids are sitting in the junkyard deciding who will go for food. The scene contains little action, and the audience emotion is not particularly high. But the scene contributes a great deal to the story in terms of other possible objectives: character background, inner motivation, inner conflict, echoing, foreshadowing, anticipation, curiosity, credibility, and theme.

Refer to this checklist with each draft of your screenplay and especially when you feel you are so close to your story and have

done so many rewrites that you have lost your objectivity. These
principles can then serve as a tool to help you identify which scenes
work most effectively, which need rewriting, which need to be
combined with other scenes, and which should be eliminated altogether.

Charting the Screenplay

For a truly left-brained exercise, chart your screenplay scene by
scene. Wait until you've done at least a couple drafts of your script
before employing this device, because if you get this organized too
soon in the process, you run the risk of eliminating all spontaneity
from your screenplay. Charting is more effective when you've exhausted the brainstorming possibilities of your story and feel too
close to your writing to come up with anything new. The chart can
then give you a new perspective to stimulate creativity.

Begin by numbering the scenes in your screenplay. (This is for
your own use only; don't number the scenes in the final draft for
submission.) Then, using index cards, notebook paper, a computer, or a large sheet of newsprint, make the following chart,
creating a column for each of the scenes in your script:

	1 ( )	2 ( )	3 ( ) . . . etc.
Description			
Hero			
Romance			
Nemesis			
Reflection			
Major secondary			

	1 ( )	2 ( )	3 ( ) . . . etc.
Other secondary			
Identification			
Structural devices			
Color code			

Begin filling out the chart by putting the appropriate page number after each scene number at the top of the page. For example, if scene 19 begins on page 104 of your script, the top of that column should read: 19 (104).

Next put the name of the appropriate character at the beginning of each of the character rows. If your hero is Jerry and your romance is Charlotte, the first two character rows should be labeled accordingly: Hero JERRY and Romance CHARLOTTE. The romance character is listed second on the chart because, if there is such a character, she is probably the second most important character in the movie.

Of course, if you have more than one primary character in any of the categories, you must add a row for each of them.

After the scene numbers and primary character names are added to the row and column headings, go through each scene and fill in the appropriate blanks for each row, as follows:

In the Description row, write a brief description of the scene—enough so you will be able to identify which scene you're outlining.

In the primary character rows, describe exactly what each of the characters does in each scene, in the appropriate column.

If there is a character who doesn't fit into any of the primary character categories but is significant enough that it seems logical to outline that character specifically, devote one of the Major secondary rows to that person. Add as many of these rows to your chart as you feel is helpful and put those characters' actions into each of the columns, just as you did with your primary characters.

In the Other secondary row, put only the names of the secondary characters who appear in each scene. You don't have to outline what they do in each scene; giving their names is sufficient.

Let's say you were charting the screenplay for *Stand By Me*. Here is how the chart would look so far:

	1 (1)	2 (1)	3 (6)
Description	*Adult Gordy in car*	*Kids in treehouse*	*Vern under porch*
Hero GORDY	*Narrates; sees headline*	*Card game; teases Vern*	
Nemesis ACE			
Reflection CHRIS		*Leader; teases; "thought he'd turn out bad"*	
Major secondary TEDDY		*Gets teased; "I'm French"*	
Major secondary VERN		*Runs with news; gets teased*	*Looks for money; hears about body*
Other secondary			*Charlie; Billy*
Identification			
Structural devices			
Color code			

There are blank spaces for each of the characters because none of them appears in all three of these scenes. Ace, the Nemesis, isn't introduced until scene 8 or 9, so he isn't on this chart at all yet. Even though Vern and Teddy would not be defined as reflection characters (they are not as important as Chris in supporting Gordy's overall outer motivation), they are significant enough secondary characters that each is given his own row. Charlie and Billy, who are far less important to the script, are only mentioned by name in the secondary character row in scene 3. And because there is no Romance character in this movie, that row has been eliminated from the chart.

Continuing with these first three scenes, you would now fill out the Identification and Structural devices rows by listing all of those techniques (see Chapters 3 and 5) you employ in the appropriate boxes. For example, both the narrator and Vern create superior position for the audience. We know that Gordy will survive whatever happens to tell about it, we know that an attorney's murder is in that day's headline (Chris' name is not in the headline in the original screenplay, though it is in the movie), and we know that Vern has heard about Ray Brower's body. But at least some of the characters in the movie don't know these things.

Similarly, in the Identification row, all of the boys in the tree house are the victims of some undeserved misfortune, particularly Gordy. Gordy is also likable, in a familiar situation, and as the narrator is the first one on the screen and acts as the eyes of the audience.

The color code row gives you an opportunity to "graph out" such elements as action, humor, and exposition in your screenplay by designating a different color marking pen or symbol to each of those elements as they occur within each scene.

Since we're not about to add color to this book just for this one chart, we'll do it the cheap way and say that the symbol for action is !!!!!!!!!!, the symbol for exposition is XXXXXXXX, and the symbol for humor is HAHAHAHA. We can then draw a line for each scene to indicate how much of each of these components is present in that particular scene. A scene with a lot of action would have a long line of !!!!!!!!!!, little action would mean few of those symbols.

This is obviously subjective, relative to the amount of action occurring in the screenplay overall. And you can add other symbols for any other qualities in your script you wish to measure, such as character growth or theme.

The completed chart for the first three scenes of *Stand By Me* would now look like this:

	1 (1)	2 (1)	3 (6)
Description	Adult Gordy in car	Kids in treehouse	Vern under porch
Hero GORDY	Narrates; sees headline	Card game; teases Vern	
Nemesis ACE			
Reflection CHRIS		Leader; teases; "thought he'd turn out bad"	
Major secondary TEDDY		Gets teased; "I'm French"	
Major secondary VERN		Runs with news; gets teased	Looks for money; hears about body
Other secondary			Charlie; Billy
Identification	*1st char. introduced; eyes of aud. (Gordy)*	*Undeserved misfortune; likable (all)*	*Funny; jeopardy (Vern)*
Structural devices	*Superior position; curiosity*	*Curiosity*	*Superior position; curiosity; anticipation*
Color code	*XXXXX*	*XXXXXXXXX !!* *HAHAHA*	*XXX !!!!!! HAHA*

In the color code row, scene 1 provides some exposition, but is devoid of action or humor. The treehouse scene has quite a bit of humor, little action, and lots of exposition as the characters are introduced. Scene 3 has exposition (information on the missing Ray Brower and on Vern's buried bank), action (scrambling and hiding under the porch), and humor.

The rest of the screenplay for *Stand By Me* would be charted in this fashion, adding columns for each of the scenes in the entire script.

So what is the point of all of this? What good does this huge chart do you?

The interesting thing about charting your screenplay is that such a detailed, left-brained exercise results in a very right-brained tool. The chart allows you to step back from your screenplay and get an overall look at the development of your story. It is an excellent device for noting problems with your screenplay which may have escaped you.

Begin with the entries for your hero. He must appear in almost all of the columns on the chart, because by definition the hero must be on screen most of the time. This usually won't be a problem, because you will tend to focus on the hero of your story as you are writing. It is in analyzing the development of the *other* primary characters that the chart can be particularly useful in revealing unnoticed weaknesses.

But before leaving the Hero row of entries, look below on your chart and make sure that you are making full use of the identification devices for your hero. You must employ at least one of the three strongest methods of establishing identification: sympathy, jeopardy, or likability. Using two or three of these is even more effective. And these should be supplemented by as many of the other identification devices as is practical to strengthen the reader's emotional connection to the hero. Finally, these devices must be employed within the first few scenes. Remember, you must establish identification with your hero before revealing major flaws that could reduce sympathy. The chart can help ensure that you've done that.

Now move on to the entries for the other primary characters, and make sure the following needs are met:

1. Are your Romance, Nemesis, and Reflection defined in terms of the Hero's outer motivation *when they are introduced?*

2. Are all of your primary characters introduced by the beginning of Act 2?

3. Once a primary character is introduced, are there any long gaps on the chart where the character doesn't appear? This is a danger signal. A primary character must appear regularly throughout the screenplay unless the character dies. Otherwise, the character is not fulfilling her necessary function.

4. Is there an "arc" to each primary character's story? In other words, do your Nemesis, Reflection, and Romance all possess clear outer motivations, and are those desires built up and resolved by the end of the screenplay?

5. Do the primary characters other than the hero interact? This won't always occur, but as a general rule, your screenplay will be stronger if your reflection, nemesis, and/or romance confront each other. Such scenes will provide opportunities for added conflict, humor, and character revelation and will help prevent a monotonous story line involving only your hero.

6. Does each of your primary characters have at least one "big moment"? It's nice if you can create a particularly dramatic, funny, or revealing scene or two for characters besides your hero. As with the previous item on this list, such moments will add depth, texture, and emotional involvement to your screenplay.

Such scenes can also help commercially, when it's time to cast the movie. Charles Durning and Teri Garr like to chew up the scenery as much as Dustin Hoffman does.

In the row or rows for secondary characters, make sure that each provides the desired logic, humor, conflict, and so on, but that you haven't overloaded your screenplay with more minor characters than is necessary. And don't leave any of those characters dangling; the reader shouldn't wonder what became of one of your secondary characters unless that character is to reappear later in the script.

In the row for character identification, have you established sympathy to some degree for your reflection? Is the romance someone we can fall in love with as the hero does? Why? Even the nemesis must be given qualities that will make him unique, interesting, and perhaps sympathetic. This row on the chart will help ensure that there is the necessary emotional connection between the reader and all of your primary characters.

The structural device row will help you focus on the events you have chosen for your story and the order in which you have arranged them. Begin by marking the two points in the story where the hero's outer motivation changes. These points signal the beginnings of Act 2 and Act 3. If the motivation doesn't change twice in the manner outlined in Chapter 5, then your story lacks the necessary three acts.

When you have identified the three acts of the story on your chart, check the page numbers of the scenes where they occur. If the changes don't occur ¼ and ¾ of the way through the screenplay, your act breaks are misplaced. For the story to effectively elicit emotion, it *must* follow the ¼–½–¼ pattern.

Now go to the checklist of structural devices in Chapter 5 and make sure that you have employed as many of those principles as possible throughout your screenplay. Is the screenplay repeatedly creating anticipation? Do you reverse expectations occasionally to surprise the reader? Is there frequent use of superior position? Curiosity? Jeopardy? Echoing? And most important of all, *does each scene relate to the hero's outer motivation?*

Use this row to ensure that the characters behave logically and believably within each scene. If you feel any scene might be hard to believe, the solution might be to go to an earlier scene to provide the necessary background or foreshadowing to *make* the action believable. Similarly, look at the color coding to see which scenes contain the most action. These are usually the scenes involving the biggest hurdles the characters face. Then use the structural device row to ensure that the characters' abilities to overcome those obstacles have been effectively foreshadowed.

The color coding can reveal several other qualities of the screenplay:

1. The action lines must get generally longer as the story progresses, with the longest and most frequent lines occurring in Act 3. This indicates the necessary accelerated pace.

2. Similarly, the exposition lines should usually disappear about halfway through the script, because giving the audience information slows down the pace. The exception might be a denouement where the solution to a crime or the explanation of the story resolution occurs after the climax, as in a murder mystery.

3. Make sure there is occasional humor in your screenplay, no matter how serious or dramatic the subject. And if you're writing a comedy, the humor symbol, or color, should occur in at least half of the scenes.

4. Both the action and the humor lines should be alternately long and short: one to three scenes of heavy action or humor, followed by a few quieter or more serious scenes. This indicates the necessary peaks and valleys to the emotional level of your story.

You can add as many other colors or symbols or rows to this chart as you feel would be helpful in rewriting your screenplay. Character growth, theme, and even dialogue could be broken down in a similar fashion, if you find that process helpful.

The key to the chart is this: If you look at this device and declare, "I didn't get into screenwriting to become a CPA!" then simply don't use it. All of the principles employed in the chart are also contained in the checklists and methods outlined earlier in this book. If you truly believe that turning your screenplay into a spread sheet will rob you of your creativity and fun, then use the other methods to evaluate and rewrite your script.

Most of my past students who were initially resistive to this process, however, tried it anyway and were surprised at how helpful it was. The chart can provide you with a fresh look at your screenplay just when you're starting to believe your creative well is dry.

The rule is always this: *If it doesn't work, or if it blocks you, don't do it; if it works, keep doing it until you discover a method that's even more effective.*

Summary

1. There are five basic principles of scene writing:

You must create a movie in the mind of the reader.

Nothing goes on the page that doesn't go on the screen.

There are three uses for any screenplay: as a proposal; as a blueprint (shooting script); and as a record, for postproduction.

There must be nothing in the screenplay which you know you can improve.

Improper format reduces the reader's emotional involvement.

2. The basic rules of format are:

Photocopy the script on 8½ by 11 inch, white, three-hole paper.

Use a blank, plain color, 8½ by 11 inch card stock cover.

Nothing is printed on the cover.

Bind the screenplay using Chicago screws, brass fasteners, or an Acco two-piece fastener.

Include only the title page and the screenplay itself; no illustrations, cast of characters, or the like.

A feature script should be no more than 129 pages; 110 to 115 pages is best; 105 pages for a TV movie.

Omit camera directions and parenthetical directions to the actors.

Action and description paragraphs are indented 1½ inches from the left edge of the paper, 1 inch from the right.

Dialogue is indented 3 inches from the left, 2 inches from the right.

Characters names above the dialogue are written all in capital letters and indented 4 inches.

Page numbers are written ½ inch from the top of the paper, and 1 inch from the right-hand edge.

Begin the text 1 inch from the top; end the text approximately 1 inch from the bottom.

Single-space within dialogue and within an action sequence.

Double-space between action and dialogue, between one character's dialogue and another, and between scene heading and action.

Action in a new location requires a new scene and a new scene heading which identifies the new location.

Screenplays are always written in present tense.

When characters are introduced, write their names in all capital letters in the action before giving them dialogue. Their names need only an initial capital letter from then on when they appear in action paragraphs.

When writing a script for a TV series, obtain a past shooting script for that show and copy that format.

3. Write character and setting description that is concise, clever, provocative, and *detailed* and that conveys the essence of a character or setting, rather than mere physical description, which might limit casting.

4. In writing action, your primary goal is *clarity*.

5. Omit mention of the credit sequence and the musical score.

6. Ask the following questions about any scene before writing dialogue:

What is my objective?

How will the scene end?

What is each character's objective?

What is each character's attitude?

How will the scene begin?

7. With each successive rewrite, polish the dialogue so that it:

Contributes to the scene's objective and the overall outer motivation for your hero

Is consistent with the characters

Reveals character background, inner motivation or conflict, or theme, when appropriate

Is as clever, funny, original, provocative, interesting, and enjoyable to read as is appropriate

8. When the second or third draft of a scene is completed, apply the following checklist:

How does the scene contribute to the hero's outer motivation?

Does the scene possess a beginning, a middle, and an end?

Does the scene thrust the reader into the following scenes?

What is each character's objective?

What is each character's attitude?

Does the scene contain action, not just dialogue?

Does the scene serve multiple functions?

9. When the second or third draft of the screenplay is complete, chart the script using the method outlined on pages 153 to 161.

■ ■

CHAPTER 7

An Analysis of *The Karate Kid*

I now want to analyze the movie and screenplay of *The Karate Kid*, in order to illustrate all of the writing principles outlined in this book. There are a number of reasons I have selected this particular film:

1. It is a product of the mainstream American film market, which most of you reading this book are probably pursuing.

2. It was an immensely successful film, both commercially and artistically (big box office *and* generally good reviews), and generated two sequels and an animated series. Its huge profits mean that *The Karate Kid* is helping define what Hollywood will be looking for over the next few years, because the film industry always tries to replicate success.

3. It is an original screenplay and one that conceivably could have been written by a newer screenwriter. If you were trying to launch your career, this is a screenplay that could certainly have gotten you work.

4. Most important, it's an excellent screenplay and one which clearly illustrates the principles I've been discussing throughout the book. You didn't think I'd pick a script that *disproves* these rules did you? Fat chance.

Opinions of *The Karate Kid* aren't really pertinent to this discussion. If you think the movie is a piece of crap, it doesn't matter, as long as you figure out *why* you don't like the film. Ask yourself specifically which principles and methods for eliciting emotion were not met when you saw the movie. Then be certain you employ those principles more effectively when writing your own screenplay.

My primary concern here is that this analysis gives you a clearer understanding of the basic rules of concept, character, structure, and scene writing.

This chapter does not necessitate your reading the actual screenplay for *The Karate Kid*. But if you can obtain a copy of the screenplay itself, through the script library of a local film school or one of the screenplay sources listed in the bibliography, it will increase your appreciation of the movie and of the principles discussed.

Be certain, however, that you *see The Karate Kid* before reading the rest of this chapter. The ideal way to approach this chapter is to see the film twice: the first time just to experience the emotion created by the movie; the second to identify as many of the principles contained in this book as you can.

Try on your own to figure out the story concept, the identification devices used, the three acts to the story, and the structural devices employed. Use the character chart from Chapter 3 to identify the four primary characters in *The Karate Kid,* and the inner and outer motivation and conflict for each. And then use your completed chart to explore the theme of the movie.

If you give this process a shot before reading my conclusions about the movie, it will help solidify your understanding of the principles I've presented. Think of it as a pop quiz, solely for your own use, which won't affect your final grade and won't go on your permanent record.

I will now go through the various principles for eliciting emotion, as prescribed in this book, and examine how they are used in Robert Mark Kamen's screenplay for the film.

Story Concept

The concept for *The Karate Kid* can be expressed in the following sentence:

It is a story about a high school transfer student who wants to learn karate in order to stand up to the school bully, *and* who wants to have a relationship with the bully's former girlfriend. This story concept clearly defines the hero and his overall outer motivation for the screenplay.

If this were your original idea and the movie hadn't already been made, how would you evaluate it using the principles of the Story Concept checklist from Chapter 2?

1–5. Does the movie have those qualities which are absolutely necessary for a screenplay to be successful, either commercially *or* artistically? These are a hero, identification with the hero; a visible outer motivation for the hero, obstacles and hurdles to achieving that objective, and the need for physical and/or emotional courage.

The Karate Kid meets all five of these requirements: Daniel is the hero, we identify with him (through the use of various devices I will discuss below), learning karate and having a relationship are his visible outer motivations, there are obstacles to achieving those desires (getting beat up, the lessons, the dates with Ali, and so forth), and facing those obstacles requires both physical and emotional courage.

Any properly expressed story concept can be given these five necessary elements. The single sentence alone identifies the hero and the outer motivation; you can establish identification with any character using the devices outlined in Chapter 3, and obstacles requiring courage can be created for any outer motivation.

What about items 6 through 12, the primarily commercial items on the Story Concept checklist?

6. Does the story convey a high concept? Would people line up to see *The Karate Kid* just because of what it's about, regardless of the stars or reviews or word of mouth? In other words, does the story concept alone promise an audience action, romance, or humor?

The answer would be *yes,* because the karate action is implied in the title alone. For those who read the ads or saw the movie trailers, it is clear that there is romance in the movie, and some humor as well. Add to this the fact that the hero is a suburban American high school kid, always a strong commercial situation, and the high concept becomes even more attractive.

The conclusion that *The Karate Kid* possesses a high concept (hindsight being 20/20) is borne out by the fact that the opening weekend for the film was very strong, even before people had heard much word of mouth about the movie.

7. Does the concept combine originality and familiarity? Yes. We've all seen lots of movies about high school kids and lots of movies about karate. Even the story about an older, more skilled mentor teaching a new, inexperienced student is a familiar one.

The originality comes from combining these elements. I don't recall any American film in which the karate student was an everyday high school kid. Added originality comes from the particular character of Mr. Miyagi, who is a real departure from the Bruce Lee/Chuck Norris mold of karate expert.

8. Does the story possess a second level of sell and subplots? Yes. As with most love stories, Daniel's desire for a relationship with Ali is an equally important outer motivation for the hero. So it qualifies as a second level of sell.

The subplots are those involving Daniel's mother, Kreese and the Cobras, and Mr. Miyagi's background. These are not as important as the original concept or the second level of sell, but they do add conflict, realism, and texture to the story and serve to elicit additional emotion in the reader.

9. Can the audience identify with the setting of the story? Yes. High School, USA, is probably the *most* identifiable setting a movie can have for the current mainstream audience.

10. Does the movie fall into a popular category? Yes. *The Karate Kid* is a combination action/comedy/love story, all of which are among the five universally popular categories. Certainly it is not a musical, western, period piece, science fiction film, or horror story.

11. Is the movie expensive? No. There are no big special effects, huge cast, period setting, exotic locations, or inclement weather to drive up the below-the-line budget.

Based on these six items, your conclusion would be that the movie meets all of the primarily commercial considerations on the Story Concept checklist.

One might argue that the story idea isn't *that* high a concept, since the promise of action, romance, and humor is minimal. Certainly, this is no *Jaws* or *Revenge of the Nerds.* But even with a moderately high concept, the screenplay meets enough of these primarily commercial principles that the uphill battle to sell the script would not be increased.

Items 12 and 13 on the list, pertaining to theme and character growth, will be discussed in detail later in this chapter.

Character Identification

Robert Mark Kamen uses all three of the principal devices for establishing audience identification with the hero of *The Karate Kid:* sympathy, jeopardy, and likability.

The opening scene of *The Karate Kid* shows Daniel leaving his home and friends on the east coast and reluctantly forced to move with his mother to an apartment in Van Nuys, California. Already feeling an outsider, he is then beaten up by Johnny for talking to Ali. Shortly after that, Daniel is unfairly kicked off the soccer team, again while Ali is watching.

Whether we've experienced it or not, we all know of the pain of being an outsider after transferring to a new school. This undeserved misfortune establishes sympathy and identification with Daniel, which are strengthened by the pain and humiliation he then suffers at the beach and on the soccer field.

The identification established by this undeserved misfortune at the beginning of the film is supplemented by placing Daniel in jeopardy. Johnny threatens Daniel, he is chased by the gang after the Halloween party, and he is then entered into the karate tournament.

Daniel's jeopardy occurs a bit later in the film than the undeserved misfortune, so it strengthens the identification that has already been established. Some identification should be established immediately in the screenplay, certainly in the first half of act 1. Additional use of the devices can then strengthen the identification the audience already feels.

The third primary identification device, likability, is established from the very first scene. Daniel is a good person (nice to his elderly neighbor, his mother, Mr. Miyagi, and his new friend), and he is kind of funny (his trick to get back at Johnny at the Halloween party).

The one component of likability that Robert Mark Kamen doesn't employ is making Daniel good at what he does. Unlike David, the high school computer genius who's the hero of *War Games*, Daniel possesses no job or skill for which we would greatly respect his abilities. Simply being a nice kid in this screenplay is sufficient to make him likable and increase our identification.

Some additional identification devices are also used to strengthen the audience's emotional connection to Daniel: he is the first character on the screen, he is in a familiar situation (high school student), and he possesses familiar flaws and foibles (his basic awkwardness or shyness around Ali).

Originality

Does Daniel exemplify a unique hero, one that breaks the mold of the typical teenager? In my opinion, no. There is nothing about this high school kid which jumps off the page or departs from the basic adolescent male, unlike David in *War Games*, the title hero of *Ferris Bueller's Day Off*, or the kids in *The Breakfast Club*, *Mask*, and *Revenge of the Nerds*, who exhibit unique (to the movies) personality traits.

I assume that this was the screenwriter's conscious choice. Kamen wisely creates an average, everyday youth to emphasize both audience identification and the difficulty of what Daniel attempts to accomplish. If Daniel were as skilled and cocky as Ferris Bueller, our concern for his success would be reduced.

But *The Karate Kid* still serves as sterling example of character originality through its portrayal of Mr. Miyagi.

In almost all the movies and TV shows which preceded *The Karate Kid*, the standard karate expert was some variation on David Carradine, Chuck Norris, or Bruce Lee:

> Physical Makeup: Male, good-looking, muscular, imposing, 30 to 45 years old, no disabilities.

> Personality: Street-smart, quiet, fearless, tough, a ladies' man, cool, a loner, macho.

> Background: Chinese or ex-Marine, a working-class cop, soldier, spy, or private eye.

Notice how effectively these three areas are altered in creating Mr. Miyagi. He is aging, not particularly handsome, a diminutive Okinawan gardener who grows bonsai trees. He possesses a quiet sense of humor, warmth, and kindness, and he tries to avoid fights and confrontation.

Kamen skillfully emphasizes Miyagi's unique qualities by creating Kreese, who *does* fit the mold of the cliché karate expert—sort of a Chuck Norris-gone-wrong character. And by pairing Mr. Miyagi with Daniel, *The Karate Kid* employs another previously discussed method to bring out qualities in both characters that give each added dimension, interest, and originality.

Primary Characters

Using the definitions presented in Chapter 3, these would be the four primary characters of *The Karate Kid:*

1. Hero. The hero is the main character, is on screen most of the time, and is the one with whom the audience most identifies and whose outer motivation drives the plot. That would clearly be Daniel. No other character meets all of those criteria.

Outer motivation is what a character visibly hopes to accomplish by the end of the film. The hero's outer motivation answers the question, What is the movie about? It is revealed through the action, and it determines the plot of the movie.

Daniel's outer motivation is to stand up to Johnny. The first fight, running away, learning karate, entering the tournament—all are aspects of Daniel's overall outer motivation of dealing with this bully.

The *outer conflict* is whatever most strongly prevents the character from achieving his outer motivation. In this film, it would be that Johnny beats Daniel up or that Johnny knows karate or some similar expression of Daniel's initial inability to stand up to Johnny because of the latter's greater physical skills.

Because the film possesses a second level of sell, there is a second, equally important outer motivation for Daniel: to have a relationship with Ali. And the second outer conflict would therefore be that Johnny tries to keep them apart.

2. Nemesis. The nemesis is that character who most stands in the way of the hero achieving his outer motivation. In *The Karate Kid*, that character would obviously be Johnny, whose own outer motivations are to beat up Daniel (in or out of the karate ring) and to keep Daniel and Ali apart. Another way to recognize that Johnny is the nemesis is to imagine Johnny removed from the screenplay. Without Johnny, Daniel wouldn't have anyone to worry about, and there would be no one standing between him and Ali.

Kreese would not be the nemesis, even though he does provide added conflict for Daniel, because Kreese is not the one who *most* stands in the way of Daniel's outer motivation. If you take Kreese out of the script, Daniel would still be getting pounded; if you take Johnny out, you've got no movie.

Johnny's outer conflict is that Daniel is learning karate. That stands in the way of Johnny's outer motivation, to beat up Daniel, because there is a moratorium on fighting during the training period and then because Daniel has become as skilled as Johnny is in the climactic tournament.

The outer conflict to Johnny's desire to keep Daniel and Ali apart is that they like each other and want to be together.

3. Reflection. The reflection is that character whose own outer motivation supports the hero's outer motivation or who at least is in the same basic situation at the beginning of the film. Daniel's reflection is Mr. Miyagi, who helps Daniel stand up to Johnny and wants Daniel to be with Ali.

Mr. Miyagi's outer motivation is to teach Daniel karate; that is what we *see* him doing on the screen throughout the film. Miyagi's outer conflict is Daniel's ignorance. The thing that most stands in the way of Miyagi teaching Daniel is that Daniel doesn't already know what he wants him to know.

If this sounds simplistic, it should. Outer motivation and conflict is usually this basic. Often the thing that prevents us from easily recognizing outer motivation and conflict is that we look for something that is too complex.

The other frequent error in identifying outer conflict is to regard it as something *inside* the character, thus confusing outer conflict with inner conflict.

4. Romance. The romance is that character who is the sexual or romantic object of at least part of the hero's outer motivation. Ali is therefore the romance.

Additionally, Ali fulfills the other requirement for an effective romance: she alternately supports Daniel's desire and is at cross-purposes to it.

When Daniel and Ali first meet, Daniel wants them to be together, and she agrees (supportive). Then Daniel starts getting knocked around by Johnny, so he wants to stay away from her, even though she still wants to be with Daniel (cross-purposes). Then the rule against fighting is imposed, so the two want to be together again (supportive). Then Daniel thinks Ali still likes Johnny, so he dumps her (cross-purposes). When he wants to get back together, she's now fed up with him (cross-purposes again). And finally, she wants to be with him and help him win the tournament (supportive).

Notice also that the screenwriter does an effective job of getting us to fall for Ali as well: she is attractive, fun, open-minded, supportive of Daniel, and independent. This increases our emotional involvement and identification with Daniel and his outer motivation.

Ali's own outer motivation is basically to be with Daniel; that is what we see her trying to do throughout the film. Her outer conflict is the same as that for Daniel: Johnny does whatever he can to keep them apart.

Given these four primary characters, the character chart presented in Chapter 3 would so far look like this for *The Karate Kid:*

	Outer motivation	Outer conflict	Inner motivation	Inner conflict
Hero DANIEL	*To stand up to Johnny; to be with Ali*	*Johnny beats him up; keeps them apart*		
Nemesis JOHNNY	*To beat up Daniel; to keep Daniel and Ali apart*	*Daniel learning karate; Ali likes Daniel*		
Reflection MR. MIYAGI	*To teach Daniel karate*	*Daniel doesn't know karate*		
Romance ALI	*To be with Daniel*	*Johnny keeps them apart*		

I don't want to discuss the right side of the chart yet; I'll deal with the characters' inner motivations and inner conflicts when I talk about character growth and theme.

Structure

Structurally, the three acts of the screenplay are as follows:

ACT 1 is about a boy who wants to avoid a school bully and get acquainted with the bully's old girlfriend.

ACT 2 is about the boy wanting to learn karate to be able to stand up to the bully and wanting to have a relationship with the girl.

ACT 3 is about the boy wanting to face the bully in the All-Valley Karate Tournament and to resume his relationship with the girl.

Each of the three acts is expressed as a visible outer motivation for the hero, and each is a facet of the hero's overall outer motivation in the film.

The three acts of *The Karate Kid* follow the necessary ¼-½-¼ pattern. Act 2 begins when Daniel tells his mother that he wants to take formal karate training. This occurs on page 30 of the shooting script, which is approximately 120 pages long. Act 3 begins on page 89, at Daniel's birthday celebration, when he and Mr. Miyagi discuss the completion of his training, and the imminent tournament.

The screenplay employs almost all of the structural devices discussed in Chapter 5. For example:

1. Every Scene, Event, and Character Contributes to the Hero's Outer Motivation. To illustrate, simply pick any scene in the movie and ask if it moves Daniel closer to his desire to stand up to Johnny or closer to his desire to have a relationship with Ali.

All of the karate scenes and scenes with Ali obviously meet this need. But so do the bonsai tree scene (teaching him an element of karate philosophy and getting him closer to his teacher), the Halloween party (showing him standing up to Johnny in a small way and creating justification for Johnny's beating him up), and Mr. Miyagi's drunk scene (creating greater closeness to his teacher and a greater desire to keep his commitment to honor Mr. Miyagi). In other words, there are no scenes in *The Karate Kid* which don't contribute to the hero's outer motivations.

2. The Movie Creates a Question in the Reader's Mind at the Beginning, Which Will Be Answered by the End of the Film.

In this case, Will Daniel overcome Johnny or won't he? is the question that keeps the reader turning the pages.

3. Each Hurdle and Obstacle Is Greater Than the Previous Ones. Obviously, avoiding Johnny is not as difficult as the karate lessons, the lessons aren't as difficult as the tournament, and facing Johnny with a broken knee is the greatest obstacle of all.

4. The Pace of the Story Accelerates. In act 1, the conflict with Johnny is interrupted by quite a few scenes of exposition, mild humor, mild romance, and only moderate emotional involvement: the bonsai tree, talking in the hall, preparing the costume, and so on.

By the time we reach act 3, the peak emotional scenes of action and conflict are spaced much closer together, thus accelerating the pace: making up with Ali, getting admitted to the karate tournament, the early matches, the broken knee, and the final match.

5. There Are Peaks and Valleys to the Emotional Level. The peak action of the Halloween party, attack, and rescue scenes are followed by less emotionally involving conversations between Daniel and his mother and between Daniel and Mr. Miyagi. The tournament matches are interspersed with quieter scenes of coaching, plotting by the Cobras, and fixing Daniel's leg.

6. The Screenplay Creates Anticipation. We anticipate fights with Johnny, the attack after the party, the budding romance with Ali, the excitement of the karate tournament, and so on.

Notice that the tournament is introduced early in the film, long before it actually takes place. This allows the audience to anticipate that forthcoming conflict, keeping them much more emotionally involved than if the issue of the tournament were introduced at the beginning of act 3.

7. The Audience Is Given Superior Position. We know that Mr. Miyagi is Daniel's rescuer before Daniel realizes it. We know that Ali isn't really still in love with Johnny, even though Daniel thinks she is after seeing her dance with Johnny at the country club. We know, but Mr. Miyagi doesn't, that Daniel learns about

Mr. Miyagi's wife and son dying at Manzanar. And we know that the Cobras plot to break Daniel's leg before it happens.

8. There Are Surprises and Reversals to Audience Anticipation. This device isn't used too extensively in *The Karate Kid*. We anticipate a fight in the dojo between Mr. Miyagi and Kreese, and there is none. Daniel's repaired bicycle, the line about Mr. Miyagi's belt being from Penney's, the drunk scene, and the Manzanar headline are all unanticipated and keep the audience from getting lulled into a sense of anticipating everything. But reversals for the sake of humor, surprise, and fear are used minimally in this screenplay.

9. The Screenplay Creates Curiosity. We're curious about why Mr. Miyagi is having Daniel paint the fence and wax the cars, about how Daniel will be able to beat Johnny in the tournament, and about what kind of costume Mr. Miyagi has in mind to make for Daniel for the Halloween party. In each case, our emotional involvement is increased for a few scenes, enhancing the overall effect of the screenplay.

10. The Screenplay Makes the Most Effective Use of Time. There must be enough time for Daniel to receive some training in karate, or the story would lose all credibility. But the three month deadline *condenses* the time span sufficiently that the audience can stay easily involved. And the deadline creates a race against the clock to prepare Daniel for the imminent tournament.

11. The Characters Are Credible. These characters behave the way people with their backgrounds would logically behave. A kid like Daniel probably would avoid Johnny at first but want to save his dignity by finding some way to stand up to him. Ali would logically be more attracted to Daniel than to Johnny. Given the misguided instruction he's been getting from Kreese, Johnny would try to beat Daniel up and would probably try to mislead Daniel about Ali. And Mr. Miyagi's own past would probably make him reluctant, but ultimately willing, to teach Daniel.

No one does anything that a normal person wouldn't conceivably do in the situations the story creates. Johnny doesn't murder anyone, Daniel doesn't turn into a superhuman Rambo, Mr. Miyagi doesn't teach Daniel to disappear or read minds.

One question of credibility, which I'll discuss later, is Mr. Miyagi's speech. Would a man who's spent at least 45 years in the United States still speak in such broken English?

12. The Big Events of the Movie Are Foreshadowed. Examples of this abound. The most important event of the script is the tournament. The audience must believe that a kid with only three months of formal training, *and a broken knee,* can face the Three-Time-All-Valley-Karate-Champion and win.

It couldn't happen.

Yet audiences believed it to the tune of about $150,000,000 worldwide. This is because it was effectively foreshadowed.

The two most important skills that enable Daniel to win the tournament are the "crane stance" and Mr. Miyagi's healing abilities. If these two issues were introduced only at the climax of the film, the audience would feel that the story was unbelievably contrived. But the fact is that they *are* contrived. They're just *effectively* contrived.

The crane stance is introduced much earlier in the film, when we see Mr. Miyagi practice it. He tells Daniel, "When done properly, is unbeatable." We later see Daniel practice the same technique. So when he moves into the crane stance at the karate tournament, the audience subconsciously says, "Oh, yeah, we remember that. That's that unbeatable karate move."

Similarly, Mr. Miyagi's ability to rub his hands together and heal Daniel's knee is foreshadowed earlier when he does the same thing to Daniel's lame shoulder muscles.

Daniel's ability to catch a fly with chopsticks ("A person who can do that can do anything"), the scene with the bonsai tree ("If it comes from within you, it must be perfect"), and Mr. Miyagi's encounter with the tough guys on the beach are all further examples of foreshadowing characters' actions or abilities to give them credibility later in the film.

13. Echoing Is Used to Illustrate Character Growth. Each time we see Daniel attempt a karate kick, from the first instances at the apartment gate and the beach to the final kicks in the karate tournament, we see how Daniel is transforming into a more skilled karate practitioner.

Mr. Miyagi tells Daniel to close his eyes and imagine a perfect bonsai tree in an early scene of the film. In the karate tournament, Miyagi echoes the instruction to help Daniel prepare for his first match.

And the photographs of Daniel and Ali are shown three times in the movie, to illustrate the evolution of their reltionship.

14. The Opening of the Screenplay Grabs the Reader. This screenplay employs a *new arrival* opening by beginning with Daniel and his mother's departure from New Jersey and arrival at their new apartment in Van Nuys.

The initial scenes aren't as powerful or captivating as the action and humor that open *Raiders of the Lost Ark* or *Beverly Hills Cop*. But immediate action would be inappropriate for introducing an everyday kid like Daniel, and an outside action opening would probably be irrelevant to this particular story line.

Kamen chooses an opening that will introduce the hero immediately, provide a little humor, and create audience identification through Daniel's undeserved misfortune. Daniel's attraction to Ali at the beach party and his first confrontation with Johnny then increase the audience's emotional involvement.

15. The Screenplay Has an Effective Ending. The climax, the karate match with Johnny, is the final confrontation between the hero and nemesis, and it clearly resolves the hero's outer motivation. We have waited the entire film to see if Daniel will be able to stand up to Johnny, and the climax answers that question with no ambiguity.

The denouement of the screenplay is very brief. Very little tapering of audience emotion is allowed with the brief denouement provided by the cheering crowd, the hug from Ali, and the closing shot of Mr. Miyagi's face. But there is enough to constitute a denouement; the screen doesn't cut to black as soon as Daniel decks Johnny.

It is interesting that the shooting script of *The Karate Kid* contains an additional scene in the parking lot outside the arena to provide a final confrontation between Mr. Miyagi and Kreese. But the filmmakers obviously decided that it was wiser to let the audience leave the theater at the higher emotional level of Daniel's victory. If you want to see the alternative parking lot ending, just go see the opening scene of *The Karate Kid II*.

And finally, Daniel's tournament victory over Johnny is obviously the ending that is most satisfying to the audience. As predictable and *Rocky*-like as the ending was to some critics, the audience loved it.

Theme

Now here's the fun part. What are the underlying layers to this screenplay? Is *The Karate Kid* just a fun, superficial piece of fluff, or does it say something more meaningful about the human condition? (I'll give you a hint: If it didn't say something meaningful, I wouldn't be taking up all these pages analyzing it. You already knew that.)

To explore the theme of *The Karate Kid*, begin with the character chart on p. 174 and fill in the blanks for the primary characters' inner motivations and conflicts.

Inner motivation is the *reason* the character wants to accomplish his outer motivation. It is always what the character thinks will lead to greater feelings of self-worth. And while the outer motivation for any character is visible and revealed through action, inner motivation is invisible and usually revealed through the dialogue.

The inner motivation for Daniel is the reaon he wants to stand up to Johnny. It is some invisible need within him that he thinks will enable him to feel better about himself.

The key line of dialogue for determining Daniel's inner motivation is provided when he asks Mr. Miyagi to be his teacher. Mr. Miyagi says, "Depends . . . (on the) reason."

"How's revenge?" Daniel responds. Daniel thinks that if he can save face by beating up Johnny in return, he will achieve greater feelings of self-worth.

Clearly, Daniel is mistaken. The movie is obviously saying that revenge is not a proper path to self-worth. But if Daniel *thinks* revenge will enable him to feel better about himself, then it is, right or wrong, his inner motivation.

It is also evident that Daniel learns, in the course of the story, that revenge *isn't* the path to self-worth. But the *initial* reason that a character wants to achieve his outer motivation is the one which determines his inner motivation and the one that will contribute most to an effective theme. Lots of movies are about heroes who go after wealth, fame, revenge, acceptance, and status only to learn in the course of the film that those paths do not bring them the self-worth they desire.

Since Daniel possesses a second outer motivation, there can be a second inner motivation as well. The reason Daniel wants to be with Ali is that he loves her—or at least he's falling in love with her. This is the most likely inner motivation whenever you have a love story, because we all think we will feel better about ourselves —achieve greater self-worth—when we earn the love or desire of the person we love or desire.

The inner conflict for Daniel is some quality within Daniel that keeps him from achieving self-worth through the path he has chosen. So you must ask, "What is it within Daniel that prevents him from feeling good about himself by pursuing revenge on Johnny and loving Ali?"

Here the process gets a little tricky. We must look for lines of dialogue that will indicate some flaw in Daniel, some inner quality or need for growth that stands in the way of his getting what he wants.

The first indication of such an inner conflict is around the issue of revenge. When Daniel reveals his inner motivation to Mr. Miyagi, Mr. Miyagi's immediate reaction is that if Daniel looks at revenge that way, he should start by digging two graves. "Fighting always last answer to problem. . . . Karate used to defense."

So part of Daniel's inner conflict is, in Mr. Miyagi's words, his attitude; he looks at karate as a means of revenge, not defense. Daniel's inner conflict is dealt with even more fully in the birthday party scene: Daniel has just shown Mr. Miyagi his new driver's license, and the picture of Daniel and Ali from the video parlor falls out of his wallet. Mr. Miyagi looks at it and says, "Look nice together. Different but same." Daniel's immediate response is, "Different but different." Then when Mr. Miyagi gives Daniel the new car, he hands the picture back to Daniel. The dialogue here is critical: "Remember lesson of balance. . . . Not just lesson for karate. Lesson for whole life. Whole life balance, everything you do be better. Karate too."

So Daniel's inner conflict is that he lacks *balance*. He sees others (both Johnny and Ali) as "different but different." His desire for revenge against Johnny, for offensive superiority, is out of balance and will not lead to self-worth.

In Mr. Miyagi's karate instruction, he tells Daniel that he must trust the quality, not the quantity, of his knowledge, that karate must be used for defense, and that "opponent will help." These are all ways of saying that Daniel must regard Johnny as an opponent whose own energy (in karate philosophy) can be used against him defensively, by regarding his opponent as "different but the same."

Similarly, the inner conflict preventing him from realizing self-worth through his love of Ali is also a lack of balance. To Daniel, she is a rich kid from the country club and he is a working class kid from Van Nuys, so he keeps misinterpreting and rejecting her feelings for him. Until he accepts Mr. Miyagi's lesson that balance is for "whole life," he is unable to achieve either his inner or outer motivations toward Ali.

Johnny's inner motivation is to show the enemy "no mercy." Johnny's path to self-worth is to follow his teacher's instructions and to get back at Daniel for stealing his girlfriend. Anything on the chart conveying Johnny's desire to save face, live up to his teacher's expectations, or overcome his enemy, qualifies as Johnny's inner motivation.

Johnny's inner conflict is revealed most clearly by Mr. Miyagi when he comments on Kreese's dojo: "No such thing bad student, only bad teacher. Teacher say, student do." The quality within Johnny that keeps him from achieving self-worth is that he is mistaught. Even though he's an expert at the moves, Johnny possesses no clearer understanding of genuine karate philosophy than Daniel does.

Mr. Miyagi's inner motivation isn't really revealed very clearly, even in the dialogue. So if your conclusion is that the screenplay doesn't explore inner motivation for that character, that's fine. But I think we can infer a clear reason why Mr. Miyagi wants to teach Daniel karate, and since that reason will play an important part in developing the theme of *The Karate Kid*, I'll include it.

It seems fairly evident that one reason Mr. Miyagi wants to teach Daniel karate grows out of a sense of family. This is Mr. Miyagi's opportunity to pass on the gift his father gave to him. And since Daniel seems to represent the son Mr. Miyagi lost, that sense of family tradition is reinforced. So Mr. Miyagi's path to self-worth is to carry on a family tradition—to give his greatest gift to his "adopted" son.

The inner conflict for Mr. Miyagi is revealed in one brief line: "For me, rule number one, no like get involved." The quality within Mr. Miyagi which keeps him from realizing self-worth through passing his knowledge on to Daniel is Miyagi's fear of getting involved.

Mr. Miyagi overcomes this inner conflict within the same scene, as soon as he agrees to go to Kreese's dojo with Daniel. But it is still revealed as his inner conflict, and it also will contribute to theme, as we shall see shortly.

Ali's inner motivation for being with Daniel is clearly that she loves him. As was said earlier, a character always thinks that winning the love or the desire of the person the character loves or desires will lead to self-worth.

There is no inner conflict for Ali. There is nothing within Ali that prevents her from feeling good about herself by loving Daniel. She simply has to wait until Daniel evolves to her level and can look upon the two of them as "different but the same."

As was earlier illustrated by *An Officer and a Gentleman*, this is a typical pattern for a love story: the hero must overcome his own inner conflict in order to win the love of the romance character, who has no inner conflict. Ali shares that quality with Paula in *An Officer and a Gentleman*, Madison in *Splash*, and Julia in *Defending Your Life*.

The completed character chart for *The Karate Kid* would therefore look like this:

	Outer motivation	Outer conflict	Inner motivation	Inner conflict
Hero DANIEL	To stand up to Johnny; to be with Ali	Johnny beats him up; keeps them apart	*Revenge; he loves her*	*No balance; different but different*
Nemesis JOHNNY	To beat up Daniel; to keep Daniel and Ali apart	Daniel learning karate; Ali likes Daniel	*"No mercy"; to save face*	*Mistaught*
Reflection MR. MIYAGI	To teach Daniel karate	Daniel doesn't know karate	*To pass father's teachings on to new son*	*"No like get involved"*
Romance ALI	To be with Daniel	Johnny keeps them apart	*Loves him*	—

Given these inner motivations and conflicts, what is the theme of *The Karate Kid*? What universal statement is the screenplay making about how anyone in the audience can better live his life, and be more fully evolved or individuated? What does the movie say we should do to be better people?

Remember that theme emerges when the hero's similarity to the nemesis, and difference from the reflection, are revealed. Daniel's similarity to Johnny is primarily in the area of *balance*. Daniel's desire for revenge and Johnny's desire to show Daniel "no mercy" are both ways of looking at the other as "different but different." At the beginning of the film, both misunderstand the true principles of karate philosophy.

It is important to note that Mr. Miyagi never uses the term "enemy." When Daniel worries that he doesn't know enough, Mr. Miyagi tells him not to worry " . . . opponent will help." He is telling Daniel to use his opponent's energy to overcome the opponent defensively—to look upon Johnny (and the others in the tournament) as "different but the same."

Daniel and Johnny are obviously alike in other ways: they are both high school kids, both like Ali, both ride bikes, both study karate. But none of these has deeper application to the audience. *Thematically,* the main similarity between the hero and the nemesis seems to revolve around this issue of balance and looking at others as different but the same.

The theme becomes clearer if we examine the differences between Daniel and Mr. Miyagi, Daniel's reflection. These all emerge from the karate instruction: Mr. Miyagi knows karate philosophy, and at the outset, Daniel does not. So we must look at all of the underlying principles which Mr. Miyagi teaches Daniel which have broader application to everyday living and regard those as the thematic principles of this screenplay.

There are three basic principles of karate which seem most important to Mr. Miyagi and to this film thematically:

1. Inner Perfection. In the scene with the bonsai tree, Mr. Miyagi says that if Daniel's vision comes from within him, it must be perfect. The scene is then echoed for emphasis at the tournament, where Mr. Miyagi again tells Daniel to close his eyes and imagine overcoming his opponent, enabling Daniel to win his first match.

2. Commitment. When Mr. Miyagi asks Daniel if he will follow his instructions totally, Daniel answers, "I guess so." He receives this response:

> MIYAGI
> Danielsan. Walk on road. Walk left side.
> Safe. Walk right side. Safe. Walk middle,
> sooner or later get squished like grape.
> Same thing here. Either karate do yes,
> or karate do no. Karate do guess so you
> looking get squished. Understand?

Daniel must commit totally to karate is he wishes to pursue it. That idea of commitment is then reinforced when Mr. Miyagi commits Daniel to the tournament. When Daniel worries that he'll get the crap beat out of him if he doesn't learn karate in three months, Mr. Miyagi's answer is, "Either way, problem solved." Again, it is the commitment that is important for Daniel's growth, not the outcome of the tournament.

By clear implication, this is Mr. Miyagi's attitude toward Daniel's relationship with Ali as well: he wants Daniel to commit to her in spite of their difficulties or superficial differences.

3. Regard Others as Different But the Same. The most important scene in the movie thematically is Daniel's birthday party with Mr. Miyagi. When Mr. Miyagi comments on the photo of Daniel and Ali, "Different but same," he is saying that Ali and Daniel are essentially the same and that recognition of their mutual affection and commitment make them a good couple. But when Daniel answers, "Different but different," he can't see past their superficial differences: he's poor and she's rich; she's from a big house on the hill in Encino, he's from an apartment in Van Nuys; she's established and popular, he's a new kid from back East.

With Mr. Miyagi's succeeding lines, "Remember lesson of balance . . . " this single scene unites the issues of karate, balance, and looking at others as different but the same.

Now if we go back and put all these similarities and differences together into one universal thematic statement, it results in something like this: In order to succeed (or grow, or evolve, or be as good as we can be), we must recognize our inner perfection, commit it to someone or something, and look upon others as different but the same.

In other words, we can realize our full potential as human beings when we recognize not only our own inner perfection, but the inner perfection of others as well (balance) and then commit to our goals and relationships on that basis.

This theme of *The Karate Kid* is reinforced by another key scene in the film: when Mr. Miyagi gets drunk and Daniel discovers that Mr. Miyagi's wife and child died at Manzanar.

Manzanar was a U.S. internment camp during World War II for Americans of Japanese descent. It serves as a sterling example of the tragedy that results when society regards others as different but different.

As revealed in the screenplay, Mr. Miyagi was an American

fighting the Nazis in Europe and winning decorations. But because his family was orginally from Okinawa, they were regarded not as fellow Americans (different but the same), but rather as the enemy, due solely to their racial background (different but different).

The screenplay skillfully creates the character of Kreese in contrast to Mr. Miyagi to reflect that same "enemy" attitude that led to Manzanar and that is now being passed on to the kids in the dojo.

The drunk scene also makes clear why "getting involved" is such an inner conflict for Mr. Miyagi. The last time he got involved, it cost him the only family he had. In light of what happened 40 years before, Mr. Miyagi's own ability to regard others as different but the same and not to look upon them as the enemy shows what a powerful, balanced character he is.

So the beauty of *The Karate Kid* is that underneath its entertaining, funny, and emotionally involving story is a powerful statement about prejudice and human dignity.

It is unlikely that anyone viewing *The Karate Kid* for the first time would verbalize the above theme. But that doesn't mean it isn't received by the audience on a deeper, unconscious level or that it doesn't contribute to the greater depth, texture, and even popularity of the movie.

Writing Style

Using passages from Robert Mark Kamen's screenplay of *The Karate Kid*, I want to illustrate the principles of writing effective description, action, and dialogue. How did this screenwriter put the words on the page in a way that would create a vivid movie in the readers' minds and would make the process of reading this script a fast, easy, and enjoyable emotional experience?

Please note that these passages are taken directly from the shooting script of *The Karate Kid* and are not to be used as format samples for your proposed script. For example, the phrase "DANIEL'S POV" means the camera angle is from Daniel's point of view. In your proposal script, this would be considered a camera direction and therefore should be avoided.

Description

As an example of description, read the following scene from *The Karate Kid,* where Daniel first arrives at Kreese's dojo to watch Johnny and the other Cobras:

INT. DOJO - DAY

Daniel enters a trophy filled vestibule in the midst of which is a photograph of a hard eyed man in green beret fatigues with a caption below "Captain John Kreese All American Karate Champion 1970–1973." On the right wall is a large poster announcing the under 18 All Valley Championships.

A booming voice from the dojo proper draws Daniel's attention.

Daniel enters.

POV DANIEL:

The Cobra Kai students kneeling with their backs to him as KREESE prowls the ranks.

                    KREESE
          Fear does not exist in this dojo. Does
          it?

                    STUDENTS
          No, Sensei.

                    KREESE
          Pain does not exist in this dojo. Does
          it?

                    STUDENTS
          No, Sensei.

                    KREESE
          Defeat does not exist in this dojo. Does
          it?

> STUDENTS

No, Sensei.

Kreese comes to the head of the class. His hard eyes fix on Daniel for a moment sending a shiver up his spine.

> KREESE

What do we study?

> STUDENTS

The way of the fist, sir.

> KREESE

What do we study?

> STUDENTS

The way of the fist, sir.

> KREESE

And what is that way?

> STUDENTS

Strike first, strike hard. No mercy, sir.

> KREESE

I can't hear you.

> STUDENTS

STRIKE FIRST, STRIKE HARD. NO MERCY, SIR.

> KREESE

Rei!

The class bows.

ANGLE ON DANIEL, watching, entranced. KREESE'S face sweeps the line of students from left to right, fixing each one with his intense, dangerous eyes. Tension crackles in the air. Finally, KREESE'S voice breaks the silence.

> KREESE
>
> Mr. Lawrence?
>
> JOHNNY
>
> Yes, Sensei.

JOHNNY stands at attention his clenched fists are riveted in front of him.

> KREESE
>
> Warm them up.

The black belt snaps heels and arms together smartly, coming to attention. He bows crisply from the waist. KREESE bows back and steps aside as the black belt sprints to take his place.

As he turns DANIEL'S knees go weak. JOHNNY'S eyes meet DANIEL'S above the heads of the still bowing class. The slightest trace of a smile creeps across JOHNNY'S face.

> JOHNNY
>
> Prepare. Rei!

As one the students straighten up. Their bodies obscure JOHNNY'S line of vision.

> JOHNNY
>
> Reverse punch. Rei!

As one the class begins the exercise.

Robert Mark Kamen uses very brief description throughout *The Karate Kid*. But look at how much we learn about Kreese in this short passage: he was a Green Beret; he was a karate champion; he is imposing, authoritarian, frightening, and in complete command of the students.

More important, the brief scene creates a vivid mental picture of the entire situation. Rather than simply describing the room as "a karate classroom," and Kreese as a "tough teacher," the screenplay goes into *detail*. The "hard eyed man," the trophies, the photograph, the "booming voice," the "intense, dangerous eyes"—all of these increase the reader's emotional involvement and interest in the scene.

The description is supplemented by the action and the dialogue to complete the vividness and effectiveness of the scene: the pacing Kreese prowling the ranks; the kneeling students; the shiver up Daniel's spine; the automatic, subservient responses to Kreese's threatening dialogue; all contribute to the emotion of this scene.

The scene is also a superb example of how a minor sequence can contribute a great deal to the overall screenplay by employing the various identification, structure, and writing devices discussed earlier in the book. Character background; a threat to a character; curiosity; anticipation; foreshadowing; echoing; theme; detailed description and action; and original, emotional dialogue are all effectively employed in this single scene.

Sometimes the screenplay gets a bit too brief in its description, particularly as a guide for effective screenwriting. When Daniel is introduced, he is described only as "DANIEL LARUSSO, fifteen-and-a-half." Ali is simply "cute as a button." These descriptions don't really create very vivid or original images for the reader.

Often screenwriters will limit the details of the hero's description in order to keep the casting possibilities wide open and to allow the character to take shape as the action progresses. But I'll stick with my original advice: In writing your screenplay, use sufficient detail to create vivid, emotionally involving images for your readers.

Action

To see how *The Karate Kid* illustrates clear, detailed action, look at the following scene:

EXT. MIYAGI'S HOUSE - MORNING

Daniel, on his bike, approaches the front door where a large note is affixed.

CLOSE-UP: THE NOTE

> "Paint house. No up and down. Side
> side. One half left hand, one half right
> hand."

To the left, another half-dozen cans of paint are stacked. Daniel
is incensed. He rips the note off the door, crumbles it, and
flings it onto the ground. After a moment, his anger subsides.
He removes the lid on the first can of paint and begins to stir
it with a brush.

EXT. MIYAGI'S FRONT YARD - NIGHT

The house is almost finished. Daniel is slowly doing the last
strokes, breathing in and out, when Miyagi pulls up. Daniel
does a slow burn but does not turn around. Miyagi crosses the
yard, whistling happily, carrying a full string of freshly-
caught fish.

> MIYAGI
>
> You miss a spot.

Daniel's brush stops in mid-stroke.

> DANIEL
> (angrily)
> Why didn't you tell me you were going
> fishing?

> MIYAGI
>
> Not here when I go.

> DANIEL
>
> Maybe I would like to have gone. Ever
> think of that?

> MIYAGI
>
> You doing karate training.

> DANIEL
>
> I'm being your goddamn slave is what
> I'm doing. We made a deal.

> MIYAGI
> So?

> DANIEL
> So you're supposed to teach, and I'm supposed to learn. Remember. It's four days and I haven't learned a goddamn thing.

> MIYAGI
> Learn plenty.

> DANIEL
> Yeah, how to sand your deck, how to wax your cars, how to paint your house.

> MIYAGI
> Not everything is as looks, you know.

> DANIEL
> Bullshit.

He flings the paintbrush into the can and stalks off.

> MIYAGI
> Danielsan.

Daniel lifts his bike.

> MIYAGI
> (sharply)
> Danielsan.

Daniel is stopped by the edge in his voice.

> MIYAGI
> (commanding)
> Come here.

Daniel grits his teeth, but obeys, returning to stand before the
old man, sullen, distant.

                         MIYAGI
               Show me wax on, wax off.

Daniel does not move.

                         MIYAGI
                        (sharp)
          Show.

                         DANIEL
                        (defiant)
               I can't lift up my arms.

Miyagi feels around Daniel's shoulder for a moment. He rubs
his hands together back and forth, very fast, then applies them
to Daniel's shoulder, one on each side, pressing hard with his
thumbs and palms.

                         DANIEL
          Ow!

                         MIYAGI
               Now show. On, off.

Daniel does as he is told. To his surprise the ache is gone.
Miyagi corrects the angle of his elbow, tucking it in.

                         DANIEL
                        (surprised)
               How'd you do that?

                         MIYAGI
                        (stern)
               Show. Left right. Left right. Left right.

Daniel catches the rhythm, making perfect half circles. Without warning, Miyagi throws a chest punch. Before Daniel realizes it, one of his circling hands has intercepted the punch

and deflected it effortlessly. His eyes find Miyagi's. His face lights up. Miyagi remains emotionless.

> MIYAGI
>
> Sand floor.

Daniel does as he is told. Miyagi makes the right corrections so that Daniel's arms circle down. The old man shoots a half-speed kick to Daniel's stomach. Daniel's hand deflects it smoothly.

> MIYAGI
>
> Paint fence.

Now Daniel is eager, quick to comply. Miyagi makes a small adjustment, Daniel keeps painting. Miyagi throws a head punch. On the upstroke, Daniel's bent wrist catches Miyagi's punch. Miyagi throws a stomach punch. Daniel's downstroke deflects it perfectly.

> MIYAGI
>
> Side side.

Daniel needs no prompting. As he draws his hand from side to side across his body, he deflects two rapid hook punches thrown by the stone-faced old man.

> MIYAGI
>
> Look eyes.

Daniel's eyes lock into Miyagi's.

> MIYAGI
>
> Wax on.

Miyagi fires a chest punch. Daniel deflects it easily.

> MIYAGI
>
> Wax off.

Again, the block is there.

                              MIYAGI
                    Paint up.

Miyagi fires hard for the head. Daniel's snapping block is there
to meet the attack.

                              MIYAGI
                    Down.

Daniel's palm heel crashes into Miyagi's fist.

                              MIYAGI
                    Side.

He punches. Daniel blocks.

                              MIYAGI
                    Side.

Daniel's block snaps into place.

                              MIYAGI
                    Sand.

Daniel sweeps two kicks out of the way.

                              MIYAGI
                    On off.

The punches come faster. The blocks are right there. Suddenly,
at the height of the exercise, Miyagi stops. Daniel, breathing
hard, elated, waits for more. Miyagi picks up his fish.

                              MIYAGI
                    Come tomorrow.

He turns abruptly and enters the house, slamming the door
behind him before Daniel can say another word.

   Again, it is impossible to separate the action from the dialogue,
which is also extremely effective in this scene. I chose this illustra-

tion because the action is very effective on the screen but tough to convey on the page. In spite of the difficulty of presenting all these body movements in written form, the screenwriter creates a vivid, emotionally involving scene.

The language of the scene is very *simple*. The screenwriter doesn't get caught up in a lot of martial arts jargon or complicated body moves. By illustrating karate through the everyday tasks of sanding, painting, and washing, the reader is also brought into the instruction in a very basic way. We're not just watching Daniel learn karate, *we* are learning karate. And that level of emotional involvement is precisely what the screenwriter strives for.

The dialogue is minimal and very clipped so that it won't detract from the action, which is the essence of the scene.

The scene is very easy to read. It passes quickly, consistent with the pace of the action, but also allows the reader to remain emotionally involved in the story. At no point in this scene would a reader be likely to say, "Wait a minute, now what exactly are they doing here? Just how does that move work?" Instead, the scene propels the reader through the clear, exciting, concisely written action.

And with the abrupt ending, the writer leaves the readers wanting more, compelling us to turn the page and keeping us emotionally involved.

Dialogue

As an additional example of both effective dialogue and exciting action, read the following two scenes. Notice again how the action of the attack by the Cobras is conveyed in clear, simple, detailed language and minimal dialogue.

The scene that follows between Daniel and Mr. Miyagi then provides a lower emotional level to contrast with the high emotion of the fight and rescue (structural peaks and valleys). And the conversation not only provides effective, emotionally involving dialogue but accomplishes numerous character and structural goals, as you will see:

EXT. SCHOOL - NIGHT

Shedding his costume in bits and pieces DANIEL runs across
the street. Cars SCREECH to a halt, rear ending each other, as
the Cobras come rushing out.

EXT. VACANT LOT - NIGHT

Winded, tiring, DANIEL takes off across a weed-choked lot. At
the end of the lot is a chain link fence, beyond the fence is
home and safety. DANIEL reaches the fence and leaps. His
hands grasp the top as he struggles to pull himself over, he is
dragged down from behind by JOHNNY. The others catch up,
breathing hard, their faces obscured in shadow. They surround
DANIEL and with one last desperate attempt he tries to break
away, punching and kaiing loudly, but JOHNNY'S knee to his
chest ends all that.

                        JOHNNY
            You couldn't leave well enough alone,
            could you you little twerp and now you
            are going to pay for it.

JOHNNY, soaking wet and furious, lifts DANIEL by his collar
and pushes him to one of his compatriots. The Cobras push
DANIEL around setting him up for JOHNNY'S vicious kicking
technique. He is pushed around three times, JOHNNY hitting
him each time until at last he is prostrate on the ground.

                        JOHNNY
            Get him up.

The others hang back, hesitant to do more damage.

                        BOBBY
            Come on man, he's had it.

                        JOHNNY
                      (robot-like)
            A man faces you, he is your enemy. An
            enemy deserves no mercy. Get him up.

Two of the other Cobras obey, propping the almost unconscious figure against the fence. Johnny backs up, takes a running start, and leaps into the air.

DANIEL'S POV: Through blurred vision, he watches Johnny's
lethal side kick unfolding in SLOW MOTION, aimed for his
head. Too weak to move, he waits for the inevitable impact,
when out of nowhere a figure leaps the fence, pushing Daniel
to the ground. Johnny's foot hits the fence a second later with
such force a slat cracks where Daniel's head was.

DANIEL'S POV FROM THE GROUND: A small, lithe figure, obscured by shadows, poised opposite the Cobras in a low cat
stance. The first three Cobras attack. In a moment, they are on
the ground, writhing in pain, as the anonymous defender
lashes out with punches and kicks. Johnny, the last one left
standing, charges madly. The mystery figure somersaults to-
wards him, shooting his leg up into Johnny's exposed groin.
Johnny stops dead, choking, and crumbles. Daniel's vision
fades to black.

INT. MAINTENANCE SHED - NIGHT

Daniel revives, his vision clears. He looks around at a familiar
setting. A repugnant smell catches his nose. He removes an
offensive compress from his head when Miyagi appears.

                    MIYAGI
          Leave on.

He firmly slaps the compress on Daniel's head.

                    DANIEL
          It stinks.

                    MIYAGI
          Smell bad. Heal good.

As Miyagi dabs at Daniel's cuts and bruises, Daniel looks
around.

                         DANIEL
                 Where's the other guy?

Miyagi blinks. A revelation slowly unfolds.

                         DANIEL
                 You?

Miyagi bows and smiles.

                         DANIEL
                 No.

                         MIYAGI
                 Why no?

                         DANIEL
                 Because—because—

But the words will not come.

                         MIYAGI
                 Because old man?

A KETTLE WHISTLES. Miyagi rises.

He goes over to the hot plate and pours two cups of tea. Daniel
sits up slowly.

                         DANIEL
                 Why didn't you tell me?

                         MIYAGI
                 What?

                         DANIEL
                 That you knew karate.

                         MIYAGI
                 Never ask.

                    DANIEL
Where'd you learn?

                    MIYAGI
From father.

                    DANIEL
I thought he was a fisherman.

                    MIYAGI
All Miyagi know two things. Fish and
karate. Karate come from Okinawa.
Matter of fact, Miyagi ancestor bring
from China in sixteenth century, call
"Te." Hand. Later, fancy pants uncle
call karate, empty hand.

                    DANIEL
I thought it came from like Buddhist
temples and stuff.

                    MIYAGI
Watch too much TV.

Miyagi removes Daniel's head cloth, rinses it out, and reap-
plies it.

                    DANIEL
Have you ever taught anyone?

                    MIYAGI
No.

                    DANIEL
Would you?

                    MIYAGI
Depend.

                    DANIEL
On what?

                         MIYAGI
Reason.

                         DANIEL
How's revenge?

                         MIYAGI
Look revenge that way Danielsan, start
by digging two graves.

                         DANIEL
At least I would have company.

                         MIYAGI
Fighting always last answer to problem.

                         DANIEL
No offense, Mr. Miyagi, but I don't
think you understand the problem.

                         MIYAGI
Understand perfect. Friends karate
students, yes?

                         DANIEL
Yeah.

                         MIYAGI
Problem attitude.

                         DANIEL
Problem is, I'm getting my ass kicked
every other day.

                         MIYAGI
Yes. Because boys learn wrong attitude. Karate used to defense.

                    DANIEL
That's not what these jerks are taught.

                    MIYAGI
Can see. No such thing bad student,
only bad teacher. Teacher say, student
do.

                    DANIEL
                  (sarcastic)
Oh, great. That solves everything. I just
have to go down to their school and
straighten it out with the teacher.

                    MIYAGI
Now use head for something besides
target.

                    DANIEL
I was only kidding.

                    MIYAGI
Why?

                    DANIEL
'Cause I'll get killed if I show up there.

                    MIYAGI
Get killed anyway.

Miyagi has a point. Daniel stops and thinks about it.

                    DANIEL
Would you come with me?

                    MIYAGI
No can do.

                    DANIEL
You said it was a good idea.

                         MIYAGI
          For you.
                    (beat)
          For me, rule number one, no like get
          involved.

                         DANIEL
          But you're already involved.

                         MIYAGI
          So sorry.

Daniel gets up and throws the rag off.

                         DANIEL
          Well thanks for nothing. I didn't have
          enough trouble. Now I gotta carry your
          weight too.

Daniel stalks out. Miyagi's face reflects his troubled thoughts.

EXT. MAINTENANCE SHED - NIGHT

Daniel is halfway to his building.

                         MIYAGI
          Danielsan.

Daniel stops and turns, petulantly.

                         MIYAGI
          Okay, I go.

Daniel's petulance gives way to a smile. Miyagi turns to go
back to the maintenance shed.

                         DANIEL
          Mr. Miyagi. What belt do you have?

> MIYAGI
> (tugs at his belt)
> Canvas. You like?

> DANIEL
> (surprised)
> Yeah, it's very nice.

> MIYAGI
> J. C. Penney, $3.98.

Miyagi sees by Daniel's face that his joke is not understood.

> MIYAGI
> In Okinawa, belt mean "don't need rope
> hold up pants." Karate here.
> (taps his head)
> Here.
> (taps his heart)
> Not here.
> (he pulls on his belt)
> Understand?

Daniel nods.

> MIYAGI
> Good night, Danielsan.

Miyagi enters the maintenance shed and closes the door.

There is nothing about this dialogue that is particularly exciting or unusual and probably little that an audience would even remember when leaving the theater (with the possible exception of the line about J. C. Penney). Yet it is very effective dialogue.

Look at all that the screenwriter accomplishes in the scene: the language is consistent with the characters; it's original and un-clichéd; there is conflict between the two characters to heighten the emotion; it reveals character background, inner motivation, and inner conflict; it employs the structural devices of anticipation, curiosity, reversal, foreshadowing, and believability; it creates humor; and it contributes to theme. And it's an enjoyable, easy scene to read.

Remember that there must be peaks and valleys to the emotional level of the screenplay. I purposely picked the scene following the fight with the Cobras because it is one of those "valley" sequences. This scene lacks big, dramatic action, humor, or romance. But that is precisely why it can be so effective at accomplishing so many other objectives.

Even in this talk-heavy scene, the description is brief and vivid and things *happen*. The smells, sounds, and expressions of the characters; applying the compress; making the tea; bowing; Daniel storming out of the room are all action and description that increase interest in the scene and prevent it from becoming a talking heads situation.

As in all of the examples I have chosen in this chapter, action, description, and dialogue combine to maximize the emotional involvement for the reader.

Weaknesses

It's probably fairly obvious that I think *The Karate Kid* is a terrific movie. But what about it's shortcomings? Does it also serve as an illustration of any mistakes to avoid in your own screenplays?

In the fifteen or twenty seminars in which I have discussed this screenplay in detail, about 10 percent of the students polled didn't like the movie. Those students consistently pointed to certain weaknesses in the script:

1. **Predictability.** This is probably the most consistent complaint about the movie. Because of its familiar, Rocky-like plot and structure, its teenage love story, and its happy ending, many viewers felt they were seeing a cookie-cutter Hollywood fantasy.

2. **Language.** As I mentioned above, it's a little hard to believe that after more than four decades in the United States, Mr. Miyagi still wouldn't have mastered the art of complete sentences.

3. Unresolved Anticipation. When Daniel and Mr. Miyagi go to Kreese's dojo and enter the tournament, Kreese tells Miyagi, "[if] you don't show, [at the tournament] it's open season. On him . . . . and you." This creates anticipation of a final confrontation between Miyagi and Kreese. But it never happens, leaving the audience somewhat unsatisfied.

Since the shooting script for *The Karate Kid* contains the scene in the parking lot that serves as the prologue for *The Karate Kid II*, it seems evident that the scene was shot, and then excised in the editing room after it was too late to go back and reshoot the earlier dialogue in the dojo. So this is really a problem of the film rather than the screenplay. And given the effectiveness of the highly emotional climax and immediate denouement, it was probably the best decision at the time.

4. An Uninteresting Concept. A number of those who didn't care for the movie said they simply weren't interested in a movie about teenage romance and karate.

5. No Identification. Some students said they just didn't feel any emotional connection with Daniel or the other characters.

6. Slow Beginning. Many people who read the screenplay felt it took a long time for anything very interesting or exciting to happen. The opening of the film isn't really captivating, and there is quite a stretch before Mr. Miyagi starts teaching Daniel.

Personally, I believe items 2, 3, and 6 are the most valid, or are at least the ones that I felt as well. But all of these opinions can serve as guides to your own writing, because each relates to principles we have previously discussed.

From now on, don't look at any movie as a waste of seven bucks, even if you don't like it. Instead, analyze *why* it failed to involve you emotionally. Figure out which of the principles of concept, character, structure, and scene writing are weak and then check your own work in progress to be sure you haven't fallen into the same traps.

The first criticism listed above relates to both story concept and structure. One of the principles from the Story Concept checklist is to combine familiarity and originality. For some people, *The Karate Kid* is too long on familiarity and too short on originality.

Similarly, reversal in expectation is a principle of effective structure. Those who felt they were always able to guess exactly what was going to happen lost their emotional involvement with the story.

Item 2 above, Mr. Miyagi's language, is also a structural weakness, violating the principle of credibility. Remember to ask yourself, "Do my characters behave the way people *with their backgrounds* would normally behave?"

The third criticism reflects a misuse of the principle of anticipation. Don't create anticipation in the audience if you can't pay it off.

The story concept itself failed to attract those people who didn't care about teenagers or karate. You'll never come up with a story idea that appeals to everyone, and sometimes audience members bring their own emotional baggage to a movie that prevents them from enjoying the story. But be certain to choose story concepts that you believe will appeal to at least the majority of the mainstream audience, especially when launching your career.

Those who didn't identify with Daniel may have simply been uninterested in any story about a high school boy. But use those kinds of comments to emphasize the necessity of establishing immediate emotional involvement with your hero, particularly through undeserved misfortune, likability, and jeopardy.

And finally, those who criticized the opening of the screenplay point up the need for grabbing the audience, and the reader, as quickly as possible.

It will be immensely helpful to your own screenwriting if you begin reading screenplays for the current movies you love, especially if they are also commercially successful. Then subject those scripts to the same kind of analysis outlined here for *The Karate Kid*. Use the principles and checklists from this book to determine exactly how the screenplay creates such effective emotional involvement. And then apply those principles to your own screenwriting.

PART III

THE BUSINESS OF SCREENWRITING

CHAPTER 8

. . . .

Marketing Yourself as a Screenwriter

The title of this book is incomplete. It is not the sale of your screenplay that should be your primary goal in pursuit of a screenwriting career; your real objective is the sale of yourself as a screenwriter. You ultimately want to make money writing for the movies or television and to support yourself in a manner to which you'd like to become accustomed by getting paid for your work. Selling your completed screenplays is certainly one way to accomplish that. But keep in mind that *you* are the commodity. It is your talent that you are marketing, and your screenplays will exhibit that talent.

It is sometimes difficult to accept, but the majority of films produced by Hollywood do not originate with completed screenplays. "Spec" scripts—screenplays written speculatively, which are completed before any deal is negotiated—account for less than a third of the movies seen on the big screen, and almost none of the movies or episodes shown on television. This will be discussed in detail in the section on the development deal.

It is far more important that your screenplay indicate your talents and abilities as a screenwriter than that your script be sold outright. The sale of your screenplay is always a goal, and it is wonderful when it happens, but you must also use your screenplay as a calling card and a writing sample which will enable you to get additional work as a screenwriter.

In other words, this section of the book is about launching your *career* as a screenwriter and not just about selling individual screenplays.

I'm talking here about *selling*. Good, old-fashioned, pavement-beating, door-knocking, phone-dialing, Fuller-Brush-Man-type salesmanship. If your goal is to support yourself as a screenwriter, you can't spend all your time in the closet writing. You must accept the fact that part of your job entails risking rejection, frustration, and discouragement by putting yourself on the line and selling yourself to the people who can help get your movies made.

The Three Keys to Marketing Yourself

Once you've decided that you're willing to put yourself out there with the determination of Rambo in order to launch your career, there are three principles to keep firmly in mind:

1. Try Everything. Talk to ten working screenwriters, and you'll hear ten different stories of exactly how they broke into the business and reached that first rung of success. Anything that doesn't hurt anybody should be attempted, even if at times it stretches the limits of your courage and chutzpah. The method outlined here will give you the principles that all of the success stories share, plus a foundation approach which you should expand and modify into the scheme that works for you.

2. Don't Listen to Statistics. All of those stories about the number of screenwriters who are out of work or the thousands of unsold screenplays the Writers Guild has registered or the impossibility of getting an agent only serve one purpose: to dissuade you from your goal.

If you're pursuing screenwriting because you think it's easy, then you haven't been reading very carefully. Selling yourself as a screenwriter involves some formidable hurdles. But show me one thing in life worth pursuing (besides sleep) that doesn't require risk, fear, commitment, and perseverance.

You shouldn't pursue a screenwriting career in blissful ignorance of the realities of the marketplace. But once you decide that your dream, your path to personal fulfillment, is through screenwriting, then you must focus on those methods and attitudes which will enable you to realize your goal. *The fact that someone else failed to achieve the same goal has nothing to do with you.* You must continually reject rejection and reject the things that diminish your courage and resolve in going after your dream.

I know that all sounds a bit dreamy and *Man of La Mancha*-ish, so if you're determined to hear some cold, hard statistics, here are some to consider very carefully:

100 percent of the screenwriters who now have agents at one time didn't have agents.

100 percent of the screenwriters who are now working at one time weren't working.

100 percent of the screenwriters who have made money at screenwriting at one time hadn't made a dime.

And in addition, if you had any notion of the quantity of absolute garbage that's floating around Hollywood between script covers, you'd never again wonder if you could compete for talent. In all my years of meetings and negotiations and interviews and seminars, I have never *once* heard any producer or agent or star or executive say, "We are no longer looking for good screenplays or good screenwriters."

The problem is not that there is already enough talent to meet Hollywood's needs. The difficulty you face is that wherever there is so much garbage, there has to be a filtering system. And that's why God made the reader.

That's also why so many of those same producers and agents and stars and executives *do* say that they won't *read* any more "unsolicited" material. Your goal must be to penetrate that filtering system and get your work read by the people (including readers) who can help launch your career.

3. Knowledge Is Power. It is insufficient to assume that somewhere out there somebody is looking for a screenplay and maybe it's yours they will buy. You must know specifically *who* the people are who are getting movies made, *what* they are looking for, and *where* you can reach them.

Acquiring Information

So to begin pursuing your career as a screenwriter, you must ignore all negative statistics, find the courage to put yourself and your work out there in the marketplace in any way you can, and begin acquiring loads of information. And there are two ways to find out the things you need to know:

Contacts

The first source of information is primary research. Or, in the current vernacular, *contacts*. A contact is anyone you know. It is not just anyone in the film business, not just anyone who has ever written a screenplay, not just anyone who lives in Hollywood. It is anyone you know, period. Your gardener's sister's cousin's girlfriend's daughter might be the agent in Hollywood who will be willing to read your screenplay or the financier who will want to make your movie.

The process of meeting two people and having them each introduce you to two people who in turn each introduce you to two more is known as *networking*. By continually pursuing this process, you eventually will have a massive pyramid of names that will lead you to the specific people who will pay you for your work. What you are actually acquiring from each person in that chain, each individual in your network, is information: information about (or introductions to) other people, or information about that particular individual's screenwriting needs.

Once you regard everyone you encounter as a contact, you will become increasingly effective at expanding your base of operation and at obtaining information. There are numerous situations for meeting people in order to promote your career: attending film classes, joining writers' groups and professional organizations in the film industry, contacting city or state film commissions, volunteering on student films or independent productions, even switching your job to one in the movie industry.

This last suggestion does not mean quitting your job as a commodities broker to become a grip on the local TV station's farm report. But if you are working as a secretary at a bean cannery, why not see if you can obtain the same position for a film production company? It will give you additional information about the film business and will greatly increase your contacts.

Another well-known source of contacts is the social gathering, which brings us to the myth of the Hollywood Party. Particularly in Los Angeles, there seems to be a notion that unless you're invited to Warren Beatty's house regularly, you really haven't got much of a chance of being a screenwriter. Being invited to Warren Beatty's house would probably be a lot of fun. *I'd* like to be invited to Warren Beatty's house. But the truth about Hollywood parties is that either (1) people who meet there for the first time are just making contacts; or (2) people who close deals there are just continuing discussions and negotiations that probably began in someone's office or over the telephone earlier that week. It is pretty rare that someone meets a mogul for the first time over cocktails and closes a deal for their screenplay before the party's over. Lots of successful screenwriters never even go to parties.

Starting today, make the pursuit of contacts a part of your screenwriting efforts until it becomes second nature. When anyone asks you what you do for a living, say you're a screenwriter. Later on you can mention that you're a neurosurgeon on the side. You must give people an opportunity to connect with your pursuit and give you whatever information they have.

The key to using contacts is this: Don't be afraid to ask for a favor, but never depend on one. The film business, like most other businesses, revolves around favors. When you ask for something, assume your contact is enough of a grownup to say no if he really doesn't want to do it. And you must not be offended if he does say no. This is a key principle of honest, assertive behavior.

But your career will grind to a halt if you ask one person for a favor and then sit back and wait until he delivers as promised. The favor you have asked may be high on your list of priorities, but it won't be high on his. The best thing you can do is ask politely for the favor, be very appreciative when it is promised, and then go on to your next contact to get additional information or ask for more help. Then, if the first person delivers as promised, you're in terrific shape, and if he doesn't, you haven't lost ground through laziness or cowardice.

The Media

The other source of information is traditionally known as secondary research. In other words, The Media. It's all that stuff they talked about on Library Orientation Day in junior high school, when you were ogling the cheerleaders or passing notes instead of paying attention.

Books, magazines, the trade papers, the daily newspaper, television, and radio are among the sources of information that must supplement your contacts. Given the multitude of articles, interviews, programs, and publicity events that are generated by the film industry, the media offer a wealth of information to aid in the pursuit of your career.

Let's say you're watching *Entertainment Tonight,* and you hear that *Stakeout* was the biggest box-office hit of the 1987 summer releases. An interview with Richard Dreyfuss follows, in which he reveals he has a deal with Disney Studios for future projects and he wants to do something more serious next.

You have now learned who is hot, what he's looking for, and where he is. If the hero of your dramatic screenplay could be played by Richard Dreyfuss, you can call Disney Studios, ask for the name and number of Richard Dreyfuss' production company, and pursue that company with your screenplay, in the manner outlined below.

The bibliography contains a list of media sources. But *all* contacts and media are potential sources of the Who, What, and Where information you need to launch your career as a screenwriter.

The Four Paths to a Deal

Four categories of people will enable you to secure a screenwriting deal: the *agent,* the *producer,* the *element,* and the *financier.* Within each of these categories, you must determine *who* are the individuals with power, *what* they are looking for in a client or a project, and *where* you can reach them.

Usually you will need at least two of these people attached to you or your project in order to secure a deal. For example, you might get an agent, who in turn will submit your screenplay to a production company, which will attach an element (a star or director) to it and will then set up a production deal for your film with a financier (studio, investor, or the like). This is a logical, familiar process for many first-deal screenplays, but it is only one of many possible combinations and sequences.

You should approach all of these people on your own, *simultaneously.* We will discuss the way you determine the who, what, and where for each of these categories and how you approach each one of them later in this chapter. But before reaching that stage of the process, you must be sure you have the *essential* item for pursuing your career: a good screenplay.

In order to market yourself as a screenwriter, you *must* have a completed screenplay. This is absolutely critical. It will not suffice to have book rights, a treatment, a hot idea, interest from a star, or anything else short of a complete screenplay. You can use those other things to pursue producing but not to become a screenwriter. The exceptions to this are so rare that they are best ignored. Take it as law that until you complete a screenplay, you cannot begin pursuing any of the avenues toward your ultimate deal.

Not only must you have a completed screenplay, but it must fall into the category you're pursuing: half-hour situation comedy, one-hour episode, or feature-length film (feature film or TV movie). And two completed screenplays in your area of interest are more than twice as good as one. Each additional screenplay will be better than the previous one, increase your chances of success, and show your contacts that you are committed to your goal.

Don't consider writing a miniseries or a pilot for an episodic series that does not yet exist. These two television forms are almost always written by established screenwriters who have already proven themselves in the episodic series or TV movie arenas.

When you have completed your screenplay, before you submit it to any of these categories of people, you have to make sure it's good enough. Unfortunately, you can't trust your own judgment in this regard. Of course *you* will think it's great; you've been working on your screenplay so long and hard by now that *Plan Nine from Outer Space* would seem great to you if it was your creation. So to get a more objective sense of the quality of your script, follow this process:

When you finish what you believe is your final rewrite, put your screenplay in a drawer for a couple of weeks, just to get some emotional distance. Otherwise you'll be so relieved to have completed it that you'll have no objectivity about it at all. Then give it one final polish, making certain, as honestly as you can, that your script meets all the requirements outlined in this book for an effective screenplay. Go over it carefully for typos and grammatical and spelling errors and put it in the best form you possibly can. It's usually an even better idea to have someone edit it for you *just* for such errors.

When your screenplay is as good as you can possibly get it, make eight copies and distribute them as follows:

1. Put the original someplace safe so that if your house burns down at least you'll have your screenplay left.

2. Keep the first copy.

3. Register the second copy for a copyright with the Copyright office in Washington, D.C. Register of Copyrights, Library of Congress, Washington, D.C. 20559.

4. Register the third copy with the Writers Guild of America. The current fee for nonmembers of the Guild is $20.00. For information on this process, call (213) 205-2500.

5. Give the last five copies to five people whose judgment you trust and ask them to read it and give you their suggestions. You can trust their judgment if they are intelligent, know something about film, and preferably have read screenplays before or work in the film business. It doesn't hurt to give an extra copy to your mom, just so you can be certain of one good response. But the other five should go to people who you know will be honest, neither falsely sensitive to your feelings nor falsely critical.

One of these last five people might be a professional evaluator of screenplays, who for a fee will critique your screenplay and give you recommendations for a rewrite, feedback on its suitability for submission, and so on. The fees for such services in Hollywood range anywhere from $50 to $500 for a feature-length script. The names of these people are available through various film schools and the *Hollywood Scriptwriter* (see bibliography).

When you ask a friend or contact for her opinion, it's a good idea to provide a colored pen to mark up the copy and some specific questions to focus on. This will encourage the reader to be critical and direct and help overcome the natural reluctance to mark up a fresh, clean copy of your creation.

When these five people have responded to your screenplay, you face one of the toughest stages of the entire process. If you get back five responses of "Have you ever considered going into animal husbandry?" then you know your screenplay isn't ready to show. As emotionally wrenching as such a decision is, you must either go back to square one with your story concept and use all of the principles you know and all the feedback you got to start over, or you must realize that you did as much as you could with that particular idea, and now you're going to trash it and go on to a new story concept possessing greater potential.

Either path is excruciating for a while. But take courage in knowing that every writer faces this decision sometime in her career, that your next script or your next rewrite will *always* be better, and that the process up to this point has been both fulfilling (probably) and educational (certainly).

Never bypass this objective evaluation stage. To submit a weak screenplay to people with the power to get you a deal is worse than submitting nothing.

Let's say, for example, that through your contacts you are able to get your script to Sydney Pollack, and in your eagerness to take advantage of this good fortune, you send him a screenplay that isn't ready. So he politely rejects it. Then you write your next screenplay, which *is* terrific. How eager is Sydney Pollack going to be to read another script from the same guy who a few months ago sent him a piece of junk? It's better to get some substantiation for your own enthusiasm before you waste your contacts on a mediocre script.

Now let's assume, more positively, that out of the five people who read your script, at least two had a strong positive response. If at least two out of the five people think that your screenplay has strong potential and is ready or nearly ready to show, then you can move forward. You'll never get five people to all agree on anything, including your script, and two out of five is a positive enough reaction that you should prepare the script for submission.

Use both the positive and negative comments from all five people to complete a final rewrite and polish of your screenplay. Then copyright and register the new version. It only costs $20 to do both, and it's the only real protection you have. Now you're ready to pursue those four categories of people in power.

Begin by purchasing a three-ring binder and set of dividers. (Do this even if you haven't yet started writing your screenplay.) Designate a section of the notebook for each of the four categories of people mentioned above, plus a fifth section for general contacts.

Each time you obtain a new name through your contacts or the media devote a new piece of notebook paper to that person, adding their page to the appropriate section of the binder. Put the person's name at the top of the page, along with his address and phone number if you have it. Then put the date, any additional information you obtained, and the source. Whenever you obtain additional information on this person, add it to the page with the appropriate date.

If you begin this process now, by the time your screenplay is ready to show you will have an extensive list of potential contacts in all five categories.

To recap the process of marketing yourself so far, you must:

1. Immediately:

Begin writing your screenplay.

Obtain a three-ring binder with dividers for recording information on agents, producers, elements, financiers, and general contacts.

Make contacts by participating in situations involving other writers and filmmakers and by spreading the word that you're a screenwriter.

Obtain as much information as possible about the necessary Who, What, and Where through the media.

2. When you complete your screenplay to your own satisfaction:

Put it away for awhile to get some distance and objectivity.

Give it one more polish based on all the principles in this book.

Make eight copies.

Register and copyright your script.

Give copies to five honest people whose judgment you trust and ask for their opinions and recommendations.

Based on their feedback, either start over, scrap the concept, or give your screenplay one final rewrite and polish.

3. When your screenplay is ready to submit:

Start making copies.

Begin pursuing the four categories of people in power in the manner outlined below.

I will begin by discussing how you research and pursue agents with your screenplay, and then I will go on to the other three categories of people who can lead you to a deal, to outline how the process differs for each.

The Agent

The agent category includes anyone who represents you as a screenwriter, anyone whose job is to help you find work and negotiate your screenwriting deals. This could be either a literary agent or an attorney. A literary agent represents you in return for 10 percent of your income as a screenwriter; an attorney will usually be paid an hourly fee for representing you, regardless of the outcome. Established writers often have both: the agent finds work and negotiates deals; the attorney represents the writer legally, perhaps gets involved in negotiation, and finalizes the contracts.

If you a beginning writer, you will certainly want to pursue agents. But keep in mind as I outline the process that you are pursuing the other three categories (producer, element, financier) *simultaneously*. Should you get an offer from a producer or financier, and you have no literary agent, you can hire an attorney to negotiate your deal. There are well-established screenwriters who are only represented by lawyers.

Any agent is going to look for three things in a prospective client:

1. Someone Who Will Make Money for the Agency. An agent's only income is 10 percent of his clients' earnings. If you don't write scripts that sell, an agent can't afford to represent you.

2. A Writer with Career Potential. An agent knows that the sale of a first or second screenplay will seldom command major monetary figures by Hollywood standards. But an agent also knows that each successive screenplay will earn a greater amount of money, and an established career can be lucrative for all involved.

3. Someone Who Won't Add to the Agent's Problems. Agents do battle all day long with executives, producers, business affairs departments, attorneys, and other agents. They don't want to do battle with their own clients as well.

This means if you are positive, energetic, and committed to your writing, the agent will maintain a higher level of enthusiasm representing you than if you are constantly bemoaning the sorry state of your career and your life. Repeatedly blaming the agent or the film industry for making you one of life's victims is a great way not to get your phone calls returned.

You are also looking for three things in a potential agent:

1. Someone Who Will Look Out for Your Career. You don't want an agent who is just out to make a fast 10 percent by selling your script. Such an attitude would be rare among established, credible agents anyway. You want someone who is enthusiastic about you as a writer, not just about your single script, and who will work with you and guide your career toward fulfillment of your own desires, talents, and goals.

2. Someone Powerful. Power in the film business can take two forms. The first is *clout:* high standing in the Hollywood community; the influence that comes from a stable of major writers; the backing of a big agency; the ability to get anyone in town on the telephone.

If your agent represents William Goldman, John Hughes, James Cameron, and you, then your agent should have no trouble getting through to the people who can give you work. This is the advantage of representation by Hollywood's biggest agencies: their ability to reach the top studio and network executives and to package your project with the major stars and directors they also represent.

But there can be a negative side to this kind of clout. If your agent also represents William Goldman, John Hughes, and James Cameron, how much time will be spent on your behalf? Those other writers pull down $750,000 per script at least, and you're struggling to get a $20,000 rewrite deal. This is why clout is not the only form of power to consider.

The second form of power is *commitment:* energy, enthusiasm, perserverance, and determination expended on your behalf. If your agent is not one of the biggest in Hollywood but is sincerely enthusiastic and devoted to you as a writer and will get out there and dog after the work for you, you may have found your best representative.

Remember, it is an agent who will represent you, not an agency.

The backing of a powerful company can be helpful, but your primary relationship is with the individual agent.

3. Someone Who Can Negotiate. This is probably the least important of the three qualities, particularly at the early stages of your career. There is a common misunderstanding that agents spend all day negotiating deals, when in fact the majority of their time is spent actively attending meetings and making phone calls to market their clients and their clients' work. It is almost impossible to know in the initial encounters with an agent just what their negotiating power is anyway, and the first two qualifications should take much higher priority.

There is often a feeling of discouragement and frustration among unrepresented writers that follows the old Groucho Marx line: "I wouldn't want to belong to any club that would accept me as a member." It sometimes seems that any agent who would be willing to take you on in the early stages of your career must be hard-up for clients and therefore not have much power or clout. Conversely, an agent who really has the ability to represent you well is not looking for new clients and will not be a possibility.

This sort of Catch 22 reasoning is not only unproductive, it isn't even true. Even major agents lose their screenwriter clients from time to time and might be willing to take an unproven but talented writer into the agency. And whatever the agent's standing in the industry, the critical consideration is the relationship you establish with your agent, how he or she feels about you, and how much the agent will actively and aggressively promote your career.

Just as you may be a new, hungry, but talented and hard-working writer, there are new, hungry, talented, and hard-working agents coming into the picture all the time. I have known a lot of new agents who at the beginning of their careers were working out of their apartments, taking on new, unproven writers, and busting a gut trying to get those clients work. Now the clients are rich, and the agents aren't looking for new writers, because the original relationships grew together.

Researching Agents

To learn the necessary Who, What, and Where regarding agents, begin, as always, with your contacts. Every time you meet someone who says he has or knows or is an agent, pump the person for information. Who is the agent? How do they like the agent? Who else does the agent represent? Does the agent handle both TV and features? Will the person introduce you?

Then supplement this firsthand information with secondary research. Begin with the Writers Guild of America list of literary agencies which are signatories to the Guild agreement. This list can be obtained for $1 from the Writers Guild (see the bibliography) and will provide addresses and phone numbers for agents' names that you acquire from other sources.

The Writers Guild list also indicates agencies willing to accept unsolicited manuscripts. Certain agencies will consider your script even if you haven't been referred by someone they know. So the Guild list provides you with at least a dozen agencies to approach on that basis alone.

Those agencies which are willing to read your screenplay unsolicited are certainly worth contacting, but you should never limit yourself to only those agents. Even if an agent has said that she won't read unsolicited material, she should still be approached.

There are various directories of literary agencies available which are similar to the Writers Guild list. Several of the publications in the bibliography carry them, and the *Hollywood Scriptwriter* has an annual issue devoted to agents.

Screenwriting credits for movies and TV episodes can lead you to additional names of agents and agencies. Begin recording screenwriters names from the credits of features and TV movies. Or if you're interested in writing episodic series, start writing down the names of the screenwriters, story editors, and producers of the shows you like, or for the shows which are closely akin to the kind of material you hope to write.

Whenever you accumulate the names of up to three writers, call the Writers Guild of America, West—(213) 550-1000—and, through their "agency" department, ask which literary agent represents each of the writers on your list. (Three is as many as they will provide in one phone call.) Then look up that agency name on the Writers Guild master list to get the address and telephone number. This process not only provides you with names of additional agents, it gives you specific information about who they represent, which can form the basis for a more personal approach.

By continuing this entire process, you will develop a lengthy list of agents to approach when your screenplay is ready to submit.

Approaching Agents

As soon as your screenplay is ready to go, you will begin contacting the agents whose names are now spilling out of your notebook. *Do not send them your screenplay.* It will cost an immense amount of postage, it will usually be returned unopened, and it will at best be placed unnoticed at the bottom of a very large pile. It is cheaper, more professional, and more productive to first establish direct contact with the agency in the hope of persuading someone to take a look at your work.

There are several ways this can be done, so I will begin by detailing the letter of approach and then outline the variations on that method that the others entail.

The Letter of Approach.   The goal of a letter of approach to a potential agent is to stimulate interest in reading your screenplay. It is a brief, professional letter describing you and your screenplay and laying the groundwork for a future conversation.

The letter is never more than one page long and is written clearly and concisely in your own words. Don't make it overly formal or "cutesy." (Cutesy letters have the words "ha ha" in parentheses. I hate cutesy letters.) Your letter should be polite, direct, and to the point, neither cocky and full of hype nor groveling and apologetic.

When you ask agents, or anyone else, to read your work, you are imposing on their already overloaded schedules to request their time, effort, and expertise. So you should be very appreciative when someone is willing to consider your screenplay. But never take the attitude that you are crawling on the ground, begging for the slightest nod toward your creation. An attitude like that will defeat you and shatter the enthusiasm and determination about your career that you must maintain.

Be polite, professional, and positive in your approach and make the following sentence one of your daily affirmations: *I am a good professional screenwriter, and I am giving people the opportunity to make money from my work.* Seeing *Conan the Barbarian* before talking to an agent might also put you in the proper frame of mind.

Your letter of approach to a potential literary agent should include the following:

1. The Purpose of the Letter. State clearly and concisely that you have just completed a screenplay for a feature film, movie for television, or series episode and that you're now looking for representation. Don't beat around the bush with lengthy introductions; get right to the point.

If the screenplay you are writing is your second or third completed screenplay, then say so. This will show that you are not a dilettante and are determined to pursue your screenwriting career.

2. A Personalized Comment. Try at least to make your letter more personal than those for the Publishers' Clearinghouse Sweepstakes. If you're writing to this particular agent because of a friend's recommendation or because the agent represents a specific writer, then say so. Nobody gets excited about a form letter.

3. A Description of the Screenplay. The extent to which you describe your screenplay is really up to you. A high concept story line can peak the agent's interest, but it can also create a greater risk of getting your idea ripped off. Agents are not sitting around waiting to steal concepts for their clients. But story ideas sometimes do get plagiarized, so use your own judgment.

At the very least, if the screenplay falls into one of the commercially attractive categories (comedy, drama, love story, action adventure, or suspense thriller), then say so: "I have just completed a feature-length romantic comedy." If the screenplay falls into one of the less popular genres (western, musical, or period piece), then either don't mention what your story is about or tell the agent what grabbed *you* about the idea.

4. Reference to the Script as a Writing Sample. If you refer to your screenplay as an excellent writing sample, it tells the agent that you are astute enough to realize that his main concern will be getting you work, not just selling this one script.

5. An Offer to Sign Release Forms. A release form is basically a written agreement that if the agency (or production company) is ever involved in a film that is similar to your story, you won't sue them. So many agencies and production companies require these forms that if you are not willing to sign them, your attempts to market your screenplay will be extremely limited.

My tendency would be to sign any of the release forms they require, give them my script, and if they really do rip me off, then sue them anyway. But *this is not legal advice.* I would never presume to give legal advice. I could get in big trouble giving legal advice.

6. Your Background. Briefly give the agent any information about your background that will indicate potential as a screen-writer. If you've ever been published; have been paid for your writing in any arena; have received any writing awards or honors; have ever produced, directed, or written a film; or have a degree in film or writing, then say so. If your background gives you particular insight into the subject of your screenplay, that also bears mention-ing. But if you're the ambassador to Uruguay, don't bother men-tioning it, because it doesn't indicate any particular writing talent.

Even if you have extensive writing experience, do not go into lengthy detail about it. Just mention the high points in order to pique the agent's interest and let it go at that. And don't enclose a resumé with your letter, unless specifically requested.

7. Your Location. Because agents aren't keen on representing writers who are unavailable for meetings with producers, if your return address is more than 100 miles outside of Los Angeles, then include a sentence or two similar to the following: "I am currently working on my next screenplay in Metropolis, U.S.A. I can, how-ever, return to Los Angeles whenever necessary."

We will discuss the issue of screenwriting while living outside of Los Angeles in Chapter 10. But for right now, acknowledge your distant residence in this way and continue your pursuit.

8. Future Contact. Close your letter in such a way that the follow-up contact is left your own hands. "I will be contacting you in the next few days to discuss this further," would do the job.

Do not say, "If you would like to read my screenplay, please give me a call," because they wouldn't and they won't. The purpose of this letter is only to lay the groundwork for a telephone call.

Close the letter politely, sign it, and record the date in your notebook. And again, *do not send your screenplay to anyone yet.*

The Follow-Up Call. It is best if your letter arrives in the agent's office on a Tuesday, Wednesday, or Thursday, although this is a small detail. Most people are too busy on Mondays to deal with minor (to them) correspondence and too eager to go home on Fridays to give it their full attention. Allow an extra day or two (but no longer) for the letter to arrive, then call the agent's office and ask to talk to him. Sometimes it is wise to make your call so that it will arrive after 6:30 P.M., because often an agent's secretary will go home at that time and the agent is answering his own phone. Most often, however, you will deal with the agent's secretary.

This brings up a cardinal rule of marketing your screenplay: *Be nice to secretaries* for at least three reasons:

1. They deserve it. Secretaries work very hard and are given the thankless job of screening out calls like yours.

2. If you don't get the secretary on your side, there is no way you're ever going to persuade the agent to read your screenplay. Piss off a secretary, and you'll be put on indefinite hold.

3. In many cases a secretary is trying to work his own way up the show business ladder to become an agent or story editor himself. And one of the first extra duties he'll take on is reading unsolicited scripts. In other words, you may be talking to the very person who will end up reading your script anyway.

In fact, if you are unable to get through to the agent, ask the secretary to read your script. If the secretary likes it, you can be sure the agent will hear about it.

When you get the secretary on the phone, ask to talk to the agent. When the secretary asks why you are calling, be direct. You can begin by saying that the agent should have received your letter and will be expecting your call. But don't tap-dance around your motives. Tell the secretary that you have completed a screenplay and want to discuss it with the agent.

The stock answer many secretaries are instructed to give is simply that the agency does not accept unsolicited material. Here is where you must use whatever combination of salesmanship, persuasion, and charm you can muster to try to get through to the agent. If that's simply impossible, ask if there are other agents at the agency who might be willing to talk to you. Or ask the secretary if he will read your screenplay. Or at least try to come away with another contact: ask if there are any other agencies or individuals the secretary can recommend you approach.

Remember that your object is not necessarily to get the specific agent you approached to read your screenplay but to get *anyone* at the agency to take a look at it.

As a final objective, leave the door open for future communication. End the conversation with the statement, "Perhaps I'll call back in a month or so to see if the situation there has changed at all." If you're nice and if you keep calling back periodically, eventually you may get enough sympathy from the secretary, or create enough guilt, that someone will take a look at your work.

There will be lots of instances when you won't be able to accomplish any of these things, and your relationship with the agency will dead-end right there. But if the process gets your screenplay read even once out of every 10 attempts, then at least 10 out of the more than 100 literary agents in Hollywood will eventually look at your script. Since you scored at least two out of five with your screenplay earlier in the process, you should have a 40 percent chance that these ten agents will like it, too. And having four agents in Hollywood like your work would be a wonderful situation.

The business of pursuing agents is a numbers game, and it requires perseverance to find the one agent who is right for you. Never allow yourself to get discouraged to the point of quitting. Remember, you don't *have* to have an agent at all. You're pursuing the other three categories *at the same time,* and you can always hire an attorney to do anything an agent does.

Talking to Agents. When you are able to get an agent on the telephone, the first question you are likely to hear is, "What is your screenplay about?" It makes less than a great impression when you answer, "Well . . . uh . . . I don't know . . . you see, there's this guy . . . and he . . . well, no . . . first there's this girl . . ." and so on.

It's understandable that you willl have a hard time being succinct about your script. You've just spent months or years of your life carefully constructing 120 brilliantly intricate pages. Now someone is asking you to convey them in a single sentence.

To prepare for this challenge, compose two or three powerful sentences which clearly convey your story concept and its potential for grabbing an audience. Then put this captivating description on an index card and tape it to your telephone. Until you've memorized these three sentences, simply read them to anyone who wants to hear your story concept.

If you have difficulty doing this, go back to your original, one-sentence story concept (It is a story about a _____ who wants to _____), and expand that into a slightly more detailed summary of your plot. Then modify that paragraph into one that conveys whatever grabs *you* emotionally about your screenplay.

After asking about your story concept, the agent's next question will probably concern your living outside of southern California (if indeed you do). At this point you can say that you are prepared to move to Los Angeles if necessary, when there is a definite prospect of work or income by doing so, and reiterate that you can be in L.A. whenever necessary. But right now not only are you working on your next screenplay in your current home town but you also have a job, a home, and security, there.

It is OK to admit that you just can't move to Los Angeles, giving up your entire support system, unless there is a definite prospect of income to replace your current living situation. You must, however, make clear that you are willing to fly to Los Angeles at any time to meet with a prospective agent or to meet with potential producers of your screenplay.

There is also nothing wrong with admitting poverty when approaching an agent. All agents have worked with writers who at one time in their careers were waiting tables.

Some agents are simply not going to be willing to discuss your project with you or read your script until you have moved to Los Angeles. But others will look at your material to see what kind of potential you have and to see if there is interest in representing you, even though your current residence is outside of southern California.

Whatever direction the conversation takes beyond this, your goal is to get the agent, or someone else at the agency, to read your screenplay.

When the agent or secretary agrees to read your screenplay, then politely end the conversation. Immediately mail a copy of your script along with a brief cover letter reminding the agent (or secretary) of the conversation, thanking him for his time, and expressing your eagerness to get his response to your work. Be sure to keep a copy of all correspondence for your records. Don't use the cover letter to resell the agent on your script. You've already won an agreement to read your work; now let the screenplay stand on its own merits.

If you want to get the screenplay back, enclose a self-addressed, stamped envelope. Usually a script is good for about two or three submissions before it's too dog-eared or coffee-stained to send out. Psychologically, you always want your screenplay to look like it's hot off the presses so each agent subconsciously feels that she's the first to read it. And a clean copy also reflects greater respect for your own work.

After sending the agent the screenplay, wait a few days and call the secretary to make sure it arrived. Or enclose a self-addressed postcard acknowledging receipt.

Then wait a month or so for a response to the screenplay. It's always impossible to say how long it will take to get your material read by any agency. Turnaround time is sometimes immediate if the agency has a staff of readers, but other times a reaction can take endless months. Understand that your unsolicited screenplay always goes to the bottom of a very large stack of scripts and is always superseded by scripts from the agent's own clients.

If the agent pays a reader to read and evaluate your screenplay, the reader will give the agent a *synopsis,* or *coverage,* of your screenplay (or of a play or novel), plus comments and recommendations,. which frees the agent from having to read everything submitted.

Don't worry that your script might not be read by the agent himself. Most readers are very conscientious and long to come across a good script they can recommend to their bosses. If your screenplay does a good job of eliciting emotion in a reader, the agent will hear about it.

Synopses are sometimes confused with treatments. A synopsis is always written after the completed screenplay and hardly ever by the screenwriter himself. Avoid attempting synopses of your own work and let your screenplays stand on their own merits. Story analysis (the formal term for the job of a reader) requires a different kind of talent and is almost impossible to do well for your own work. Don't write synopses unless a potential agent or producer specifically requires one with your screenplay.

Treatments, which are prose versions of film stories written prior to the screenplay, will be discussed in Chapter 9.

Monthly calls to check on the status of your submission are the best. A month is long enough that you're not badgering the agency but soon enough to be assertive. There is no advantage in getting angry and asking for the script back if it hasn't been read as soon as you'd like. Even if it takes the agency a year, by then you might have already acquired and dropped another agent and will again be interested in this first agent's response.

If any of these calls reveal that the agency has read the screenplay and isn't interested, and if you did include a stamped envelope, then ask them to return your script.

The key to this process is the rejection of rejection. Gird yourself for a lot of refusals before getting that positive response. Remember that (1) every successful writer had to go through the same thing; (2) it's a numbers game, and there are a hundred-plus literary agents in Los Angeles, and dozens more in New York; (3) you are concurrently pursuing the other categories of people to get a deal; (4) you can hire an attorney to negotiate for you when the need arises; and (5) the entire time that you're pursuing these people you're also working on your next screenplay. When it's completed you can go back to all of the same people with an even better writing sample.

In addition to the letter of approach, there are at least three other methods of getting agents to read your work: the cold phone call, dropping in, and recommendations from your contacts.

The Cold Phone Call.   Another way to approach agents is to skip the letter of approach and go directly to the phone call. Obtain the name of a potential agent, using the methods discussed, get the appropriate phone number from the Writers Guild of America list, and phone the agency with no prior letter. If you can weave spells with your voice, this method is more direct and saves time and postage. You risk having the agent or secretary hang up on you, but you also stand a chance of being persuasive enough for someone to agree to read your script, if for no other reason than to get you off the telephone.

From that point on, the method is identical to the letter of approach. The object is to get someone at the agency to read your material. Use whatever tricks seem appropriate to get through to the agent, then succinctly explain that you have a good commercial screenplay and are looking for representation. Be prepared to answer whatever other questions the secretary or agent might have regarding your experience, your story concept, and so on.

As you begin pursuing agents (as well as the other three categories of people), try both the letter of approach and the cold phone call, until you see which method works better for you.

Dropping In.   Another method, which requires a bit more chutzpah, is to come to Los Angeles, make 20 or 30 copies of your screenplay, and go directly to the offices of the agents you're pursuing. When you appear in their offices, you say, "Here I am. I've just written a terrific screenplay. Would someone here be willing to take a look at it?" Most agencies do not hire bouncers to get rid of people using this method, although you may get a cold shoulder now and then. But I've heard more than one beginning screenwriter report a high success rate using this method.

Recommendations.   The final approach to agents is by far the best: a personal recommendation from someone the agent knows, especially a producer or one of the agent's own clients. If you meet someone who has an agent, or has a good professional relationship with an agent, and the contact is willing to at least introduce you, then you stand a much better chance that the agent will be willing to read your screenplay. If your contact reads the screenplay and then *recommends* it to the agent, that is the best approach of all.

Combine all of these methods of pursuing agents until you find your own best approach. The goal is always to get as many agencies as possible to read your screenplay in hopes that someone will emerge who likes it and wants to represent you.

If an Agent Is Interested in Representing You.   What happens if you finally get an agent to read your screenplay and she loves it? What if a literary agent wants to represent you?

First of all be pleased, proud, and excited that what you knew all along was a good screenplay has now gotten the approval of someone in the business. At the same time, don't let your relief and excitement allow you to jump into a working relationship just because this agent is the first one who comes along. You must talk at length with the agent, preferably in person, to see what kind of potential the relationship holds.

An agent will probably want the same kind of encounter to measure your potential as a client. Remember that you are looking for the three qualities discussed earlier in this chapter (career guidance, power, and the ability to negotiate), and the agent will be looking for three important qualities in you (the ability to make money, career potential, and a positive attitude).

In this mutual interview with any prospective agent, listen closely to your instincts and gut reaction. The conversation will give each of you a better chance to get acquainted on all levels, and you must trust your feelings about the agent as much as you trust the factual information you obtain.

I recommend asking the agent the following two questions in order to focus on the qualities you're looking for:

1. What did you think of my screenplay? This will give you some idea of how the agent really feels about you as a writer and how you might work together as agent and client. Don't assume that negative comments about your screenplay are a bad sign. If an agent seems to share your vision of your screenplay but offers extensive criticism which hadn't occurred to you, it indicates the potential for a strong, complementary relationship. Constructive criticism can be preferable to unending praise.

2. Who are your other clients? This question should give you a sense of how established the agent is, how much clout she wields, and whether the agent represents primarily television or feature writers.

Don't be embarrassed if you have to ask what the agent's clients have written. Few people recognize the names of any screenwriters other than Neil Simon.

Voice your other questions and concerns during this meeting as well, both to satisfy your own curiosity and to establish some rapport with the agent.

The agent, of course, will be weighing your potential as well, and will want to know about your career goals, your other story ideas and screenplays, and so on. Be honest and direct about all of these matters. Don't hide the fact that you're unwilling to write television or that you eventually want to direct features or that your goal is to be a staff writer for *The Cosby Show*. Misunderstandings at the outset can lead to major dissatisfaction later on, and if the agent won't represent you because of your objectives, the relationship wouldn't have worked even if you had kept them secret.

This discussion with an agent is not unlike a job interview, except that you are both acting like potential employers. The agent will technically work for you, but everybody knows that you're the one who *feels* like a job applicant. You are each entering a partnership, and you must approach the relationship with that kind of concern, enthusiasm, and equality.

Remember, the first agent who knocks on your door isn't necessarily the best agent for you. As difficult as this might be, sign with an agent only when both your head and your heart tell you it will be a mutually rewarding relationship.

When you finally choose an agent, you will sign a contract that conforms to the Writers Guild of America rules, even if you are not yet a member of the Guild yourself. You are then obligated to stay with that agent for a minimum period of time, but if any period of ninety days passes in which the agent has not gotten you work, you then have the right to end the relationship with the agent and go on to another agency.

It is possible to have one agent for your screenwriting and a separate agent for your fiction, or the same agent may represent you for both. But you may never be represented as a screenwriter by more than one agency at a time.

As soon as you sign with an agency, it takes over the marketing of your talent, and you concentrate on writing. It's important to continue making contacts and gathering information on the film business, but you don't want to make end runs around your own agent by pursuing deals on your own.

An agent who represents you as a screenwriter gets 10 percent of everything you earn as a screenwriter, even if you are the one responsible for finding the deal. Rarely will you begrudge your agent his 10 percent commission. A good agent will negotiate much more than an additional 10 percent for you in any deal. And remember as well, that this is the guy who stood by you during those lean months or years, when he was getting 10 percent of zip.

Finding an agent is much like finding a mate. You search extensively, meet some prospective candidates, go through periods of courtship, and after a few temporary relationships, you finally settle on the person who will be with you for life.

Pursuing Other People in Power

The underlying principles for pursuing the other three categories of people with the power to get you a deal (producers, elements, and financiers) are the same as those previously outlined for the agent category:

1. Using contacts and the media, obtain information on who the people in power are, what they are looking for, and where you can reach them.

2. When your screenplay is good enough to submit, approach these people with letters, phone calls, in-person encounters, or introductions from one of your contacts, hoping to persuade the people in each category to read your script.

3. If any of the people in power are interested in attaching themselves to you or your screenplay, meet with that person to decide if the relationship is one you want to establish.

4. Refuse to become discouraged or to accept rejection, and instead play a numbers game by continuing to pursue as many people as possible in all four categories *all at once*.

5. Never let your business activities interfere with your writing. Maintain your writing regimen, adding extra hours for marketing yourself, so that when your next screenplay is completed, you can begin the process again with an additional sample of your writing talent.

Using these principles, I will now outline the process of research and approach as it applies to producers, elements, and financiers.

The Producer

The key difference between a producer and an agent is that an agent is looking for writers to represent, and a producer is looking for movies to make. While an agent's interest is in your talent and overall career prospects, a producer's is in your completed screenplay or your ability to write a specific project.

I'm referring here to independent producers who *develop* material: their companies are putting up money for projects which can be made into movies. Another function of a producer is to see that the movie actually gets made after it's developed and financed. This is known as *line producing*.

Many producers perform both functions, line producing the films they themselves have developed. But there are line producers who are hired by the studios only to see that a project gets made after the studio decides to finance it. Since they aren't actively developing new projects, they will have no interest in your screenplay, either for production or as a writing sample. Stick to companies and individuals who get involved in projects prior to financing.

It is much easier to obtain information concerning the Who, What, and Where for independent producers than it is for agents. While there is no source one may use to learn the names of an agent's clients, it is very easy to acquire information on a producer's credits. This tells you who the working producers are and what type of material is apt to interest them.

In your career notebook you should have a section devoted to producers and production companies, just as you have sections for agents and the other categories. Each time you encounter a producer's name through your contacts and the media, devote a page to that individual or production company.

Simply looking through ads for the movies of the past couple years will provide the names of dozens of producers. Lists of the top box office films will provide a more targeted list of the producers who are strong in Hollywood. Producers also do interviews with magazines and newspapers to publicize their films. And the Margaret Herrick Library at the Academy of Motion Picture Arts and Sciences (see bibliography) has reference files on hundreds of producers and elements.

There are also several sources listed in the bibliography which can provide you with business addresses, phone numbers, and filmographies for producers and their companies. Or you can obtain a production company's location by contacting the distributor of the producer's most recent film.

As the Producer section of your notebook begins to thicken, you will begin to see which production companies would be most appropriate for your particular screenplay. Let's say you discover that Debra Hill was the producer of John Carpenter's early films (*Halloween*, *The Fog*, and so on), then went on her own to produce *Clue* and *Adventures in Babysitting*. You can probably conclude that she wouldn't be the producer to approach with your *Room with a View*—type script.

But don't pigeonhole producers too narrowly with your research; *A Room with a View* might be the very thing that Debra Hill would now love to produce. Most producers grow weary of one particular genre, and if you're the only one bringing a producer something that isn't a clone of his last five films, you might be the writer he notices.

When you are ready to begin approaching any particular producer, call that person's production company and ask for the name of the head of development. She is responsible for acquiring and developing new screenplays and projects. Her title may be vice president of development, director of creative affairs, executive story editor, or something else nondescript. She is the person to approach, not the producer, unless a contact gets you directly to the producer with an introduction or recommendation.

Once you have determined the appropriate individual at the production company, your approach is the same as for an agent. The only important difference is that you are not contacting the producer or head of development for representation but with the hope that she will read your screenplay for consideration as a project to produce or will consider working with you as a screenwriter on other projects.

Again, the strongest approach to a producer is with the recommendation of another trusted professional. Never underestimate the value of your contacts.

Always be prepared to discuss your story concept and screenplay with everyone you approach in order to persuade them to read your work. And do not let rejection thwart your efforts.

If, after reading your screenplay, a producer is interested in your work, then the result can be either the option of your screenplay or a development deal. Both of these will be discussed in detail in Chapter 9.

The Element

Elements are components of a package deal: stars or directors with sufficient clout that their willingness to participate in the movie of your screenplay will increase its chances of getting made. In other words, Eddie Murphy, Farrah Fawcett, Sally Field, Stephanie Zimbalist, Peter Strauss, Sydney Pollack, Randa Haines, and Rob Reiner are all elements.

The majority of major directors and stars (both feature-film and television stars) have their own independent production companies to develop projects. They will therefore be approached as producers, through their heads of development, in the manner described above. The difference is that you are approaching the elements with a project that you think would be of interest specifically for them to star in or direct, not simply produce.

If the star or director does not have an independent production company, then you must find another means of getting your screenplay to him. Recommendations or introductions by your contacts are again the best method. You can also reach an element through his own personal manager, agent, or attorney. This is usually a difficult approach, since the agent will primarily be looking for money offered up front. It's worth a try, even if you have no money committed, but it's a long shot.

You can also try to reach stars and directors by using those bizarre methods you hear about in film seminars: becoming a Western Union messenger to deliver your own script; taking up tennis to get invited to the star's home court; skydiving onto the set of the star's next film.

The basic rule is that if it makes sense and doesn't hurt anybody, it's worth a try. And even if it doesn't seem to make sense, you still might want to give it a whirl.

The Financier

This category includes anyone who might put up money for the film of your screenplay: studios, networks, private investors, and grant-funding agencies (private foundations or the U.S. government).

Begin by omitting studios and networks from your pursuits entirely, unless you have a direct introduction to someone at the level of story editor or higher. Otherwise your screenplay will at best go to the bottom of a huge hopper and, with no one to champion it, will eventually get rejected. It is far better to approach independent producers, get them involved in your project, and let them approach the studios and networks with whom they have deals or relationships.

To research the Who and Where for other financiers in this category, begin, as always, with your contacts. Anytime you hear about a film project which was independently financed, start asking questions. Or any time you meet someone with dough, get friendly.

Your media research should include information on any independently financed films you hear or read about. Take advantage of city and state film commissions, which will have information on movies financed and shot within their regions and which are eager to support local film activity. And film magazines often have articles on low budget and independently financed features.

Libraries are loaded with publications on foundations and agencies and how they are approached for money, including some books on writing grant proposals to finance films. You will certainly want to research foundations which have awarded grants to filmmakers in the past.

What the people in this category are looking for, besides emotionally involving screenplays, is a good or worthwhile investment. In addition to evaluating your screenplay, any potential investor will want to know the bottom line: how much an investment in your film will cost, how likely a return on the investment is, and when the profits will be paid. It is therefore important to have a financial prospectus for the project, including a basic budget breakdown of your screenplay, before approaching investors.

If you don't know how to do this, you can find people with production and investment experience to do it for you. In return, you will probably have to pay the person directly, offer her a flat fee or percentage of the investment contingent on obtaining financing, or attach the person to your project in some way.

As discussed in the earlier chapter on story concept, the lower your proposed budget and the greater the chance of immediate profit, the more attractive the project becomes to an investor.

This is one avenue where you're at an advantage if you live outside of southern California. Most investors in L.A. are already tapped out or are too shrewd to invest in motion pictures. But there are rich people everywhere, and the glamour of the movies and the possibility of huge profits can often lure potential investors in your own hometown. This is especially true if your screenplay is set in the investors' home state. Knowing their investment will be churned back into their local economy when the movie gets shot is an added incentive to many financiers.

Grant-funding agencies look for different qualities in prospective screenplays than do private investors, since generally speaking, profit cannot be accrued by tax-exempt foundations or U.S. government agencies. While a grant-funding agency will still need to know, "How much will it cost?" their other pertinent question will not be, "How much money can this make?" but rather, "What information or point of view is being presented by this film?"

These organizations' concerns will either be that the movie of your screenplay advance the state of the art of film (as with the National Endowment for the Arts), that it present information of a general educational or cultural nature (the National Endowment for the Humanities), or that it serve a particular area of need which the foundation supports. For example, if your screenplay concerns a rape crisis center, foundations awarding grants in support of women's issues will certainly be worth pursuing.

Grants as a source of financing are usually more appropriate if your screenplay is for a short film. But occassionally feature films or TV movies for PBS get foundation or government support for production. *Stand and Deliver, Testament,* and *El Norte* were all partially financed in this way.

Once you have your screenplay, budget breakdown, and prospectus ready to show, begin approaching financiers concurrently with the other three categories, using the same basic methods. Don't let the mystique of high finance deter you from this avenue. Getting even partial financing committed to your film can greatly increase the interest of the people in the other three categories.

To discuss independent financing in detail would take a book all by itself. The key is always the same: Through contacts and secondary research you need to learn about as many sources of funding as possible. Then, using the same methods outlined above for the other avenues, pursue possible financiers concurrently with the other three categories.

Remember, you never approach people one at a time. You can have your script out to a hundred people at once. The goal is to persevere, maximize your chances, reject the rejections, and keep writing.

Summary

1. There are three keys to marketing yourself as a screenwriter:

Try everything

Don't listen to statistics

Knowledge is power

2. There are two sources of information regarding who the people in power are, what they are looking for, and where they are (or how you can reach them):

Primary research (contacts)

Secondary research (the media)

3. Four categories of people in power can lead you to a deal:

Agent or attorney

Independent producers who develop projects

Elements (major stars or directors)

Financiers (studios, networks, investors, and grant-funding agencies)

4. You must approach all four categories of people simultaneously.

5. Before approaching anyone with your screenplay, be sure it is good enough to present by getting a positive response to it from at least two out of five people whose judgment you trust.

6. Research agents using contacts, the media, the Writers Guild of America list of agencies, other published lists of agents, and the Guild's agency department.

7. Agents look for three things in a potential client:

A writer who will make money

Someone with career potential

Someone who won't add to their problems

8. You will want three things in a potential agent:

Someone to guide your career

Someone with power in the film business

Someone who can negotiate

9. Approach agents with:

A recommendation or referral

A letter of approach

A cold phone call

Dropping in to the office

10. The object of approaching an agent is to get someone at the agency to read your screenplay.

11. If an agent is interested in you as a writer, meet with the agent, and at least ask the following two questions:

What did you think of my script?

Who else do you represent?

12. If you sign with an agent, he receives 10 percent of all your earnings as a screenwriter.

13. An attorney can be hired to represent you instead of an agent, usually for a fee rather than a percentage.

14. Use the same process for *concurrently* approaching producers, elements, and financiers.

15. Research producers through articles, interviews, published directories, film credits, and contacts. Then approach them through their heads of development.

16. Most elements have their own production companies, and are approached in the same way as other independent producers. Otherwise go through their representatives or obtain personal introductions.

17. Do not approach studios or networks at lower than the level of story editor.

18. Approach other financiers with your screenplay, a budget breakdown, and a prospectus or grant application.

19. Never let your business activities interfere with your writing.

. . . .

Chapter 9

The Screenwriter's Deal

Now the exciting part. What happens if you hit pay dirt? What if one of the producers or financiers discussed in the previous chapter has read your screenplay and now wants to make a deal with you?

There are three ways that a screenwriter can earn money for her work:

Outright sale of the screenplay

The development deal

The salaried or staff writer position

In this chapter, I will discuss all of those situations, the way each occurs, the components of each deal, and how much money is involved.

Sale of the Screenplay

Sale of the film rights to a complete screenplay is almost always based on an *option/purchase deal*. Rarely will the film rights to a screenplay be purchased by a producer outright; usually, those film rights will be optioned first.

An option in the film business is the same as an option in real estate or any other area of negotiation: It is the exclusive right to purchase property for a predetermined amount of money over a finite period of time.

Option money doesn't pay for the right to make the movie of your script; an option buys the right to *purchase* those film rights at a later date, exclusive of anybody else. What is actually being paid for is the exclusivity. This gives the person optioning your screenplay time to raise the money to produce the film, during which time no other person can offer more money and make a separate deal.

If you option your script to a producer today for $10,000, and tomorrow George Lucas offers you $50,000, you have to say, "Sorry, George, but the rights are now controlled by another producer."

The following example will illustrate how an option/purchase deal works. The figures used are arbitrary, because everything is negotiable. I just chose these amounts because they're nice round figures and are easy to divide.

Let's say a producer makes this offer: a $10,000 option against a purchase price of $100,000 for one year, renewable for a second year for an additional $10,000. This means that if you agree to the deal, you will be paid $10,000 by the producer to option the film rights to your completed screenplay. This deal gives the producer one year to pay you the remaining $90,000 toward the total purchase price. (That is why it is referred to as $10,000 *against* $100,000.) If, at any time during that year, the producer pays you the remaining $90,000, then he owns the film rights to your screenplay forever. If the producer fails to raise the other $90,000 during that year, you keep the $10,000, and you can then make a new deal with someone else.

The renewal clause means that if, before the first year expires, the producer does not pay you the remaining $90,000, but instead pays you an additional $10,000, then he has exclusive rights to your screenplay for an additional year. If, during that second year, he pays you the $90,000 (usually the second-year renewal fee is not deducted from the total purchase price), then he owns the rights to your screenplay forever. If the second year elapses and the producer hasn't purchased the script, then you keep the $20,000, and you can shop your screenplay elsewhere.

The producer has spent his $10,000 or $20,000 for the *exclusivity* of the deal. No other deals can be made during the original producer's option period.

In addition to the option amount and the purchase amount, all other elements of the deal are usually negotiated at the outset as well. The following are some of the elements to a deal which you might negotiate prior to signing an option/purchase agreement:

1. Exclusivity. This would guarantee that you would be the only screenwriter on the project; no other screenwriter could be brought in to rewrite your script. Only the top screenwriters in Hollywood get this clause in their contract. Unless you're up there with Neil Simon, you're likely to opt for the next clause as an alternative to exclusivity. . . .

2. Rewrites. The more rewrites of the screenplay you can be guaranteed before another writer can be hired, the more control and input you will have on your project. This clause will set the fee you would receive for any rewrites you do, as well as the number of paid rewrites you are guaranteed, should they be needed. The producer may negotiate for a certain number of rewrites (usually one rewrite and one "polish") to which he is entitled as part of his purchase price. In other words, the producer will want as many free rewrites as possible.

Obtaining a guaranteed number of rewrites, at a certain fee, doesn't necessarily mean you will do them. They may not be needed, or the producer or director may want to bring in a new writer even if you haven't written the number of rewrites you're entitled to do. But you still must be paid for that number of rewrites before another writer can be hired.

3. Bonuses. You might negotiate for a bonus if no other writer is *needed* to rewrite the script. Then some of the money the producer would have had to pay a second screenwriter goes to you for writing such a good script in the first place.

You may also get a bonus if and when the movie goes into

production, is completed, or is released. In other words, if your screenplay is good enough that the movie actually gets made, you get rewarded. This clause is more likely in a development deal (see below). In an option/purchase arrangement, the option is not usually exercised until the producer is certain that the movie is going into production.

4. Percentage of the Profits. Even on your first sale, it is reasonable to negotiate for 2 percent to 5 percent of the net (never gross) profits of the film. Of course, how net profits are actually defined is what keeps all those lawyers getting all those fat fees. And big distributors seem to have a way of never going into profit with their films, but somehow staying in business. But it's always good to negotiate for net profit participation, just in case your film turns into such a blockbuster that there's no way to hide the profits.

Net profit participation can be especially important for an independent, low budget feature. Often your fee for writing such a film will be far less than for a studio deal, so the profit share is the only way you can hope to make a comparable amount of money. And just imagine having even a tiny piece of *Friday the 13th*.

5. Sequels, Spin-offs, and Remakes. You might want to negotiate for the opportunity to write the screenplays for any sequels, television series, cartoons, and so on which are spun off from the movie of your original script. This would be a "first right of refusal": you don't *have* to write the sequel, but you must be given the opportunity to do so, at a fair fee, before any other writer can be hired.

You will certainly want a piece of the action on any of these sequels and spin-offs and any future remakes of your screenplay, for the same reason you want a percentage of the net profits of the original film.

6. Ancillary Rights. Ancillary rights enable you to participate financially in income generated by your movie in other arenas: record albums, toys, posters, neckties, key-chains, and cocktail napkins. In other words, you want to share in as much of the income that originated from your screenplay as possible. Just remember, every time somebody buys a *Star Trek* lunch box, Gene Rodenberry puts another penny in his pocket.

There may be additional elements to your option/purchase deal which you will want to negotiate. The clearer the deal at the outset, the less the danger of misunderstandings, confusions, and broken promises later on.

Sometimes only the major aspects of a deal will be negotiated in the original contract, and the rest will be left until later, so that everybody doesn't have to pay a lot of big legal fees right off the bat. Then the phrase, "to be negotiated in good faith at a later date" is added to the contract. The "in good faith" means that when it's time to work out the rest of the deal, no one can stonewall the negotiations and the fees must be consistent with standard movie industry amounts at that time.

Throughout this list, I've been saying "you" negotiate this or that. By "you" I actually mean your agent or attorney. *Never negotiate for yourself!* If a producer or financier offers you a deal, and you have no agent or attorney, get back in touch with all those agents who wouldn't read your screenplay before. An offer on the table can make you a much more attractive possibility. If they're still not interested or if you still can't find an agent you like, then hire an attorney to negotiate this deal for you.

If an offer is on the table, you can't find an agent, and you can't afford an attorney, at least get as much information as possible before you agree to anything. And somehow scrape up enough money to at least have a lawyer check over the contract before you sign. Writing, not negotiating, is your talent.

Negotiating for yourself can also strain your relationship with the producer. After locking horns over fees and profits, friendly, creative story conferences are harder to achieve. It's better to let your agent take all the heat and be nasty on your behalf.

The amount of money involved in any option/purchase deal varies greatly. Ultimately it will be whatever the traffic will bear.

If you are a member of the Writers Guild of America or if the financier you're dealing with is a signatory to the Guild agreement, then your deal must at least meet the minimums set by the Guild. Most feature film deals with studios will exceed the Guild minimums. And if more than one studio is bidding for your screenplay, your price can climb to more than a million dollars.

If neither you nor the financier is connected to the Writers Guild, then the monetary amounts are completely negotiable. The law of supply and demand is the rule. The hungrier the financier is for your screenplay, the more you will be able to get.

To give a very general sense of the kind of money involved, a studio feature deal, even for a first-time writer, will usually carry a purchase price of at least $100,000 to $150,000. It isn't always that much, but a hundred grand has a nice ring to it, doesn't it?

In television, the fees will run much closer to the minimums set by the Writers Guild. The average purchase price for a two-hour TV movie will currently run around $60,000. Series fees for new writers will usually be only slightly above Guild minimum. A booklet of current Writers Guild minimums for feature films and television is available from the Guild (see bibliography).

The sum for a one-year option is often calculated at 10 percent of the purchase price. But that, too, is totally negotiable. The current standard for option/purchase deals with a studio for a completed feature screenplay is about $10,000 to $20,000 against a $150,000 purchase price. But again, it's whatever the traffic will bear.

If could well be that you will accept a $10 option on your screenplay. In other words, a *free option*. This might sound like a bum deal at first, but if the producer offering you ten bucks is also offering a higher purchase price on the back end, if she's the only one knocking on your door, and if you really think she has a good shot at getting your movie made, then you might want to accept the offer.

The time period for the option is also completely negotiable and can range from six weeks to three years. If the producer wanting a free option requests a year, you might negotiate for only a six-month option, so your screenplay won't be tied up for such a long period of time without any remuneration. The renewal clause can then include a significant payment, so the producer will have to come up with some good faith money within six months, to prove her sincerity and abilities.

You might also reject the free option offer, but give the producer *permission to shop* your script wherever he is strongest. If you turn down the free option and the producer responds, "But I'm a close personal friend of Robert Redford, and this is just what he's looking for!" then you might tell the producer to take it *only* to Robert Redford. If the producer can make a deal with the star, then the producer is locked into the project. But he can't take it to any other element or financier without again getting your OK.

The Development Deal

Now that you understand how the option/purchase deal works, I should mention that it almost never happens. Most of what you see on the big screen and almost everything on television is *developed*.

Before I got involved in the film business, I used to assume that movies and TV shows got made in the following way: a writer would slave away on his typewriter until he had created a complete screenplay for a movie, which would then be purchased by a studio. The studio would hire actors, director, and the like and the screenplay would be turned into what we saw on the screen.

This process is obviously too simple, straightforward, and logical for Hollywood. Thus was born The Development Deal.

Developing a screenplay simply means paying a screenwriter upfront to put a film story on paper. The screenwriter is a hired gun, and the script belongs entirely to the producer, studio, or network who's paying for it. The principle is much the same as for an inventor who creates something as an employee of General Electric. He may get salary, royalties, and a bonus, but GE owns the invention.

The path to a development deal might go something like this:

You've been pursuing the four categories of people in power in the manner outlined in Chapter 8. Then one day a producer calls you and says, "I read your screenplay, and I loved it. But I don't want to make that movie, because it's too expensive/familiar/out of my arena/hard to sell/hard to cast/arty/soft/all of the above. But I would love to work on something else with you. Have you got any other ideas?

In other words, now that the producer (or story editor or executive or investor) has seen your talent, he is willing to consider putting another project in the works for you to write. This is why having a completed screenplay is imperative. No one is going to risk paying you to develop a screenplay until you have proven your ability as a screenwriter.

Once you have proven yourself to a producer, you can present him with other stories for possible development. Then, and only then, is when treatments and pitches come into the picture.

Treatments

A *treatment* is a prose version of a film story, usually 5 to 30 pages long. Shorter treatments are sometimes called outlines. As with a complete screenplay, your primary goal is to elicit emotion in the reader.

A treatment looks like a short story because it's written in paragraph form, uses quotation marks for dialogue, and omits the format devices of a screenplay. However, a treatment is always written in present tense and abides by the principle that nothing goes on the page that doesn't go on the screen. Thus a treatment can have no interior thoughts of the characters, author's asides, or editorial prose. Treatments consist entirely of action, description, and dialogue.

A treatment follows all the basic principles of concept, character, and structure: a hero with whom we identify, motivation and conflict, other primary characters, three distinct acts based on the hero's outer motivation (although the acts are never labeled), and the use of as many of the structural principles and devices as possible.

With a treatment, you outline only the broad strokes of the story; minor scenes, secondary characters, and most dialogue can be omitted. Comedy treatments will require enough dialogue to convey any verbal humor and to illustrate your ability to write hilarious lines in the eventual screenplay.

The shorter your treatment is the better; five to ten pages is ideal. A 30 page treatment is so detailed and takes so long to read that it might as well be written in screenplay form. The best treatments grab the reader immediately, clearly outline an emotionally involving story, and leave the reader wanting more.

A sample treatment is included in Appendix B.

Pitches

A *pitch* is a verbal presentation of your proposed film story. It is, as the name implies, a sales pitch. You meet with the producer, element, executive, or financier who is familiar with your writing and tell your story idea to that person in power. The object is to captivate the listeners, keep them emotionally involved, and persuade them that your potential screenplay is worth financing.

Pitching a story should take about fifteen to thirty minutes, and again, shorter is usually better. You are simply telling your story idea in such a way that the artistic and commercial (especially commercial) potential of the movie is clear.

A pitch will usually begin with a detailed opening to grab your audience, followed by the highlights of the story. Again, the principles of concept, character, and structure are identical to those for a complete screenplay.

In pitching a story, pull anything you can out of your bag of tricks to get the listener excited. Be sure that you have rehearsed the pitch thoroughly before presenting it to an executive. Notecards taken to the meeting are OK if they enhance your ability to tell the story. Some writers perform scenes from the script, do stand-up routines for their comedies, and yell, scream, and jump up and down if necessary to get the listeners' juices flowing. You must do whatever works best for you.

Opportunities to pitch your story will be less frequent at the beginning of your career, particularly if you live outside of Hollywood and aren't available for lots of meetings. If your talent is much stronger on paper than in person, treatments and completed scripts will probably serve you better. But if you can weave magic as a teller of tales and are willing to do whatever is necessary to convey the emotional potential of your story, then pitching can be your best avenue to a development deal.

So, what if a producer asks to see your ideas but you've been working on your next screenplay and have no treatments? What do you do?

You go to the little notebook you bought way back in the chapter on story concept and look over all of the ideas you have been recording on a daily basis since you began this whole process. You brainstorm, combine ideas, and select the one or two or three concepts that you believe would appeal most to the potential producer.

You then put the best of these ideas in treatment or pitch form, depending on the producer's desires. And you present it, or them, to the producer in the hope of securing a development deal to write the screenplay.

Do not write treatments until they are requested. Until you have proven yourself to an executive who is *asking* to see your ideas, treatments will be of no value. And after presenting your treatment or pitch to a person in power, go back to writing complete screenplays until another executive asks to see your material or until you are offered a development deal.

I am referring here only to treatments written for submission. If you find it helpful to outline your own story ideas before converting them to complete screenplays, of course you should do so. It can also be wise to get a critique of your story idea in treatment form before you tackle the complete screenplay. But don't stop when the treatment is done in the hope that it alone will attract a producer. *The way to become a screenwriter is to write screenplays.*

Some established screenwriters never write treatments because they want that first draft to be theirs alone. Treatments give others a hand in your creation before you've had the opportunity to do it your own way. Dealing only in completed screenplays at least allows you to realize your own vision on paper before everybody else starts to change it.

Development deals do not always grow out of your own concepts. If a producer is really enamored of your work or if you are an established screenwriter, you may be given the opportunity to write (or rewrite) a concept or novel or true story or screenplay which the producer already owns. Then you simply decide whether you wish to pursue the project, and negotiate the deal.

Elements of the Deal

The money you are paid for a development deal is your fee for writing the screenplay, not a purchase price. Otherwise, a development deal includes the same basic elements that an option/purchase agreement contains: a percentage of the net profits; a cutoff point, prior to which no other writer can be hired; sequel, spin-off, and remake participation; ancillary rights; and so on.

You will usually be paid far less for a development deal than for the sale of a completed screenplay, particularly in the feature film arena. With an option/purchase arrangement, the producer is getting a known quantity and is only gambling on the outcome of the finished film. With a development deal, there is the added risk that when you complete the script, the producer still won't be able to acquire financing to produce the film. But you must be paid your fee for writing the screenplay no matter how good or bad it turns out to be.

While the purchase price for your complete screenplay might be $150,000, a development deal resulting in the same script might only be $60,000. But then, if the movie gets made, you would probably receive a bonus of an additional $100,000, taking the total up to the equivalent of an outright purchase. If the movie doesn't ever go into production, you still get to keep the sixty grand.

For network TV movies, development deals currently pay about $35,000 to $40,000, with a bonus of $10,000 to $20,000 if the movie gets produced.

A development deal can include an option on the story itself, which works the same way as an option on a complete screenplay. The producer options your story for X amount of dollars over Y period of time. During that period, you can't set up a deal for your story anywhere else; again, the producer is paying for exclusivity. During that period, the producer will try to raise the money to pay you to write the screenplay. If he does, you get paid to write the script; if he doesn't, you keep the option money, and you can option your story elsewhere.

Development deals will often be "step deals." Your story is optioned, then you are paid to write a treatment based on the producer's input, then you are paid more to write a screenplay, then the producer is entitled to a negotiable number of rewrites, and then you are paid more for additional rewrites.

The point in this process where you can be cut off is negotiable. In other words, the producer may have the right, if that's the deal you've agreed to, to pay just for your treatment and then hire another writer to write the screenplay. You obviously hope to get a cutoff point that is late in the process; the more established you are and the more somebody wants your idea, the better your chances of getting it.

Usually your payment schedule in a development deal will be ⅓ to begin the screenplay, ⅓ upon completion of the first draft, and ⅓ upon completion of the rewrite. When your obligations are completed and the financier has paid you the full amount, the financier owns the film rights to the screenplay forever.

There is an escape clause to this issue of "forever." If, within a certain period of time, the producer has failed to go into production on the screenplay you wrote, it enters what is known as *turnaround*. In turnaround, you have the right to pursue a deal for the screenplay with other producers and financiers. If you locate another producer who wants to acquire the rights to the screenplay, the producer who intially purchased or developed it must sell them. However, the initial producer is entitled to all of the development money spent on the project. This includes not only your fee but legal fees, office expenses, salaries, and anything else that can be legitimately attributed to the development of your script.

Sometimes this figure is negotiated down. The initial producer is often pleased to recoup even some of the costs of a project that is dead in the water. But he is only *required* to turn over the rights if the total verified expenses are met.

The great news about development deals is that they create a lot more work than is evident. The networks develop at least three TV movies for every one that gets on the air. And the ratio for studio feature films is anywhere from 4:1 to 20:1. This means that if 250 features and TV movies were produced last year, at least 1000 screenplays were paid for in those two arenas alone. And that doesn't include independent features, episodic series, and the stuff on cable, syndication, and PBS. So the picture isn't quite as bleak as you thought it was.

The down side of development deals is that a lot of writers don't get to see many of their scripts on the screen. A 1986 *Newsweek* article told of several established writers making a quarter of a million dollars a year or more who had *never* had a script produced.

This can become very frustrating after a while. The only solution is to cry all the way to the bank. You can buy a lot of therapy for $250,000.

There is an even greater risk to the business side of all this. It's very easy to become so wrapped up in the money and the meetings and the deals and the payments on the car phone that the joy of creation gets pushed into the corner.

There are lots of working screenwriters who get paid handsomely but are unhappily stuck in television because the money is so good, even though their dream was always to write features. Or they go from meeting to meeting and development deal to development deal, always complaining about the heartless idiot network executives who ruin their stories. But these writers haven't written a screenplay for *themselves* in years. They no longer touch the spark of their own creativity because they always serve someone else's vision.

More to the point, especially if you are just beginning your career, is the great temptation to bury yourself in concerns about The Deal. I meet lots of new writers whose only worry is, "How can I get an agent?"

Certainly pursuing the people in power is important, but it is meaningless if you don't know how to deliver the goods. The reason that most of this book is about *writing* your screenplay is that a well-written script is the key to getting paid for your talent. You can make contacts till the cows come home, but if you can't prove your ability as a writer, all the connections in the world won't do you a bit of good. And they certainly won't bring you creative satisfaction.

Trust that talent always comes to the surface. Never let this process of selling your screenplay interfere with your writing. When your first screenplay is completed and ready to submit, immediately begin work on your next script. Find other time during the day to research and pursue contacts, agents, producers, elements, and financiers.

The Staff Writer

The third method of making money as a screenwriter is as a staff writer for a television series. These jobs carry several different titles and levels of responsibility, which I will outline below, but I'll refer to them all generically as "staff writer." These are the only salaried positions available to a screenwriter of prime-time television or feature films.

In times past, studios had screenwriters on staff to churn out scripts, but those days have pretty much gone the way of the double feature and the contract player. Established screenwriters may sign exclusive or "first-refusal" deals with production companies, but those are simply variations on the option/purchase deal or the development deal. The mainstream screenwriter drawing a weekly paycheck will almost always be a series staff writer.

The staff writing positions are achieved after proving your talents by writing free-lance series episodes. When you have shown the producers of a particular series that you can deliver the goods, then you might be hired as a staff writer.

A staff writer reports to work everyday, just like in a real job, to brainstorm with the other writers on the show, contribute ideas, write or rewrite scripts for individual episodes, and rewrite them again when the directors and stars of the series have given their input. It's a dirty job, but somebody's got to do it.

There are several levels of staff writing positions on television series. A *staff writer* contributes ideas for the overall series and probably writes at least two full episodes per season. A *story editor* does the same but also rewrites other scripts commissioned for the series.

The *creator* of a series will usually have some ongoing function with the series, either as story editor or coproducer, depending on the creator's level of involvement in the week-to-week episodes.

The *producer* or *coproducer*, who oversees or contributes to all facets of a series, has reached the highest level of salaried writing positions.

With any of these staff writer positions, the money can really get dazzling.

As a staff writer on a prime-time series, your basic salary will usually be around $2,000 per week, with a guarantee of twenty weeks. Salaries are usually somewhat higher at all levels for comedy writers than one-hour dramatic writers. Your fee for the episodes you write would be calculated against that salary, but you would receive additional royalties and residuals for the episodes that are rerun or put into syndication.

A story editor will receive a higher salary, about $3,500 per week for a guaranteed twenty weeks, and the fees for individual episodes are *in addition to* that salary.

Creators (or cocreators) of series get the same kinds of salaries and fees for their ongoing positions with the series, but in addition receive royalties and residuals for every single episode aired.

A producer on an episodic series receives more money from each of these sources (salary, script fees, royalties). The total annual income for a producer on an ongoing series can range from $300,000 to $1 million a year.

These numbers I'm tossing out here are rough averages of what salaried television writers can earn. The salaries, individual script fees, number of guaranteed weeks, and royalties must conform to Writers Guild of America minimums. But beyond that, this is all negotiable.

Let me give you a specific example of how this career path can unfold:

Once upon a time, about the same time I came to Hollywood to break into the movies, a writer arrived from back east, where he had done reviews for a small film magazine. Under his arm were five completed screenplays he had written in his spare time. He began beating the pavement, suffering many rejections from agents, until he met an agent who was impressed that the writer was committed enough to complete five screenplays. So she agreed to represent him.

He told his new agent that he eventually wanted to direct features but that, in the meantime, he would be willing to write anything she advised, television included. She had him do a spec script for an episode of one of the cop shows on the air at that time, and she submitted it to all of the active series in production.

One of the story editors for one of those series liked the script, so our screenwriter was asked to go in and pitch a half-dozen possible episode ideas for that story editor's series. The story editor liked one, the screenwriter was given a development deal. Another development deal followed, the second script was used as an episode, and the writer started getting noticed by the television industry.

This eventually led to staff writer position on *Charlie's Angels* during its final season. The writer then was hired as a story editor for another series the following year, followed two years later by a producer credit on a third series. Unlike the feature film arena, producers on television series are almost always screenwriters who have been promoted up from story editor positions.

Last season the screenwriter wrote the pilot for a new series, for which he is now cocreator and coexecutive producer. His income last year was just over $450,000.

Now before you throw away your feature script and start studying episodes of *Doogie Howser, M.D.*, understand that not all episodic writers reach the level of financial success that our friend above has. But there are about seventy-five prime time series on the four networks at any given time. And each has at least three staff writers, a story editor, and a producer. Are they all happy? Probably not. But they're all making a lot of money.

Once again, the question to ask yourself repeatedly is this: "Is writing screenplays bringing me joy?" If the answer is no, then forget the issue of money and find a more fulfilling pursuit. If the answer if yes, then go for it.

Summary

1. There are three ways for a screenwriter to earn money:

   Sale of the screenplay

   A development deal

   A salaried staff writer position

2. Sale of the screenplay is based on an option/purchase deal. An *option* is the exclusive right to purchase property for a predetermined amount of money over a finite period of time.

3. The negotiable elements of an option/purchase deal include:

Option price

Purchase price

Option period

Renewal clause

Exclusivity

Guaranteed rewrites

Bonuses

Percentage of net profits

Participation in sequels, spin-offs, and remakes

Ancillary rights

Turnaround clause

4. In a development deal, the screenwriter is hired by a producer or financier to write a screenplay based on the writer's own idea, or on a story concept controlled by the producer.

5. A *treatment* is a five to thirty page prose version of a proposed film story which adheres to the basic principles of effective screenwriting.

6. A *pitch* is a verbal presentation of a film story.

7. A *step deal* is a development deal outlining each stage in the process—treatment, screenplay, rewrites—plus the fee paid at each stage and the amount you are guaranteed before the project can be discontinued or another writer hired.

8. Staff writers, story editors, and producers for episodic television series can receive both guaranteed salaries and negotiated fees for the episodes they write, plus royalties for rebroadcasts.

PART IV

THE COMMITMENT
TO SCREENWRITING

CHAPTER 10

■ ■

The Life of a Screenwriter

Did you hear about the woman who was so dumb she tried to break into the film business by sleeping with a screenwriter?

—*Homer*

If you purchased this book to help you decide whether or not to pursue screenwriting, I would add these comments to everything else I've said. To me, there are two big advantages to being a screenwriter:

1. You Get to Work in the Movies. I love the movies, and I think the opportunity to reach people by becoming a storyteller, a creator, and a writer in the most powerful medium in the world is wonderful. Regardless of the frustrations and the discouragement and the money and the hype and the greed and the rumors and the personalities and the rejection and all the other pros and cons and success stories and horror stories, when you feel the lights go down in the theater and the rush before a new movie begins and you know that you're a part of that, that is an unequaled high.

2. Word for Word, and Dollar for Dollar, You Can Make More Money in Screenwriting Than in Any Other Form of Writing. This doesn't mean that Stephen King and Charles Schulz didn't make more than most screenwriters last year. It means that on the average, the steadily working screenwriter is getting paid quite a bundle. A staff writer on an episodic series, for example, can earn $200,000 per year or more. Such amounts of money for the working screenwriter are comfortable, to say the least.

This is not to say, of course, that everyone entering screenwriting or that every screenwriter working intermittently realizes these kinds of financial rewards. A starving screenwriter is just as unhappy as a starving poet. But once you're established and are getting paid regularly for your work, the financial rewards of screenwriting can be immense.

There are also, in my opinion, three big disadvantages to screenwriting, compared with other forms of writing:

1. You Don't Have the Opportunity to Weave Magic with Words. If the reason you wish to pursue a writing career is to revel in the beauty, glory, and depth of the English language, then screenwriting is probably not for you. If you want to make full use of everything that Noah Webster has to offer, then poetry or short stories or novels would probably be better objectives.

A screenwriter is a storyteller, and screenplays consist only of action, description, and dialogue, written at a high school reading level. Your goal is to outline the way that a story can be told and transferred to the big or small screen, not to dazzle the reader with the power of your prose.

2. A Screenwriter Is a Surrogate Mother. And you know what happens to surrogate mothers. After what is probably about a nine month gestation period, you give birth to a creation that represents your love, your passion, your sweat, your devotion, and your pain. Then you must hand over this piece of your soul to someone else, who will stomp on it with logging boots.

Occasionally your writing is treated with great respect, but you must be emotionally prepared to see your creation changed and destroyed. Your only consolations are your Mercedes, your swimming pool, and your therapist. And the fact that once you are sufficiently established, you can negotiate for greater control over your material, through directing, producing, or securing a sole screenwriter position on your later projects.

3. Screenwriters Do Not Rank Particularly High in the Hollywood Hierarchy. Even though logic and evidence would support the maxim that, "If it ain't on the page, it ain't on the stage," the screenwriter is usually given short shrift with regard to status and power. You're not necessarily low man on the totem pole, but you are rarely top dog either.

If, given all these pluses and minuses, you choose to commit to pursuing screenwriting as a career, there are several things you must do:

1. Establish a Writing Regimen. Very early in this book, I said that longtime screenwriter Art Arthur had declared two secrets to being a good screenwriter. The first was, *Don't get it right, get it written.* At last you get to learn his other secret to success: *The seat of the pants to the seat of the chair.*

Lots of us would like to *have written* a screenplay. But if you want to be a screenwriter, you have to write. Every day. No distractions. No excuses. Because it's the *regularity* of your writing regimen that will sharpen your craft and enable you to complete a salable screenplay.

If you don't already have such a writing regimen, start with a half hour a day. Don't try to bite off a three-hour-per-day writing commitment. It will end up just like exercise commitments: you'll stick to it devotedly for three days, get burned out, and give up. Instead, start slowly, so you can feel you've kept your commitment each day. Then, when a half hour is comfortable, stretch it to an hour, and keep increasing your regimen only when you're comfortable with the plateau you're on.

You'll be amazed at the amount of work you can generate in only a half hour a day, as long as, during that time, you do *nothing* but sit at the computer (or typewriter or legal pad) and work on your script.

2. Immerse Yourself in the Movies. Once you have established a writing regimen and are committed to writing each day, the next *absolutely necessary* step to becoming an effective screenwriter is to learn what's going on in the industry you are pursuing. *You must see every major release coming out of Hollywood.* In other words, you've got to start going to the movies.

I am always surprised by the large number of writers who attend my screenwriting seminar and then admit to only having seen one or two movies in the previous year. I just don't think it's possible to achieve a career in the film business without knowing what is currently being produced by the people you want to employ you.

If you aren't seeing at least fifty movies a year (that's only one a week) and your excuse is that you don't have the time, then you're just being lazy. Or else you're really not committed to being a screenwriter.

If you aren't going to the movies because you don't *like* what Hollywood's producing these days (a comment I hear frequently), then why do you want to be a screenwriter? Is it really wise to pursue a career in the film industry if you think that the stuff that Hollywood produces is crap? If that's your belief, then your screenplay is likely to be so strikingly different from current mainstream films that it will be impossible to sell. Or if you're determined, in spite of your attitude about the buyers, to write a script those tasteless morons will buy, then you'll probably end up thinking your own script is crap too. And how personally satisfying will that be?

You wouldn't want to be represented by a lawyer who hadn't been to law school or who didn't keep abreast of recent legal decisions and statutes. Well, the film industry isn't looking for screenwriters who don't know what's being produced or who don't know which of those recent releases have been successful.

The minimum of fifty movies a year means fifty current, major American releases. These should be supplemented by foreign films and older films, but your first priority must be to the market you're going to pursue.

And start seeing the good stuff more than once. Movie theaters are still the best way to experience the art of film, but the invention of the VCR has made it much easier to see all you need to see.

The same principle holds true if you want to write for television, except that you have to see not only the current feature films being released but also all the stuff on TV. You should probably see at least one episode of everything the networks show, all of the successful series in the arena you're pursuing (sitcoms or one-hour dramas), and as many TV movies as you can.

Just how tough is this recommendation anyway? All I'm telling you to do is what your parents used to tell you *not* to do when you were supposed to be doing your homework. Now seeing movies *is* your homework.

3. Be Informed about the Movies. In addition to seeing a lot of movies, you must also be aware of what's going on within the film industry. In other words, you've got to start reading about the movie business.

You must know which movies are doing well at the box office; which stars, producers, and directors are hot; what they're looking for; who the new and/or powerful literary agents are; what movies are scheduled for release in the future; and which categories of film are currently in or out of favor with the powers that be.

And you must know the same things for television.

All of this information will improve the chances of your screenplay getting produced. Remember, *knowledge is power.*

You can acquire this knowledge by reading *Writers Digest, American Film, Film Comment,* the trade papers *(Variety* and the *Hollywood Reporter)* and the entertainment pages of your local newspapers, and by watching *Entertainment Tonight* and television interviews with Hollywood personalities.

The three publications I recommend most highly are the *Hollywood Scriptwriter,* which is directed at newer writers in particular, *Premiere* magazine, which is loaded with information on scheduled releases and people in power, and *TV Guide.* Even if you're not pursuing television writing, it is crucial that you know what's going on in that arena. You wouldn't want to spend a year writing a screenplay exploring the never-before-seen issue of child pornography only to learn when you submit it that it had been done as a TV movie years ago.

You might also consider subscribing to the *Los Angeles Times.* The daily and Sunday Calendar sections contain lots of information on the business of film and television.

4. Start Making Contacts. Go to parties. Attend film seminars. Volunteer to work on someone's film. Volunteer to assist at a film festival. Hang out in theater lobbies.

And everywhere you go, tell people you're a screenwriter.

5. Join a Writers' Group. Writers' groups can be excellent sources of contacts and information, feedback on your work, and moral support. It can be a cold, lonely world out there for writers, and meeting others on the same rugged path can help immensely.

6. Pursue Other Markets for Your Work. This book is about mainstream movies and TV, because that's what I know about. But 90 percent of the film shot in this country is used outside of those arenas. If you can sharpen your talent and pay your bills writing industrial films, educational films, promotional films, training films, religious films, animated films, adult films, commercials, or audiovisual presentations, then do it. The goal of each is to create emotion in an audience, and these other markets can only sharpen your craft.

7. Consider Moving to Southern California. If you live more than fifty miles from the Universal Studios Tour, here's my best advice about moving to L.A.: *Don't do it now.*

If you're a working screenwriter, there is a decided advantage to living in Los Angeles. You are always available for meetings, you're more attractive to potential agents, and you have more direct access to what's going on in the film business.

But right now, your main concern must be to take the principles of this book and use them to perfect your craft and to pursue the people in power. And you will do a better job of writing if you remain where you already have financial and emotional support. Rather than picking up stakes and moving to some empty apartment in Tarzana, stay put.

The time to consider migrating to L.A. is when someone is offering you the likely possiblity of income if you do. If an agent convinces you that he can get you work if you move to southern California or if someone offers you hard cash to do so, then you have a decision to make. But until then, continue writing and pursuing the people in power from wherever you now live. (Unless you want to learn how to surf, too. In that case, come on out.)

You may decide that even with the promise of money, you choose to stay where you are. There are working screenwriters living all over the world. It isn't as easy, but if you're determined to succeed as a screenwriter without leaving your roots, then it can be done. And as films become more and more regional, with independent financing, location shooting, and local production facilities, moving to Hollywood becomes less important.

And finally . . .

8. Evaluate Your Goals. Every six months or so, ask yourself if being a screenwriter is bringing you joy and fulfillment. Is the writing itself satisfying and fulfilling? If the answer is yes, then keep at it.

Summary

1. There are two big advantages to screenwriting:

You get to tell stories for the movies.

You can make a lot of money.

2. There are three major disadvantages to screenwriting:

You don't get to weave magic with words.

You have no control over what is done to your screenplay after it's sold.

Screenwriters don't rank very high in the film industry.

3. If you choose to pursue screenwriting, you should:

Establish a regimen.

Immerse yourself in movies.

Acquire information on the film business.

Start making contacts.

Join a writers' group.

Pursue other markets for your work.

Consider moving to Los Angeles (but not yet).

Periodically evaluate your goals.

CHAPTER 11

■ ■

The Power of Screenwriting

From almost the first page of this book, I have been talking about the need to create emotion in a reader and an audience. For you as a screenwriter and for all filmmakers, that is the primary goal.

There are two direct paths to eliciting that emotional response in an audience. One is through the head. The other is through the glands.

The first path gets people thinking, gets their wheels turning.

The second path gets their blood racing, gets their juices flowing.

Both paths are fine. There is nothing inherently good or bad about either method. But each, if used exclusively, becomes esoteric. That is, each, when used alone, limits your potential audience.

If you go strictly with the glandular approach—trying just to get people frightened or turned on—you end up with splatter movies and pornography. And there is a limited audience for those.

If you attempt only to get people thinking, the result is at best a provocative intellectual exercise that is seen by six people in a college basement. Because there is a limited audience for those films as well.

The tragedy of the first situation is the abundance of films devoid of any apparent thought or any contribution to the human condition. The even greater tragedy of the second situation is that filmmakers with important ideas to offer humanity are unable to find an audience or even to get their movies made.

The solution to these situations is combining the two approaches. If you can see the effectiveness of getting people excited, frightened, laughing, and crying and then can use that ability to really get them thinking, then you have tapped into the immense power you can wield as an artist, a screenwriter, and a filmmaker.

That is what I call reaching people through the *heart*.

That is also what I wish for all of you reading this book.

Now be joyful, get in touch with your own power, and start writing.

APPENDIXES

APPENDIX A

....

Frequently Asked Questions

I have now taught more than 7000 writers throughout the United States, Canada, and England, and these are the questions that consistently arise. I hope the answers will help clarify the principles discussed throughout the book and will provide added assistance with individual situations you may encounter.

Where are the restrooms?

I don't know, I've never been here before, either.

You've laid out all of these rules for writing screenplays, but aren't the rules broken in **Gandhi? Ordinary People? Terms of Endearment? Roxanne? Blow-Up? El Topo? Citizen Kane? Lunch Hour at the Lumiere Factory?**

Yes, they are.

The point is this: your objective is (I assume) to break into writing mainstream movies and television in the United States, Canada, or England. That's why you picked up this book.

You can probably find exceptions to almost every principle in this book. But how does spotting the exceptions help you in your own career pursuit?

If you examine the films which break the rules, you will find that almost without exception (1) they were written by screenwriters or writer-directors who were well enough established to get an out-of-the-ordinary project off the ground; (2) even with that established background, it took the filmmakers years to get the movie made; and (3) even with the one or two rules that are broken,

279

the majority of principles contained in this book are met by the film.

Those screenwriters who *effectively* break the mold with their screenplays are the ones who already know, consciously or instinctively, what the basic rules of good screenwriting are and have chosen to break a particular rule to heighten the emotion. If that is honestly your situation, you can do that in your own script.

What I hope to prevent with this book is your breaking the rules because you don't know them, or because you're so caught up in the exceptions to the rules that you've gotten confused, or because you've chosen to ignore them so you won't be confined to a formula.

Screenwriting is formula writing. Screenplays probably have more restrictions to length, style, subject matter, vocabulary, and commerciality than any form of writing this side of haiku poetry. If you just can't stomach these parameters, then pursue some other form of writing.

If you are trying to launch a career, it will be much more helpful to find examples that *conform* to these rules and formulas for screenwriting, in order to increase your understanding of the principles and strengthen your own ability to employ them. That is what will get you work. Then, when you are established, you can start breaking the rules effectively, and the financiers will trust your judgment because of your track record.

Why do you say X, but this other author (or teacher) says Y?

Because we've each come up with a different method for creating emotion in a reader and an audience. The underlying principles of the teachers and books I respect don't differ that greatly. Bob McKee's structural approach and Syd Field's plot points and my emphasis on outer motivation aren't really contradictory; each is a possible method of laying out the story to create an effective, salable screenplay.

While the details may differ, any book or teacher might have something to offer that will stimulate and empower your own creativity. You ultimately have to draw from all the approaches you encounter and develop the method of writing that is true for you.

There is a danger in reading lots of books and taking lots of classes, however. Lots of people out there have become professional screenwriting students rather than professional screenwriters. At some point, you've got to trust that you've got enough information and just *do it*.

I recommend that when you finish this book, you write a screenplay. Then read someone else's book or take someone else's seminar and then write another screenplay. This will ensure that you haven't gotten class-happy and that the new information you glean from each successive book or teacher will mean that much more because of your added experience.

I've had students who took my class a second time after having written a screenplay who heard a whole new set of ideas and methods the second time around, because they'd had the added experience of actually writing a script.

The exception would be hands-on writing classes, where you are working on a screenplay as a part of the class. If you need the opportunity to get your work-in-progress evaluated and to get the feedback and moral support that an ongoing class or writers' group can provide, then sign up for one. Just be sure that education doesn't become a substitute for experience.

What about J.R. in Dallas? How can you call him a hero?

Television series have an advantage over feature length films in the series' ability to create heroes with lots of flaws. Over long periods of time, we can get to know all of the characters in a series, and our emotional involvement with even the villains is strengthened. J.R. Ewing, Archie Bunker, Louie dePalma, and George Jefferson can become characters we love to hate because we know them so well and have learned to see their more sympathetic, human side.

It is interesting to see the pilot episode for *Dallas,* because the hero of the series in that first episode is clearly Pam Ewing. She is the sympathetic new arrival at South Fork who is thrown in among all these greedy, conniving rich folks. It is only after successive episodes that we become equally involved with the rest of the characters in the series.

I think in very visual terms, and that is why I would like to write

movies. Shouldn't I include camera directions in the screenplay to convey exactly how I see it?

No.

How many of your students have gone on to sell scripts?

Lots.

For further discussion, reread the item in Chapter 8 entitled "Don't Listen to Statistics."

Why can't I write a pilot for a new series or the screenplay for a miniseries?

You can, but if you're a new writer trying to break in, your chances of getting work from it are so slim that I strongly recommend against it. The writers who are hired to write pilots and miniseries are those who have already established themselves strongly in television. Pilots are commissioned to those who have experience as staff writers on current series, and miniseries are written by the top TV movie writers or occasionally by well-known novelists, playwrights, or feature writers.

If I already finished my screenplay and the format isn't the way you said it should be, am I ruined?

Of course not. No one will reject your script just because your format varies slightly from the current standard.

But if you finished your screenplay before you began this book, I find it hard to believe you haven't learned some principles that will improve the *content* of your screenplay as well. If you're not willing to do a rewrite now to incorporate those new ideas and meet those new standards, then you're probably being lazy. So since you're going to be doing that rewrite anyway, why not fix the format as well?

Doesn't mailing a copy of my screenplay to myself protect my material?

If it makes you feel better, go ahead, but make sure you register it for a copyright and with the Writers Guild as well.

How do I join the Writers Guild?

To qualify for membership in the Writers Guild of America, you must have been paid for a minimum amount of work (sales, term employment, or development deals, but not options) writing feature films, television, or radio over a two-year period. The amount of work necessary is based on a point system determined by the Guild.

Once you qualify, the current initiation fee is $1,500. Monthly dues are based on your income. You must join the Guild after qualifying in order to do additional work with production entities which have signed the Guild agreement.

The WGA is primarily a collective bargaining entity for screen, television, and radio writers. The Guild will get involved in individual disputes and possible infractions against members, will arbitrate screen credit whenever two or more unteamed writers are involved in a project, and offers a script registration service to all writers, including nonmembers. The Guild never assists in securing an agent or obtaining employment for writers.

The WGA East, located in New York City, and the WGA West, in L.A., can be contacted at the addresses or numbers listed in the bibliography.

I got an agent six months ago and I can't get her on the phone. What should I do?

The underlying question here is probably, "How do I know if my agent is doing a good job for me?" When you're not getting your phone calls returned, it's one of the signs that the relationship may have soured.

I believe you have a right to expect, or request, certain things from your literary agent:

> Conversations at least once a week when your project is active, that is, when your script is being submitted or you are being sent on meetings regularly.

> Conversations at least once a month, even when nothing's going on (because you're in the middle of a new screenplay), just to touch base.

> Information about all of the places you or your work are being submitted. This could be either periodic lists of submissions or copies of all accompanying correspondence.

The return of all your phone calls within forty-eight hours. If the agent is simply too busy to get back to you, or is out of town, then you should at least receive a call from the agent's secretary to let you know what's going on or when the agent will be calling.

This is really the minimum amount of communication I would expect; some agents I know would rarely let a week go by without talking to every client at least once. But the main consideration is not the number of calls; it's whether you feel your agent is still in your corner. And there's no clear answer to that. It's like asking how you know when a romantic relationship is over. Sometimes you just know.

I also believe that an agent has a right to expect certain things of *you* in the relationship. As with any new endeavor, enthusiasm runs strongest at the outset. Remember when you began your new script, and you were all hot about its great potential, eager to get to the typewriter every morning? And remember how that feeling had dwindled by about page 72, and getting act 2 finished seemed like booking for steerage on a slave ship?

Well, agents encounter act 2s in their work as well. When you first signed on, your agent probably was high on your script and thought an offer would be on the table within a week. And you seemed like a talented, creative, energetic, and dedicated screenwriter who was loaded with money-making ideas. But after a few weeks of repeated rejections and piles of other screenplays from other clients and no new ideas or screenplays coming from you, it is understandable that your agent might not be putting in the effort on your behalf that she once was.

So do some things to hold up your end and to keep your agent's interest from waning:

1. Keep working! *Never* sit back at any point in your career and expect your agent to carry the ball. Keep writing every day and keep originating new ideas to discuss with your agent for the next script, or for possible development deals. It's your career, not your agent's, and it's up to you to keep it going. Nothing will revive your agent's enthusiasm like a new script or a strong belief that you are dogging away at your goal.

2. Never call without a real reason. Give the agent ample opportunity to get some things in motion. And if you're just calling to see what's going on, tell the secretary that, and that a progress report from the secretary will suffice unless there's something concrete to discuss.

3. Keep making your own contacts. If you encounter someone who is interested in your writing, have the agent make the actual submission. But it's still your responsibility to keep networking on your own behalf.

If all of this fails, and your agent is simply incommunicado, I would write a letter requesting a meeting to discuss the status of your projects and your relationship. If that gets no response, I'd start pursuing other agents. Don't leave the first one, though, until you've found somebody else; if a possible deal comes along, the agent who wouldn't return your calls might be better than no agent at all. And if you call your unresponsive agent with the message that an offer is on the table, you probably stand a much better chance of getting your call returned.

What about services that offer to read or represent scripts for a fee?

My personal belief is that professionals offering to *critique* your screenplay for a fee should be considered and those offering to *submit* or represent your script for a fee should be avoided.

There are a number of qualified, helpful, professional script evaluation services available, varying in cost from about $50 per script to as much as $500. These can be a good source of objective opinions and recommendations for developing or rewriting your screenplay. I have to believe this is a good source of feedback because I'm one of these people.

But before purchasing *any* evaluation of your script, check out the person offering the service: What is his background? Will he refer you to past customers? Will he show you a past critique he's done? What exactly do you get for the fee? And be sure your screenplay is registered with the Copyright office and the Writers Guild before showing it to anyone.

I'm very skeptical of those offering to *submit* your script for a fee. Just sending a script to someone is no big deal. The critical issue is how it will be received: Who is on the receiving end? How much power does she possess? What is her relationship with the submitting agency? Is she really interested in representing or producing new material? Often these services promise representation "if the screenplay meets our particular standards." Well, that's the basis on which any agent will read a script.

I don't know any agent in Hollywood who charges a fee for considering a screenplay for representation. And among all my past students, I have never heard a single person say that he was glad he paid someone in advance to represent him or that the fee paid ever led to a deal.

Some services offer to do both: evaluate your script and (perhaps) represent it. If you feel the evaluation alone is worth the cost, then I'd go ahead. Then if something more comes of it, all the better. *Caveat emptor.*

What if I have a great idea but I don't care if I write it or not and I would be willing to give it to an established writer for a share of the profits?

It is possible to be paid just for a story idea. There are people in Hollywood who are great at coming up with high concepts and make a living just by selling their ideas to producers, who then hire other screenwriters to come in and do all the work. Sounds great, doesn't it?

But before you decide that this is the niche for you, you'd better ask yourself if this pursuit is worth the effort.

Ideas in Hollywood are worth quite a bit less than a dime a dozen. *Everybody's* got ideas. It's the execution of the concept that determines whether the concept has value. So the chances of finding an established screenwriter who wants to pay you for your idea or wants to team with you on a project are slim, since they've all got drawers full of their *own* ideas that they haven't gotten made.

You might interest a *producer* in your idea and make some money that way. But the amount of money you would receive is rarely very significant—maybe a couple thousand dollars for your concept. Now I know that a couple thousand dollars probably doesn't sound bad just for selling something you came up with while you were folding your laundry. But to get that two grand, you've got to get in touch with dozens of producers, find those who are willing to hear bare ideas from an unestablished nonwriter, and get them to like it enough to pay even that much for it.

So then you've got to decide what your career goals really are. Sale of an idea can get you a little money and perhaps a shared story credit. But then what? Having sold an idea doesn't really move you very far up the screenwriting career ladder, because you still haven't written anything. And you're not going to survive that long on that $2000. At least not if you care about things like food and shelter.

If you want to be a screenwriter, trust your own abilities and use your good ideas yourself. Maybe your first script won't do justice to this great concept, but a producer might want to option your script just to use the idea, so you'd still end up as well off as if you had sold the idea outright in the first place. Only now you have more experience and another writing sample. And you'll always be able to come up with more ideas.

If you really don't want to write screenplays but you like developing ideas and want to work in film or television, consider producing. If that is your career goal, you can take your ideas to an established producer with the understanding that if the producer wants to develop one of them, you will also be involved in the project, perhaps as an associate producer or coproducer. If the project goes, you are then launched on a whole new career path.

I've just made this sound a whole lot easier than it is. There are lots of people in Hollywood competing for this goal as well, and it possesses its own set of rules. But if you like the prospect of developing ideas and working in the movies but hate putting words on paper, this might be a path worth considering.

Can I star in or produce or direct my own screenplay?

Sure.

But every extra demand you make when negotiating for sale of your screenplay encumbers it a bit more. And the more it's encumbered, the more difficult it is to get a deal. It's hard enough just to sell your script. Until you're established, going after a *Rocky*-type deal puts your chances in the one-in-a-million category.

Don't I have any control at all over what is done to my screenplay once I sell it?
     No.

Is it a good idea to work with a writing partner?
     This is like asking if it's a good idea to get married. Collaboration has the same kinds of advantages and disadvantages that any other committed relationship possesses.
     On the plus side, a writing partner is a good source of brainstorming, because you can tap into each other's creativity and feed on each other's ideas. Two heads are usually *more* than twice as creative as one in this regard.
     A writing partner can be especially helpful writing comedy because you can try to make each other laugh as a test of your funny ideas.
     A writing team can often combat block more easily as well. When one partner is getting lazy or scared, the other can insist that the team stick to the writing commitment.
     And writing, like sex, is sometimes more fun if it's shared.
     The down side of collaboration is the sacrifice of one's ego. The only way a partnership will work is if each member has the right to say, "I just can't accept this idea (or line of dialogue or character description or whatever)." And the partner has to agree to go along, giving up that particular idea, even though it would have changed the course of filmmaking as we know it.
     Collaboration can be more cumbersome, because your writing regimen has to conform to two schedules. You also have to split the money. And if you break up, anyone reading your past scripts will assume it was your partner that had all the talent. So you'll often have to write an additional spec script on your own.
     You pays your money and you takes your choice.

How can I bypass readers?
     Don't be so worried about readers. You want to approach a company at as high an executive level as you can, but your script

will usually end up on a reader's pile even if your submission was to a vice president.

Readers are, for the most part, conscientious, thorough, and dying to find a script worth recommending. If you've written a screenplay that meets the standards outlined in this book, most readers will recognize your talent, and the agents, producers, stars, and executives they work for will hear about it.

Is it worth it to go to film school?

Maybe.

If you want to be a lawyer, you've got to get a degree in law. But if you want to be a screenwriter, a degree is next to meaningless. Nobody in Hollywood really cares if you've got a certificate on your wall or what your grade point average was. All anyone cares about is your script. Having a film degree might persuade more people to look at your writing sample, but beyond that, I've never seen any evidence that the diploma made any difference to a screenwriter's success.

But this doesn't mean that film schools aren't of value. The education you get in pursuing that degree can offer you four valuable commodities:

1. Information. If you get exposed to good teachers in film school, you can develop your talent as a screenwriter to the point where you can write a salable script. The guidance and feedback of a good instructor is invaluable in learning your craft.

2. Contacts. Film school can be a great source of lasting friendships and associations tht will pay off as you all pursue Hollywood together. The classic example is the gang that came out of USC in the 60s (George Lucas, Francis Ford Coppola, John Milius, Terrence Mallick, and others) who came into their glory in the 70s, and continued to help and support each other as their careers grew. Both fellow students and professors can provide the information and introductions you need when you try to launch your career.

3. A Screenplay. Getting that degree will include writing at least one screenplay, which can then serve as your sample script when you begin pursuing your career. *River's Edge*, for example, was screenwriter Neal Jimenez's masters project at UCLA. And if you want to pursue directing, film school gives you access to equipment and a finished piece of film to show.

4. A Liberal Arts Education. Don't pooh-pooh this one. The more you know about life in general, the breadth of man's history and knowledge, and the history and forms of artistic expression (including film history), the better a writer, and possibly human being, you will be.

These four rewards of film school, or at least the first three, are essential to becoming a working screenwriter. You must have information, contacts, and a finished screenplay if you hope to achieve your career goal. And as an added bonus, film school can allow you to concentrate entirely on your film pursuit without having to worry about the real world (unless, of course, you're working your way through school or have children, in which case the real world is ever present). And as a full-time student, you have the added fun of flirting with coeds and cheering for the football team. College can be fun.

However, film school is a very expensive way to acquire that necessary information, those contacts, and a finished screenplay. Tuition, books, equipment, and living expenses could run anywhere from $8,000 to $20,000 per year or more for two to four years, depending on the school. Even without that kind of money to spend, there are other ways to pursue screenwriting.

Since the degree itself is of little importance, you can get the information you need through books and through individual seminars and classes offered by continuing education programs, free universities, and media centers around the country. For example, the UCLA Extension Writers' Program offers at least twenty screenwriting classes every term.

You can make contacts through all of the methods outlined in the chapter on marketing yourself or by volunteering to work as an unpaid intern for someone in the film business.

You can write your sample screenplay in any living or working situation.

I'm not trying to discourage you from film school, only to get you to look at it as one of several choices in pursuing your career. You may decide that the intensity and quality of education and the number of contacts and opportunities it provides make film school the best alternative for you.

In choosing a particular school, do the kind of research you would do in pursuing a job. Consider at least a half dozen possible schools. Get all their available literature and then visit the campuses you're seriously considering. Talk to the staff and members of the faculty in the media department, talk to current students, and then ask for the names of recent graduates of the program. When you talk to those former graduates, ask them for the names of some of their fellow students who may *not* have gotten film positions after graduating. And finally, call some executives and agents in the industry and ask them whether a degree from the school you're considering would increase your chances as a potential screenwriter.

How do I obtain rights to a book, play, short story, or true story?

If a work of fiction is no longer under copyright, that is, the copyright has expired because the necessary time has passed, the work is in the public domain. That means it can be adapted to the screen without securing any rights.

The same holds true for a true story if all of those depicted in the film are deceased or if the characters are only portrayed when acting as public figures. Rights pertaining to privacy and defamation basically die when the person portrayed does. So rights are not a consideration when writing a screenplay about Millard Fillmore. However, if Millard Fillmore's mistress is still alive and she is portrayed in your screenplay, her permission will have to be obtained or she must be omitted from your film.

If a person's actions are a matter of public record, these can be portrayed without danger—*but only those actions by the person as a public figure*. Once you leave the actions revealed in newspaper articles or court transcripts and move into a person's private life, rights must be obtained. In other words, you can show Ronald Reagan in the Oval Office, but not in bed with Nancy. (Of course, why would you want to anyway?)

This entire matter of rights and permissions, defamation, and invasion of privacy is a very gray area. Lawyers make big bucks preventing or participating in litigation about these issues. The best rule is when in doubt, secure the rights.

If you wish to obtain the rights to adapt a work of fiction which is still under copyright, you must first find out who holds those rights and whether they are currently under option for a film adaptation. If you phone the publisher of the novel (or play, or short story, or song, or whatever) and ask for the film rights department, they should be able to tell you who controls the movie rights.

Usually these rights will be retained by the author of the original work, but not always. Occasionally the publisher will acquire them as part of the original deal with the author. If the author holds the rights, it is best you contact him or her directly.

Doing a little detective work through your contacts, the library, or the long-distance information operator can sometimes lead you straight to an author. If those methods fail, you can always write to an author in care of the publisher and hope you eventually get a response. Reaching the author directly is usually best because the author will respond more positively than would the publisher or author's representative to your ideas, enthusiasm, and respect for the original work and may be less concerned about the money you are offering up front.

If you can't reach the author, you will have to deal with the author's representative. The publisher, unless they control the rights, will give you the name of the author's agent or attorney. This will usually be the New York literary agency which represents the author for publishing. They will often pass you on to a Hollywood literary agent who represents the film rights to the author's work.

After tracking all of these people down, you may learn that the book is already under option for film. If this is the case, try to find out who has the film rights or at least when the option expires. When that expiration date is near, call again to see if it is likely to be renewed or if the film has gone into production. Books and plays often get optioned when first released, and then the producers involved can't get a deal, and the option expires.

If the film rights to the work are available, your ability to acquire them will depend entirely on what you have to offer in the way of money, experience, enthusiasm, and the likelihood you can get the movie made.

Even if you have no money to offer up front, you still might get the rights to a work of fiction if those involved think you've got a good shot at getting the movie made, thus making them money down the road. Your chances will improve if your ideas about the novel's adaptation are consistent with the author's goals for the original creation, and if no one else is knocking on her door.

With both true stories and fiction, you can adapt an original work even without securing the rights. To my knowledge, there is nothing illegal about writing an adaptation of another work or a person's life story, as long as you don't try to make any money from it and you don't pretend it's your original creation. Then, if you can get a producer interested in the screenplay, it will be up to *her* to acquire the rights in order to make the movie.

You might even show your adaptation to the original author, hoping that he will be so dazzled by your devotion to the spirit of his original work that he will *then* sell you the film rights.

This is a risky path to take, because if the rights can't ever be obtained, you'll have a script that can never be made into a movie. But it may still have been worth it, because you'll end up with some valuable experience and perhaps a good writing sample.

Where are my chances of success greater, in TV or features?

If you live in L.A., it's probably a toss-up. Far fewer features are made each year than TV movies and series episodes, but feaure producers and financiers are often more open to unsolicited submissions than the networks and television production companies. There are really only three (three and a half with Fox Broadcasting) markets for your TV work. A feature script can be submitted to independent studios, producers, and money people all over the country.

If you live outside of L.A., features are probably your better bet, because it's very hard to get TV development deals without an agent and without the ability to meet frequently with producers and network executives.

But immensely more important than these considerations are the issues of what you want to write and what you're good at. If you rarely go to feature films, but love watching TV, it's a good indication that that is what you should write. Use the criteria above only if the two media are truly equal in terms of your desire and your abilities.

How should I go about writing an episode for a TV series?

Choose the series for which you want to write a sample episode. If you're choosing between two, pick the one that is more likely to be renewed for at least one or two more seasons (because the ratings are strong and the contracts of the stars aren't close to expiration).

Videotape at least four episodes of your chosen series. Watch the episodes the first time just as a regular viewer, to experience the emotion in a normal way.

With the second viewing, take extensive notes for each episode in the form of a *step outline*. A step outline is simply a list of the events which occur in the episode, in order. A step outline for a past episode of *Cheers*, for example, might read:

1. Frazier arrives at the bar.

2. Tells others about Rebecca's college nickname.

3. Sam says he'll kid her with it.

4. Rebecca enters and they tease her.

OPENING CREDITS

5. Neighbor of Cliff arrives and asks him to sign petition.

6. He refuses and makes fun of the guy . . .

When you have completed step outlines for at least four episodes, including indications of when the commercial breaks occur, look for the *similarities* among all the episodes. This will show you the requirements and structure for the series. Your sample episode must then conform to that pattern.

For example, repeated viewings of *Moonlighting* reveal that in almost every episode (not counting the period of Matty's pregnancy), David and Matty argue in a car, Agnes answers the phone with a rhyme, and the case they investigate reflects some current aspect of David and Matty's relationship. Therefore your sample episode of *Moonlighting* should possess these elements as well.

Never take it on yourself to write an episode that will change the course of the series. The producers of the shows will decide when they want Matty and David to get married, Cliff and Claire Huxtable to get divorced on *The Cosby Show,* or Jessica Fletcher to become a lesbian on *Murder, She Wrote;* don't *you* write those episodes.

Don't worry that the elements of the series will have changed by the time you finish your screenplay, even if you're writing a sample episode of a soap like *Dallas.* Write your script consistent with where the show is when you begin. The executives who read the screenplay won't expect you to be able to predict the future.

Your sample screenplay should be good for at least two seasons past completion, particularly if the series is still on the air.

How would I go about adapting a novel (including my own novel) into a screenplay?

I'm glad you asked that, because the process is similar to the one outlined above for writing a series episode.

Do the same kind of step outline for the novel (or play or short story or true story) you are adapting. Then put the original source material away.

Based on the step outline, choose the *single* outer motivation for the *single* hero from the original story which will serve as your basic concept. Add a second level of sell if there is a love story or a second equally important outer motivation for your hero. Even if the original novel covered three generations in the lives of an entire family, you must reduce it to one story concept.

Break that story concept into three acts, based on the three stages of the hero's overall outer motivation. Then, drawing from all the events listed in the step outline, select only those relevant to one of your three acts and eliminate the rest.

Based on the structural principles outlined in Chapter 5, combine and rearrange these possible scenes to maximize the emotional impact of your screenplay. And perhaps even invent additional scenes or characters if that helps and if you're adapting from a fictional source.

From this point the process is the same as outlined in this book. You will only return to the original novel or source material as a possible source of descriptions or dialogue.

Following this process will help you maintain enough emotional distance from your original material that you can meet the needs of an effective *screenplay*—especially if your original source material is your own creation or your own life story.

What about cable TV? Hasn't it created a whole new market for screenwriters?

Not really. All the cable networks and Fox Television combined produce less original programming than any one of the networks. And none of them are doing anything strikingly different from network fare. These are simply new production entities to pursue with your work in the manner outlined in Chapter 8.

If there are all of these rules for screenwriting, why are so many movies so bad?

Because those filmmakers haven't read this book yet.

And also because the process of making a film involves so many people, so much money, so much talent, so many egos, so many physical obstacles, and so many things that can go wrong that it's a near miracle every time a movie even gets made, let alone is any good.

I certainly believe that Hollywood's greatest weaknesses are obvious and extensive: a lack of respect for the screenplay and the screenwriter; censorship, through a lowest-common-denominator, don't-offend-anyone attitude on television or a boneheaded rating system for features; an unwillingness to pursue a modest profit from a modest investment; undue allegiance to stars and ideas only because they've made money in the past; too many fingers in the creative pie; and a general administrative philosophy of "cover your ass."

But I also think that the film industry takes the rap a bit too often for what is wrong with the world. Anytime you try to unite art and commerce, it's an arranged marriage at best, certainly not one made in heaven. I don't think the people in Hollywood have any more to answer for than those in Detroit or Wall Street or Washington or Battle Creek, Michigan. Creativity in the pursuit of money and power is a tricky undertaking.

And I certainly believe that any enterprise that results in *Manhattan*, *Psycho*, *The Sure Thing*, *The Last of Sheila*, *Hill Street Blues*, *Play it Again, Sam*, *What's Up, Doc?*, *Perry Mason*, *From Russia with Love*, *Chinatown*, *thirtysomething*, *Star Wars*, *The Omen*, *The Return of the Secaucus Seven*, *Ben Casey*, *Body Heat*, *The Big Chill*, *Airplane*, *All the President's Men*, *Run for Your Life*, *M*A*S*H**, *Bye Bye Birdie*, *Jaws*, *Tootsie*, *The Dick Van Dyke Show*, *The Wonder Years*, *Big*, *When Harry Met Sally*, *Working Girl*, *The Twilight Zone*, *Too Far to Go*, *The Sting*, *Stand By Me*, *The Graduate*, *E.T.*, *Cheers*, and *A Fistful of Dollars* has to be given a nod of gratitude for a lot of wonderful moments in the dark.

Is there sexism in Hollywood?

Yes.

Also racism, ageism, plagiarism, nepotism, homophobia, dishonesty, and brain-dead executives.

So what?

Faced with the realities of the film business, you can do one of two things.

You can say, "I don't want any part of this." And then you can choose some other path and goal which will probably involve those same hurdles and obstacles or others just like them.

Or you can say, "Screenwriting is what brings me fulfillment and a sense of worth. So I'm going to pursue it, in spite of the difficult, negative, unfair people and practices I will have to face as part of choosing that particular game. I won't be naive about it, but I won't use those obstacles, or any of the 623 others out there in Hollywood as excuses to feed my fear and keep me from pursuing my dream. I'll accept the consequences of my choice as long as being on the path of screenwriting brings me joy."

And then you go for it.

APPENDIX B

. . . .

A Sample Treatment

The following is a sample treatment for a project I developed a few years ago. The true story is based on the book *The Sylmar Tunnel Disaster,* by Janette Zavattero, a journalist and author who was the sister of the story's hero.

My company acquired the material for possible production as a docudrama. I wrote the story in treatment form as a selling tool for packaging and possible development.

If you reach the stage in your writing career where you are asked to provide treatments, this provides an example of the proper layout. Remember that treatments are written in present tense, dialogue is minimal (with a bit more included in most comedy treatments), only the major scenes and characters are included, and that all of the principles of concept, character, and structure apply. And the shorter the better; always leave the reader wanting more.

Sylmar!

a treatment by

Michael Hauge

from the book

The Sylmar Tunnel Disaster

by Janette Zavattero

On the night of June 24, 1971, in an irrigation tunnel beneath the town of Sylmar, California, seventeen miners were blown to bits. This is the story of that tragedy, and of the one man who saw that those responsible were brought to justice.

It is another world; a place of total silence, and total darkness. The strings of bare electric lights which extend for the full three mile length of the tunnel give it the feeling of outer space, rather than a huge, man made cavern seventeen stories under the earth.

As the small cage carrying the men to their jobs descends into the earth, the miners laugh and talk about the bonuses they will get from Lockheed if the irrigation tunnel is finished ahead of schedule. The men are highballers, working stiffs who have spent half their lives under the ground, in mines and tunnels like this. And always in their voices is the slight trace of unspoken fear at what can happen in so foreign a place.

Wally Zavattero picks up the ringing phone before he is fully awake; this is not the first such midnight call the forty year old safety engineer has received. The California Division of Industrial Safety has placed him in charge of monitoring the Sylmar tunnel. Zavattero is a former highballer himself, a short, blunt man whose compressed energy seems to keep him constantly in motion. His wife Mercedes watches anxiously, once again, as Wally listens to the phone and climbs out of bed.

"That was Loren Savage," he tells her. "It's the Sylmar tunnel. There's been a flash fire."

"Was anyone . . . ?" She doesn't let herself finish the question.

"I don't know, Mercy," he replies. "Loren said they've got it under control. But they've said that before."

"Why do these things always happen in the middle of the night?" she asks, hiding her fear with anger.

Zavattero smiles at her. "That's a good question. From now on I'll ask them to schedule their accidents during normal working hours." The anxiety is apparent in his voice as well as he rushes out the door for Sylmar.

It is near dawn when Zavattero confronts the tunnel management team in the trailer that serves as headquarters for the Sylmar tunnel. Across from him is Loren Savage, the project manager and Zavattero's friend. Savage's easygoing nature covers a sometimes cynical attitude that Zavattero doesn't possess. Also in the trailer are Bob Ree, the project engineer, a short, nervous man who always seems to sweat, and whose collar always seems too tight, and David Finkle, the crafty young lawyer for Lockheed who looks as if his surfboard is still tied to the roof of his car.

"I'm yellow-tagging the tunnel," Zavattero tells them. His penetrating eyes tell them that this won't be debated. "There's no trace of gas in the tunnel now, but if the meter registers even a molecule, you shut down."

"Don't worry, Wally," says Finkle. "Lockheed isn't about to take any chances."

"Don't bullshit me, OK Finkle?" Zavattero snaps back. "I was at the Angeles tunnel, remember? Four men were hurt here today, and I don't want any more injuries."

As the men leave the trailer, Savage takes Zavattero aside. "I'm glad you didn't red-tag us, Wally."

"I would have, but you know Lockheed would have the tag pulled in a half hour with one phone call. How come you're pushing so hard on this tunnel anyway? You're way ahead of schedule. Those must be some bonuses Lockheed is promising you."

"Don't worry, Wally," Savage tells him. "It's under control."

Late that evening, just as the graveyard shift is set to come on, the meter records traces of gas at the tunnel face. Ree and Savage look at the readings, then Savage goes inside the trailer to phone

Lockheed. The door closes behind him. Several minutes later he emerges from the trailer. "We're going ahead," he tells the crew boss. "It's only surface gas, and the readings are clear now." The highballers begin descending into the darkness below.

There are eighteen men in the mine at 2:30 AM when the face of the tunnel explodes into an inferno of fire and flying rock. The blast will be felt as far as fifty miles from Sylmar. Above the tunnel, Loren Savage can feel the rumble of the earth. "My God," he says.

Inside the tunnel, those closest to its face have been obliterated by the explosion. As the flames and gas spread up the length of the tunnel, men try hopelessly to flee the fire. Their screaming echoes through the tunnel. . . .

When Zavattero arrives on the scene, it is a madhouse of miners, firemen, reporters, and spectators. He is just in time to see Loren Savage, his face blank and white with horror, being driven away from the confusion by his wife. Zavattero finds Bob Ree, who screams at him that the fire department is keeping the miners from going in to rescue their co-workers. "They're getting out their *hoses*, for God's sake!" shouts Ree. "You can't fight a gas fire with hoses!"

Zavattero sees that the confrontation between firemen and miners will turn into a fight at any moment. He marches up to the fire chief.

"This tunnel is sealed off," announces the chief.

"No it's not," replies Zavattero firmly, pushing a blunt finger against the chief's chest. "Your men don't know the first thing about tunnels, and the miners are going after anyone who might be alive down there, whether your firemen are in the way or not." The fire chief merely nods in the face of Zavattero's rage, and the firemen back away from the tunnel entrance.

The miners are outfitted with breathing apparatus, which gives each of them only forty minutes in the smoke-filled tunnel. Soon the first of them emerges from the tunnel entrance carrying the body of one of the men. As others continue the search in the tunnel, they find other bodies, or sometimes only parts of bodies, belonging to their friends. As they move closer to the face of the tunnel, a weak voice penetrates the blackness.

"Hey, what about me?" It is Ralph Brisette, a miner who has

crawled into an air duct of the tunnel. The excited miners lead him to the surface, and his rescue gives renewed hope to the men above. But Ralph Brisette will be the only survivor. . . .

The entire operation of retrieving the bodies takes more than forty-eight straight hours. When Zavattero is finally driven home, he is numb. Mercy sees the grief and anger that are buried under his exhaustion, and she knows not to ask anything.

Wally peels off his blackened clothes that smell of smoke and death, and sits on the edge of the bed. "When we first went in after the bodies," he says weakly, "I saw something lying near the dolly tracks. It was a man's liver. It didn't seem horrid, or awful or anything, just very strange. I remember thinking, 'This was once a part of a man,' so I carefully put it in a bag and set it aside. . . . By this morning we had found so many pieces of so many men it was impossible to identify anyone, and I was just putting the remains in piles. . . . " As he sits silently with these thoughts, Zavattero begins to cry softly.

"They're going to pay this time, Mercy," he tells her at last. "This time Lockheed's going to pay."

A short time later Zavattero has collapsed in sleep on the bed. Mercy picks up the clothes he was wearing, takes them out to their trash barrel, and quietly burns them.

Over the next two weeks, Zavattero waits with increasing frustration for an investigation into the explosion to be announced. His written request for prosecution is ignored, and there is no mention in the papers of the $250 million loan guarantee that Lockheed Construction is trying to secure from the government—a loan that will be seriously jeopardized by any bad publicity. When he finally hears that a public hearing on the explosion has been cancelled, he storms into the office of Jack Hatton, the head of the California Division of Industrial Safety.

Jack Hatton is a large, doughy man who looks as if he has been desk bound for too many years. He is a public official who has learned that the secret of hanging on to an appointment by the Governor is to avoid making waves or grandstanding at all costs. Jack Hatton is also a former executive for Lockheed Construction Company.

As Zavattero paces angrily in front of his boss's desk, Hatton tells him to calm down, that the incident is being looked into. "These things must follow their normal course, Wally," he tells him. "Besides," he adds, "even if there was negligence, it's only a misdemeanor."

With this comment, Zavattero explodes. "A MISDEMEANOR?! That's the same thing Lockheed's attorneys are saying! Well, I've seen enough misdemeanors in this state. In seven years of working in mine safety I've seen men maimed, crushed, electrocuted, scraped to the bone by lousy equipment and just plain killed. And you know why? Because some smart lawyer figured out how to spread a few bucks around and turn manslaughter into a misdemeanor. What happened at Sylmar wasn't even manslaughter. It was murder. And I'm going to see to it that somebody's going to pay, because I'm the one who wrote the safety orders!"

Zavattero is still shaking when he gets home, and he starts yelling at Mercy about how they are going to cover it all up. She tries to calm him down, then finally screams at him in desperation. "Stop taking your anger out on your family, and on yourself. If you've got to do something, then DO IT!"

He stares at her a long time, then quietly walks into the bedroom and phones the *L. A. Times.*

The next day's headline, LOCKHEED VIOLATES SAFETY ORDERS IN DEATH OF 17 MINERS, begins what will ultimately be a two year ordeal for Zavattero and his family.

Zavattero's first obstacles come from his own department, when Jack Hatton refuses to let him off his other duties in order to concentrate on the Sylmar investigation. This results in long hours of arduous questions and documentation every evening with George Bane, the determined but inexperienced young attorney who has been assigned to the case. The strain begins to show, and tensions rise between Wally, Mercy, and their two teenage daughters. Then when Wally attempts to retrieve the gas meter from the Sylmar tunnel, which will prove that gas was present in the tunnel prior to the explosion, he discovers that Lockheed has substituted a different meter in an attempt to cover up their own negligence. Shortly after confronting a Lockheed attorney with this accusation, he receives an anonymous phone call threatening his life. He decides not to tell Mercy about the threat.

When the California Senate finally begins hearings into the Sylmar explosion, he is relieved that someone will at last be on his side. So he is totally unprepared at the grilling he gets from the committee chairman when he takes the stand. Jack Fenton, a Democratic senator, wants to show that Governor Reagan's budget cuts and appointments have made the Bureau of Safety ineffectual. But the result is that Zavattero is accused of near murder and negligence in allowing the miners back into the tunnel prior to the explosion. Mercy is shocked and angered as she watches from the gallery while Wally is dragged across the coals by the senator's verbal barbs. And their twelve-year-old daughter Gina is so infuriated that she accosts the senator later in the hallway and screams at him for calling her father a murderer.

After Wally reveals to the hearing that his life has been threatened, the tension that has been building at the Zavattero home finally explodes. "Your obsession with bringing down Lockheed, or appeasing your own guilt, or whatever you're trying to do, has blinded you to your own family," Mercy cries at him. "One of your daughters is getting badgered by the kids at school because her father was practically accused of murder, and the other is out every night 'til all hours, wants to get married, and I can't even talk to her. You're already exhausted, you've got an ulcer, and you're starting to drink too much. And now I find out that your life's in danger."

As Mercy breaks down in his arms, Wally doesn't answer her, just holds her quietly for a long time. Later that evening, he tells her, Gina and Paula, their older daughter, "I know you've been going through hell, and I haven't been much of a father lately, and I'm sorry. I promise I'll be there for you from now on. But I can't stop what I'm doing. I'm the only hope for those seventeen miners' families right now, and I've got to fight for them. I've got to try to see that this won't happen again.

Just as the time grows close for Lockheed to be brought to trial, George Bane gives the Zavatteros some shocking news. "I've been fired," he reveals with a half smile. "I guess we've been pushing poor little Lockheed a bit too hard." The next day Wally meets the new prosecutor, who couldn't be more opposite from his predecessor: Roosevelt Dorn is a tall, dignified black man with graying temples who carries a pearl-handled cane and speaks with quiet, powerful conviction. But in one way he is identical to the young lawyer he follows: he is determined Lockheed will pay.

When the trial finally begins, the courtroom is a three-ring circus of attorneys, witnesses, spectators and press. The army of lawyers defending Lockheed, Savage, and Ree fill a dozen chairs; on the prosecution side are only Dorn and Zavattero. But as Zavattero begins to testify, and the evidence emerges, the history of negligence, inaction and coverup overwhelm all of Lockheed's legal minds: dozens of requests for prosecution against Lockheed and other contractors that Jack Hatton and the Bureau of Safety have ignored . . . numerous injuries and deaths that went unpunished . . . Lockheed's attempt to switch the gas meter at Sylmar . . . Lockheed's attempt to "hide" Bob Ree in Seattle so he couldn't testify . . . the threat to Wally's life.

When Jack Hatton finally comes to testify, he enters the court a broken man, reads a prepared statement to the jury, and announces his resignation.

Then Ralph Brisette, the only miner to survive the Sylmar explosion, takes the stand, and for the first time the courtroom is silent. In a soft, shaken voice, Brisette quietly breaks down as he recalls the screams of the miners trapped inside the tunnel, and the agony of hearing his friends die while he wondered if he would be rescued. There is no cross-examination when he finishes his testimony, only silence. Ralph Brisette shakily gets up from the stand and slowly, quietly walks out of the courtroom.

Through all of the hearing and trial, Zavattero has maintained his friendship with Loren Savage, in spite of strong objections from Roosevelt Dorn that it could jeopardize the case against Lockheed. When Wally and Loren discuss the case over late-night drinks, they joke about the endless political and legal maneuvers that mystify and anger them both. It is clear that even from opposing sides in the courtroom, they are still closer to each other than either of them is to all the lawyers who are now running the show. But the strain it is putting on their friendship is also clear. When Wally finally asks his friend what really happened that night at Sylmar, *why* he let the miners back in the tunnel, Savage won't answer. "Maybe someday, Wally," he shakes his head sadly, "but not now."

After months of testimony, arguments, appeals, and legal maneuvers, the trial finally ends and the jury is sent to render its verdict. Walking out of the courtroom for the last time, Wally sees Loren Savage sitting alone. "Well, it's finally over," Wally says quietly.

"Thank God," his friend replies.

"I guess some good will come of it all," Wally says. "Maybe next time companies like Lockheed will be a little more cautious. Still I wonder if somewhere along the line, with all the politics and legalities and money, those seventeen men weren't forgotten."

The two men sit quietly for a moment, each with his own thoughts, and then they say goodbye. It is the last time the two friends will see each other.

When Wally arrives home that evening, he tells Mercy, Paula and Gina that he has requested a transfer to a new division, north of San Francisco. The girls seem pleased, and Mercy's face lights up with hope and relief. "Maybe we can start to put all this behind us," he tells them.

Word of the verdict reaches Zavattero as he drives past a newsstand and spots the headline: LOCKHEED GUILTY! He screeches to a halt and grabs the paper off the counter. Lockheed has been found guilty of a wrongful death misdemeanor, and has been fined the maximum in real and punitive damages. In addition, the families of the seventeen miners have received the largest civil award in California history: a total of 9½ million dollars. Savage and Ree have also been found quilty, but their sentences suspended.

In a sidebar of the newpaper, a separate article reveals that Senator Jack Fenton has spearheaded passage of a bill increasing the possible penalties for wrongful death employer negligence. From now on, incidents like the one at Sylmar will be felonies, not misdemeanors.

The fight is over.

Wally pulls away from the curb and snaps on the car radio just as the station is playing "John Henry." Zavattero smiles and begins to whistle the tune softly to himself as he heads home to his family.

Bigliography

The following list of source material includes other current books on writing and the film industry, plus publications, organizations, and script services which can assist you in pursuing information and potential contacts.

BOOKS

Aristotle: *Poetics*, Oxford University Press, 1968.

Burger, Richard: *The Producers*, Burger Publications, 1985.

DiMaggio, Madeline: *How to Write for Television*, Prentice Hall, 1988.

Egri, Lajos: *The Art of Dramatic Writing*, Citadel Press, 1968.

Field, Syd: *Screenplay*, Delacorte, 1982.

————: *Screenwriter's Workbook*, Dell, 1984.

————: *Selling the Screenplay*, Dell Publishing, 1989.

Goldman, William: *Adventures in the Screen Trade*, Warner Books, 1983.

Hunter, Lew: *434: Becoming a Screenwriter* (work in progress).

Jaffe, Jewel: *How to Write Situation Comedy and Laugh All the Way to the Bank* (work in progress).

Josefsburg, Milt: *Writing Comedy for Television and Hollywood*, Harper & Row, 1987.

King, Viki: *How to Write a Movie in 21 Days: The Inner Movie Method,* Harper & Row, 1988.

Kozak, Ellen M.: *Every Writer's Guide to Copyright & Publishing Law,* Henry Holt & Co., 1990.

Litwak, Mark: *Reel Power,* Morrow, 1986.

Root, Wells: *Writing the Script,* Holt, Reinhart and Winston, 1979.

Sautter, Carl: *How to Sell Your Screenplay,* New Chapter Press, 1988.

Seger, Linda: *Making a Good Script Great,* Samuel French, 1987.

————: *Creating Unforgettable Characters,* Samuel French, 1990.

Stempel, Tom: *FrameWork: A History of Screenwriting in the American Film,* Continuum, 1988.

Trottier, David R.: *Correct Format for Screenplays and Teleplays,* The Forbes Institute, 1990.

Walter, Richard: *Screenwriting: The Art, Craft and Business of Film & TV Writing,* Plume, 1988.

Wolff, Jurgen, & Kerry Cox: *Successful Script Writing,* Writers Digest Books, 1988.

The following are two other books that have nothing directly to do with movies, but which are appropriate nonetheless, and which will greatly enrich the quality of your journey:

Bolles, Richard: *What Color Is Your Parachute,* Ten Speed Press, 1991.

Peck, M. Scott: *The Road Less Traveled,* Touchstone, 1985.

PERIODICALS

Acquisitions & Development Directory: Omni Artists Management Group, Inc., 12021 Wilshire Boulevard, Suite 459, Los Angeles, CA 90025-1021.

Daily Variety: Daily Variety, Ltd., 1400 North Cahuenga Boulevard, Hollywood, CA 90028.

Feature Film Producers: DVE Productions, 3017 Santa Monica Boulevard, Suite #149, Santa Monica, CA 90404.

Hollywood Agents Directory: 451 Kelton Avenue, Los Angeles, CA 90024.

Hollywood Creative Directory: 451 Kelton Avenue, Los Angeles, CA 90024.

Hollywood Reporter: 6715 Sunset Boulevard, Hollywood, CA 90028.

Hollywood Scriptwriter: 1626 North Wilcox, #385, Hollywood, CA 90028.

Los Angeles Times: Times-Mirror Square, Los Angeles, CA 90053.

Overall Deals at the Studios: DVE Productions, 3017 Santa Monica Boulevard, Suite #149, Santa Monica, CA 90404.

Pacific Coast Studio Directory, 6331 Hollywood Boulevard, Hollywood, CA 90028.

The TV Producers: DVE Productions, 3017 Santa Monica Boulevard, Suite #149, Santa Monica, CA 90404.

SCREENWRITERS' RESOURCES

Samuel French Books carries all of the titles listed, plus thousands of others on film and theater, as well as an extensive selection of screenplays: (800) 722-8669 within California, or (800) 822-8669 from anywhere else.

Larry Edmonds Books specializes in film and television books, periodicals, and screenplays: 6658 Hollywood Boulevard, Hollywood, CA 90028, (213) 463-3273.

Script City offers a huge list of screenplays, plus screenwriting and film books, etc: 1765 North Highland #760AF, Hollywood, CA 90028, (213) 871-0707.

The Writers' Computer Store has a complete line of computer hardware, plus all available software appropriate for screenwriters: 11317 Santa Monica Boulevard, Los Angeles, CA 90025, (213) 479-7774.

Davenport Productions has a long list of audiotapes on fiction and nonfiction writing, including "How to Write and Sell Your Screenplay," a 90-minute audiotape of my essential principles, edited from my weekend seminar: Department MH, 3 Casa Verde, Austin, Texas 78734, (512) 261-6183.

ORGANIZATIONS

The Academy of Motion Picture Arts and Sciences, Margaret Herrick Library, 333 South La Cienega Boulevard, Beverly Hills, CA 90211, (213) 247-3020.

The Freelance Scriptwriters FORUM is a member-driven organization assisting screenwriters in securing products and information. Membership includes a bimonthly newsletter: P.O. Box 7, Baldwin, MD 21013.

Writers Guild of America, East, Inc., 555 West 57th Street, New York, NY 10019, (212) 245-6180.

Writers Guild of America, West, Inc., 8955 Beverly Boulevard, Los Angeles, CA 90048, (213) 550-1000.

Index

Primary character
    four categories of, 59–65
    The Karate Kid and, 171–74
    scene chart and, 158–59
Primary research, 214–15
Princess Bride, The, 12, 59–60
Privacy, invasion of, 291–92
Prizzi's Honor, 104
Producer, 238–40
    of television series, 260
Professional evaluation, 219–20,
        236, 285
Profits, percentage of, 250
Prologue, 104
Proposal script, 114
Prose version of film story, 254
Protagonist (*see* Character; Hero)
Psycho, 297

Quest for Fire, 47
Quotation marks, 126

Radio, 18
Radio Days, 45
Raiders of the Lost Ark, 95, 102–3,
        179
Rain Man, 34
Rambo, 46, 91
Raw Deal, 46
Reader, 288–89
Reading of scene, 148
Recommendation to agent, 235
Reflection
    character and, 61
    The Karate Kid and, 173
    An Officer and a Gentleman and,
        67, 78
    scene chart and, 159
Registration of screenplay, 218
Rejection, 233
Release form, 228

Remakes, 250
Renewal clause, 248
Research
    of agents, 225–26
    character and, 50
    financier and, 241–42
    primary, 214–15
    secondary, 216
    story concept and, 43
Resolution
    act III and, 86
    lack of, 150
Return of the Secaucus Seven, The,
        297
Revenge of the Nerds, 169, 170
Reversal
    of anticipation, 94–95
    The Karate Kid and, 177
Rewrites, 249
Rewriting of dialogue, 143–
        48
Right-brained method, 5–6
Rights
    adaptation and, 16–17
    ancillary, 250
    film, 292–93
    music, 137
    obtaining of, 291–92
    true story and, 17
River's Edge, 290
Road Warrior, 91, 92
Robocop, 45
Rocky, 11, 41, 60, 71, 102, 107
Romance, 61–62
    The Karate Kid and, 173–74
    An Officer and a Gentleman and,
        67–68
    scene chart and, 158–59
Romancing the Stone, 12, 98, 103
Room With a View, 240
Roxanne, 34, 58, 61, 91, 279

About the Author

Michael Hauge is a screenplay consultant, independent producer, and screenwriter who has worked in the Hollywood film industry for fifteen years and has taught screenwriting for more than eleven. He was formerly executive story editor for Henry Jaffe Enterprises and Waterman Entertainment, director of creative affairs for Zev Braun Pictures, and staff producer for Robert Guenette production. He is now president of his own company, Hilltop Productions, and is actively developing feature films and movies for television. He is also completing a computer software program based on his screenwriting principles.

Mr. Hauge has taught screenwriting at UCLA, the American Film Institute, and the University of Southern California, and has presented his two-day intensive screenwriting seminar to more than 7000 writers and filmmakers in major cities throughout the United States, as well as in Canada and England.

He also offers a screenplay critique and consultation service to writers and producers through his offices in Sherman Oaks, California.

Prior to entering the film business, Mr. Hauge taught Head Start in his home state of Oregon. He has a bachelor of arts degree from the University of Oregon and a master's degree in education from the University of Georgia.

Reader Comments, Suggestions, and Questions

I would love to hear any comments, suggestions, or questions you have for future editions of this book. Please direct them to me in care of my office:

Michael Hauge
Hilltop Productions
P.O. Box 55728
Sherman Oaks, California 91413

Please contact me as well if you have any questions regarding my seminar and teaching schedule or my consultation service. And let me know when you sell your screenplay. I love success stories.